4343

5- 2 X 00
1 st
Service

THE MAKERS OF
CLASSICAL
ARCHAEOLOGY

THE MAKERS OF CLASSICAL ARCHAEOLOGY

A Reference Work

LINDA M. MEDWID

Humanity Books

an imprint of Prometheus Books
59 John Glenn Drive, Amherst, New York 14228-2197

To Marvin,
for your love and for your infinite patience . . .

Published 2000 by Humanity Books,
an imprint of Prometheus Books

The Makers of Classical Archaeology: A Reference Work. Copyright ©
2000 Linda M. Medwid. All rights reserved. No part of this publication may be reproduced, stored in a retrieval system, or
transmitted in any form or by any means, digital, electronic,
mechanical, photocopying, recording, or otherwise, or conveyed
via the Internet or a Web site, without prior written permission
of the publisher, except in the case of brief quotations embodied
in critical articles and reviews.

Inquiries should be addressed to
Humanity Books
59 John Glenn Drive
Amherst, New York 14228–2197
VOICE: 716–691–0133, ext. 207
FAX: 716–564–2711

04 03 02 01 00   5 4 3 2 1

Library of Congress Cataloging-in-Publication Data

Medwid, Linda M., 1952–
    The makers of classical archaeology : a reference work /
Linda M. Medwid.
        p. cm.
    Includes bibliographical references and index.
    ISBN 1–57392–826–7 (cloth. : alk. paper)
    1. Classicists—Biography. 2. Archaeology—Biography.
3. Classical antiquities—Bio-bibliography. I. Title.
DE9.A1 M43 2000
930.1'092'2—dc21
[B]   99–462362
                                               CIP

Printed in the United States of America on acid-free paper

CONTENTS

FOREWORD

I was honored and somewhat surprised when Dr. Linda Medwid asked if I would write a foreword to her book. The 119 men and women Linda has chosen to include are a virtual who's who of some of the most influential individuals in the field of Classical (Greek and Roman) archaeology, broadly defined: the period from the Aegean Bronze Age through the Roman period, well over two millennia. Most of these intrepid people lived in the nineteenth and twentieth centuries, but a few were from earlier times. Some cannot truly be considered Classical archaeologists in the traditional sense of the word; Linda's compendium includes at least one Egyptologist, influential laypersons, collectors, compilers of information, draftsmen, linguists, numismatists, and art historians. Yet, their contributions laid the foundations for and formed important building blocks of our discipline. We would not be where we are in the profession today were it not for the pioneering efforts, sometimes ridiculed and criticized by contemporaries, that they made both in the field and in their writings. Mistakes were made and lessons were learned, and in the course of time we have vastly improved our ways of coaxing from the pots, stones, and bones of the ancients the stories they tell us of the past.

Classical archaeology is a relatively new and ever evolving branch of the humanities which has so many distinguished fields with much longer pedigrees than ours. Ours, too, is an area which has made enormous strides in bringing together a number of disparate fields to help in the excavation and understanding of what we have found. We have come a long way since some of the nobility of Naples tunneled into the ruins of Pompeii to search for antiquities to decorate their palaces or since the avid amateur archaeologist Heinrich Schliemann's first years at Troy. The important, often ground-breaking contributions made by many of these men and women have shaped our ways of excavating, interpreting what we "dig up," indeed our very way of looking at the ancient world.

While most of those who lived and excavated over a century ago would not recognize many of the more "scientific" advances in archaeology—and the list includes radiocarbon dating of organic finds, thermoluminescence of pottery, underwater archaeology, aerial photography, the use of landsat imagery to locate or interpret ancient sites often invisible on the ground, DNA analysis or use of modern forensic techniques to tell us what a long dead individual actually looked like in life—I think that they would be pleased by what we have done to further our knowledge of ancient Classical civilizations. They would recognize that we are following in their footsteps.

Because of the nature of our work, what we do is viewed by many as a science and, indeed, we rely more and more on scientific tools and techniques to squeeze the tiniest bit of information from the objects we recover. Ours remains, however, by its very nature a humanistic discipline and, being such, no amount of scientific application can ever transform what we do from an art form into a purely laboratory exercise. We are, after all, dealing with our ancestors who were as human as we with all the inconsistencies, shortcomings, and amazing accomplishments which make examination of the past truly a study of ourselves many generations removed. We try to maintain an analytical, scientific approach to our work, but the exciting "find" or unexpected ramifications it has for our interpretation of the past make ours, in the final analysis, very much a humanistic field of study.

The view that Classical archaeology has as its raison d'être the search for valuable artifacts is one still current in the minds of many nonarchaeologists and, I dare say, of some who call themselves archaeologists. Who is not excited about the accidental discovery of a hoard of gold coins or of a beautiful statue? Yet these are really only the exceptional finds and, in the end, they tell us precious little about the day-to-day lives of most of the people of the ancient world who will forever remain anonymous. Classical archaeology is much more than the discovery of dazzling artifacts; it is, rather, the search for our past and one which reading the ancient authors alone cannot fulfill. The golden statue may be beautiful, the sweeping account of wars and conquests by an aristocrat writing two thousand years ago is certainly gripping, but can they tell us anything about the daily lives of the bulk of the people whose civilization created them?

Increasingly, nonarchaeologists might view ancillary fields such as the study of ancient floral and faunal remains as rather "esoteric" and remote from their view of archaeology. Far from it. These bones and seeds and remains of wood and related objects found in excavations formed the bases of the daily lives of all ancient peoples; their study, while perhaps not glamorous, provides the really interesting news of what these people and their animals ate and the often very perishable building materials they used. These are the truly "exciting" discoveries. Collectively, over years of study and quantification of such mundane "residue" of the ancient world, one can slowly form a picture of daily life for the average person, not just the nobility and royalty. For the most part, it is slow, methodical detective work which eventually forms the answers to key questions about life in antiquity and which allows us to rewrite history.

The reader will appreciate that Linda Medwid has undertaken a great deal of work to produce this very useful and informative introduction to the trailblazers in Classical archaeology, their major contributions to the field, and their most significant publications. It should become a standard reference work for Classical archaeologists and a good introduction to some of the formative pioneers in our field for interested nonspecialists.

Steven E. Sidebotham
Newark, Delaware
February 2000

INTRODUCTION

I

One might wonder how the idea for this work came about. During my early days as a graduate student I had read something of Carl Blegen's work at Korakou and wanted to learn the names of other sites that he had excavated, together with their attendant publications. I went to the reference section of the university library and discovered that beyond Blegen's works which were actually part of the library's holdings, there was no reference in which to find a more complete list of his major excavations and publications. My next move was to research the scholarly journals. Surely, I thought, I would find a detailed obituary which would encapsulate Professor Blegen's career and which would include at least some reference to the information that I needed. I went to the *American Journal of Archaeology*, but in light of the fact that it has only issued fifty-year indexes and one has not been brought out since the approximate date of Professor Blegen's death, the first problem I came up against was "When, exactly, did Professor Blegen die?" I was able to find the year of his death from the library's data entry listing for one of his works, but when I started looking through back issues of the *AJA* I was again disappointed (and somewhat astounded) to find that no obituary on Carl W. Blegen had ever appeared in the *Journal*. I have since discovered that necrologies in journals are often "spotty." It may take up to three or four years for an obituary to appear in a scholarly journal and then, as in the case of Professor Blegen (for whatever reasons), one may not appear at all. Obituaries are also uneven in the information that they provide. Some are written by close friends of the deceased, often dwelling on personal reminiscences, and may not provide substantive information on his or her contributions and publications. And finally, obituaries are often not listed in the annual indexes of scholarly journals though they may in fact have appeared.

In short then, there was no quick reference source that I could go to in order to look up the contributions of Carl Blegen, or any other significant figure in Classical archaeology. While there are several very useful reference type publications which deal with the archaeological history of sites (e.g., the Noyes Press series of publications by Doris Leekley [with coauthors] and Richard Stillwell's *Princeton Encyclopedia of Classical Sites*), the focus of these works is on the sites themselves; none includes archaeologists' names in its index or detailed lists of major publications. In addition, the Stillwell publication does not concern itself with prehistoric sites.

Other available sources of information on contributors to Classical archaeology are narrative works on the history of the field. It would seem that archaeology has reached a plateau; after the major developments of the early part of the twentieth century and those of the last thirty years, archaeology is beginning to reflect upon its past. As a result, a fairly large number of publications on the history of archaeology have appeared (e.g., Glyn Daniel's *A Hundred and Fifty Years of Archaeology* [1975, 2d. ed.], William H. Stiebing Jr.'s *Uncovering the Past* [1993], and Lesley J. Fitton's *Discovery of the Greek Bronze Age* [1995]); but while these are informative, they are necessarily general in their approach, major figures are consequently often given only a few lines of consideration if any at all, and the titles of publications are usually not provided. Another problem with these histories is that if one wishes to research the contributions of someone from a closely related field, for example, J. D. Beazley, one would be likely to find no reference to him at all, a fact which necessarily leaves large gaps in the total picture, though it makes sense from the point of view of a history of archaeology per se.

Recently a new publication appeared which at first sight seems to fill the very gap in Classical archaeological scholarship that I have been discussing. This is Nancy Thomson de Grummond's *Encyclopedia of the History of Classical Archaeology* (*EHCA*), which was published in 1996.

While the *EHCA* is indeed useful in obtaining general

information about archaeological sites, artists, and scholars, it is uneven in the breadth of information it gives on any two topics (it has 171 contributors), and in most cases is typical of an encyclopedia in that it is synoptic and does not deal in specifics. The entries do not for the most part deal with past (and present) issues in Classical archaeology; for example, there is no discussion of how particular problems of chronology, archaeological method, technique, and so forth, were ever developed and/or reconciled.

In the present compendium, the researcher is made aware of the developmental process, or the unfolding of Classical archaeology: one learns who influenced whom, who directly learned from whom, what information was derived from what sources to contribute to new hypotheses. One is also made aware of the ramifications of new theories. The current work serves to convey the contributions of each person by discussing his work in a "nuts and bolts" fashion, dealing with specifics and not simply providing general statements.

In addition, in the present work it is possible to look up specific subject areas in the index. For example, if one were interested in finding out who were contributors to the study of aqueducts, domestic architecture, or even to a more obscure topic such as *ostraka*, one can do so; this is not possible in the *EHCA*, as it provides only a proper name index. A last point: entries in *EHCA* often do not include more than a few of the publications of the scholar being discussed and usually provide a similar number of references in the bibliographies.

In view of the foregoing, it seems that a reference work of the present sort, confined to Classical archaeology and to individual contributors to the field, is sorely needed not only to provide a ready reference to those who have made major contributions (together with a comprehensive list of their most significant publications) but also to stand as a testament to the achievements of these great men and women whose work has enabled us to form the picture of ancient Greek and Roman civilization that we have before us today.

II

There are a number of basic problems in preparing a work of this sort, such as the question of whom to include and whom to leave out. How does one establish a set of criteria for inclusion? What should be the historic parameters of such a work? Which fields of study should be included? Scholars who cannot be considered to have been archaeologists proper have nonetheless made significant contributions to Classical archaeology; but which should be considered under the general heading of "Classical Archaeology?"

In determining whom to include, one basic question was asked: "Did this person, through his or her work in Classical archaeology, make what could be considered a significant contribution to our understanding of ancient Greek and Roman civilization?" Throughout the work a special effort has been made to give a sense of the state of Classical scholarship at the time of a specific individual's appearance and to show how that person's work succeeded in deepening our knowledge and understanding of the Classical world. Each individual discussed in this work was instrumental in changing our awareness, attitude, or knowledge of the Classical world in some important way. In the end such a determination is necessarily subjective; there will be those who feel that some very important contributors have been neglected while others less important have been included. Nonetheless, this work provides the reader with information on those individuals who stand out as being among the relatively few who have succeeded in making significant contributions to the field.

Regarding the historic parameters covered in the work, it will be seen that individuals from as early as the late sixteenth century through the 1990s are discussed. It is believed that persons who were instrumental in the development of antiquarian studies in seventeenth- and eighteenth-century Europe were as important to the progress of our knowledge of the Classical world as are their more contemporary colleagues. For example, the vast numbers of Classical figures (especially Greek sculpture) acquired by Thomas Howard, second earl of Arundel (1585–1646), represented one of the earliest collections of large Classical sculpture to appear in Britain. This collection served as a catalyst in the formation of societies which concentrated on the serious study of Greek and Roman antiquities; one such organization which formed in London as a direct result of Arundel's collection was the important and influential Society of Dilettanti which would later fund the scholarly efforts of James Stuart (1713–1788) and Nicholas Revett (1720–1804) in Athens, the travels of

William Gell (1777–1836) in Asia Minor and Greece, and a large number of other scholarly expeditions to Mediterranean lands. Thus it was considered important to include these earlier figures, as these individuals provided the initial interest from which later scholarship evolved.

In determining what fields of study should be considered in this work it was decided that its scope should be extended beyond the field of archaeology proper (as touched upon above). The core of the work is indeed made up of archaeologists in the pure sense of the term; that is, men and women who went out into the field and actually dug, uncovering ancient structures and artifacts and later making observations and developing theories about those discoveries. While it is true that archaeologists have provided the largest pieces of the jigsaw puzzle that make up our picture of the civilizations of ancient Greece and Rome, it is also true that large gaps in that puzzle have been filled in by scholars from related disciplines; individuals who may not have actually toiled for long hours under burning Mediterranean skies, but who have studied the artifacts procured by archaeologists and who have advanced our knowledge in great measure. It is important that these contributors not be forgotten, and the present work strives to acknowledge Classical archaeology's debt to all those who have contributed significantly to the field, including the work of art historians, numismatists, epigraphers, and cultural theorists, among others.

III

The term "Classical" archaeology is here used in its broadest sense to include the study of all Greek and Roman history, from the earliest phases of the prehistoric period to the Late Roman Empire. No geographical constraints were placed on the subject matter; all names included in this work contributed significantly to our knowledge of ancient Greek and Roman civilization, whether they were concerned with the civilizations of Magna Graecia, the Greek mainland, the Hellenistic East, or Roman Britain.

Because of the difficulty involved in obtaining information about the careers and publications of foreign-born archaeologists, an effort has been made to ensure that individuals from countries in addition to the United States and Great Britain be represented; these include scholars from Greece, Italy, Germany, France, Sweden, Russia, and Australia.

Each entry provides the full name of the individual, together with dates and places of birth and death. This is followed by information on education, professional appointments and awards; a list of excavation sites and dates (when available) is provided if appropriate. The largest part of the entry is devoted to listing the individual's most significant publications and to providing an account of his unique contribution/s to the field of Classical archaeology; again, special attention is given to evoke the historical/archaeological context in which the person lived so that the reader can gain a greater appreciation of his work. Anecdotal information has been kept to a minimum and extra effort has been made to provide the reader with information which deals specifically with archaeologically related matters. Lastly, a list of sources is provided from which additional information may be obtained. The format for the abbreviations in this section follow that set out by the Archaeological Institute of America in the *American Journal of Archaeology* 95 (1991): 1–16.

A proper name and subject index is provided at the end of the work and has a number of uses: if one wished to research the major publications of an author, one could do so by looking up the name either in the index or the contents page; if one were interested in learning about those who have contributed to the field of Cycladic archaeology, one would simply look up the term "Cycladic" in the index for the appropriate references; if one wished to find out more about a particular archaeological site one would locate the name of the site in the index to find all references to it which appear in the text (including the major figures who had dug there, together with a summary of their work and relevant publications on the site). In addition, all individuals who have entries devoted to them are printed in full capitals if they appear under another entry. For example, in Adolf Furtwängler's entry, it is said that his work later provided the foundation for the work of Carl W. Blegen. This reference to Blegen would appear as CARL W. BLEGEN in the text under Furtwängler, so that the reader would be alerted to the fact that there is a separate entry on Blegen to which he or she can readily refer by going to the contents page.

IV

This work is designed to be used as a reference tool by teachers and students of Classical archaeology as well as by scholars from other areas of Classical studies. It is hoped that it will also serve as a useful reference for those with interests that range further afield. Some of the problems experienced during our unfolding of the history of ancient Greece and Rome have been long and involved, and it has been impossible (as well as undesirable) not to discuss some of these at length and in archaeological terminology. A short glossary has been provided to assist readers who are less familiar with terms such as Helladic, Dorian invasion, Linear A, and so on.

In addition to providing a ready reference to the careers and accomplishments of contributors to the field of Classical archaeology, a primary goal of this work has been to elicit a sense of the often painfully slow progress made in this field, particularly prior to the end of the first quarter of the twentieth century. In archaeology courses students come to know the names and contributions of the "giants" such as Heinrich Schliemann, Arthur Evans, Carl W. Blegen, and individuals of the calibre of Michael Ventris. However, what they often fail to gain is a sense of (and thereby an appreciation of) the very slow and often piecemeal way in which our current knowledge was acquired. This knowledge is not simply the product of the work of the few "giants" in the field, but represents the fruit of many individuals' efforts—people like Sir William Hamilton (1730–1803), who initiated the production of the first catalog of Greek vases and so gave birth to the serious study of these ancient artifacts; Adolf Furtwängler (1853–1907), who first recognized that the chronology of a site could be ascertained through the careful study of the patterns found on pottery sherds; and individuals like Esther Boise Van Deman (1862–1937), who was a pioneer in the study of Roman brick and concrete construction and upon whose work our current dating of Roman buildings in Italy rests. Our knowledge of the Classical civilizations of Greece and Rome did not progress in leaps and bounds brought about by the chance discoveries of a select few; the achievements of the "giants" in the field rested squarely on the foundations provided by those major contributors who came before them. It is hoped that this compendium will provide a testament to those whose work has contributed most to our knowledge in the field of Classical archaeology.

MANOLIS ANDRONIKOS

b: October 1919.¹ Prousa (modern Bursa), Turkey.
d: March 30, 1992. Thessaloniki, Greece.

EDUCATION

Aristotelian Univ. of Thessaloniki, 1952 (Ph.D.).
Oxford Univ., 1954–56.

APPOINTMENTS AND AWARDS

Greek Archaeological Service; Univ. of Thessaloniki: Lecturer (1957–64), Professor (beg. 1964). Member: German Archaeological Institute; Society for the Promotion of Hellenic Studies; Archaeological Society of Athens. Hon. Foreign Member: Archaeological Institute of America. Awards: Olympia Prize (Onassis Foundation); Grand Phoenix Cross (Greece).

EXCAVATIONS

Veroia; Naousa; Kilkis; Dion; Thessaloniki; Vergina (early Iron Age tumulus, 1952–61 with Ph. Petsas), "great tumulus" beg. 1976 (Director).

PUBLICATIONS

Vergina, The Prehistoric Necropolis and the Hellenistic Palace, Lund: C. Bloms Boktryckeri, 1964; Βεργίνα I: Τὸ νεκροταφεῖον τῶν τύμβων, 1969; *Vergina: The Royal Tombs and the City,* Athens: Ekdotike Athenon, 1984.

Manolis Andronikos excavated in the area of Vergina for forty years. His discovery (1977–78) of three "royal" tombs

21

supported his idea that the ancient Macedonian capital of Aegae occupied present-day Vergina and not Edessa as some had thought. Andronikos proposed that Tomb II at Vergina was the final resting place of Philip II, father of Alexander the Great. Among the other important finds at Vergina were the first complete wall paintings of the Hellenistic period. Andronikos also made a major contribution to our understanding of the Iron Age chronology of Macedonia in his 1969 publication (listed above).

SOURCES

Eugene N. Borza, "Manolis Andronikos, 1919–1992," *AJA* 96 (1992): 757–758; Leekley and Efstratiou, *AECNG*, 1980; Stillwell, *PECS*, 1976; *NYT* (March 31, 1992).

NOTE

1. There would appear to be no record of Professor Andronikos's exact date of birth due to the difficult political climate in Prousa (present-day Bursa, Turkey) in 1919.

J(OHN) LAWRENCE ANGEL

b: March 21, 1915. London, England.
d: November 3, 1986. Washington, D.C.

EDUCATION

Choate School (Connecticut).
Harvard Univ., 1936 (A.B.), 1942 (Ph.D.).

APPOINTMENTS AND AWARDS

Univ. of California, Berkeley: Instructor (1941–42); Univ. of
Minnesota: Asst. Prof. (1942–43); Thomas Jefferson Medical
College: Faculty Member (1942–62), Prof. of Anatomy and
Physical Anthropology (1962); U.S. Naval Hospital: Con-
sulting Surgeon of Anatomy (1953–62); Smithsonian Institute,
National Museum of Natural History: Curator, Physical
Anthropology (beg. 1962); Consulting Forensic Anthropologist:
F.B.I., U.S. Army, U.S. Air Force, U.S. Navy, Washington, D.C.
Police Dept. (beg. 1962); American Board of Forensic Anthro-
pology, President (1980–85). Award: Pomerance Medal,
Archaeological Institute of America (1983).

PUBLICATIONS

"A Racial Analysis of the Ancient Greeks," *AJPA* n.s., 2,
No. 4 (1944); "Skeletal Material from Attica," *Hesperia* 14
(1945): 279–363; "Social biology of Greek culture growth,"
AmAnth n.s., 48 (1946): 493–533; *Troy: the Human Remains*,
Supplemental monograph to: C.W. BLEGEN (editor) *Troy
Excavations Conducted by the University of Cincinnati, 1932–1938*,
Princeton, N.J.: Princeton University Press, 1950–58; "The
basis of paleodemography," *AJPA* 30 (1969): 427–37; "Pale-

odemography and evolution," *AJPA* 31 (1969) 343–53; *The People of Lerna: Analysis of a Prehistoric Aegean Population*, Princeton, N.J.: American School of Classical Studies at Athens, 1971; "Health as a crucial factor in the changes from hunting to developed farming in the Eastern Mediterranean," in M. Cohen and G. Armelogos, eds., *Paleopathology at the Origins of Agriculture*, Vol. 3, New York: Academic Press, 1984.

J. Lawrence Angel was a physical and forensic anthropologist who was an expert in Classical anthropology and well known for having produced pioneering demographic studies on the ancient populations of Greece, Cyprus, and Turkey. By comparing genetic variations in human skeletal remains with archaeological data he was able to confirm established theories (as well as to propose new hypotheses) with regard to the prehistoric populations of these areas.

Angel moved from Britain to America at the age of thirteen and derived his interest in the Classics from his mother who exposed him at an early age to ancient Greek art and literature.

While earning his doctorate at Harvard University, his interests became focused upon skeletal anatomy and Classical anthropology (he did not become involved in forensic anthropology until the early 1960s). His doctoral studies included visits to Greece and Turkey, and he was to make a total of eleven visits to the Mediterranean area during his career, examining and photographing hundreds of skeletal remains in order to determine their age, sex, race, diet, injuries, and diseases. His greater objective was to study the complex relationships between culture and biology over a long period of time with special interest in the role of health and disease as major determining factors in human microevolution.

Angel's historical interests were not confined to the Mediterranean area; he carried out a number of examinations of human remains in America dating to the Colonial period, and was consulted for his forensic expertise in a large number of murder investigations.

SOURCES

Ubelaker and Scammell, *Bones: A Forensic Detective's Casebook*, 1992; Winters, general editor, *International Dictionary of Anthropologists*, 1991; Grmek, *Diseases in the Ancient Greek*

World, 1989; *WWWA* 1985–1989, Vol. 9: 11; Don Brothwell, *AJA* 76 (1922): 333–334; *NYT* (November 5, 1986); *WP* (November 5, 1986).

THOMAS ASHBY

b: October 14, 1874. Staines, England.
d: May 15, 1931. London, England.

EDUCATION

Winchester School, 1893.
Christ Church, Oxford, 1895 (Mods.), 1897 (Lit. Hum.).

APPOINTMENTS AND AWARDS

Craven Travelling Fellow (1897); British School at Rome: Assistant Director (1903–06), Director (1906–25); Archaeological Institute of America: Norton-Loeb Lecturer (1926); Christ Church, Oxford Univ.: Research Student (1930–31). Fellow: Society of Antiquaries (1901); British Academy (1927). Hon. Associate: Royal Institute of British Architects (1922). Member: German Archaeological Institute (1913); Pontifical Roman Academy of Archaeology (1914).

EXCAVATIONS

Caerwent, Wales (1899–1910); Malta and Gozo, 1908–1911; Italy (topographical surveys).

PUBLICATIONS

Excavation reports on Caerwent can be found in *Archaeologia* vols.: 57 (1901), 58 (1903), 59 (1905), 60 (1907), 61 (1909), 62 (1911); *Forty Drawings of Roman Scenes by British Artists*, 1911 (text); *Turner's Visions of Rome*, London: Halton and T. Smith, Ltd., 1925; *Spiers's and Anderson's The Architecture of Greece and Rome* (Vol. 2, *The Architecture of Ancient Rome*),

(1927), Freeport, N.Y.: Books for Libraries Press, 1971; *The Roman Campagna in Classical Times* (1927), Westport, Conn.: Greenwood Press, 1971; *Some Italian Scenes and Festivals*, London: Methuen and Co., Ltd., 1929; *Rome, the Eternal City*, 1929; *Topographical Dictionary of Ancient Rome*, Oxford: Oxford University Press, 1929 (Revision of S. B. Platner's work); *Aqueducts of Ancient Rome*, Oxford: The Clarendon Press, 1935 (edited by I. A. Richmond, published posthumously).

Thomas Ashby was introduced to the city of Rome as a child when his family moved there in 1890 (his father was to become a close friend of RODOLPHO LANCIANI). At Oxford one of Ashby's tutors was J. L. MYRES. From the very beginning of his studies Ashby concentrated on the subject of Roman topography.

Ashby was the first student of the British School at Rome (then known as the British School of Archaeology, History and Letters of Rome) which opened in 1901. He was made director in 1906 and was its first director after its incorporation in 1912. As such he was largely responsible for its early development and direction.

After leaving the British School in 1925 Ashby produced a number of major publications. A work on the topography of Rome had been planned as a joint project with S. B. Platner, but due to World War One Platner had almost completed it alone. While on a journey to meet with Ashby to discuss further collaboration, Platner died and the manuscript was then given to Ashby for completion.

Another major accomplishment was Ashby's work on the Roman Campagna (above). This book summarizes more detailed discussions that he had published earlier in various journals (see *PBA* 17 [1931]: 533 for specific topics and publications) and is primarily concerned with the ancient roads that ran through the Campagna region. It is still considered a standard work on the subject.

In addition to his work in Italy, Ashby carried out important and lengthy excavations of the Roman town of Venta Silurum (present-day Caerwent) in southeast Wales. This site comprised a walled town of some fifty acres; excavations revealed a forum, temples, an amphitheater, a basilica, and domestic architecture.

Ashby was greatly interested in sixteenth- and seventeenth-century illustrations of Rome and produced several publications on this and related topics.

SOURCES

A. J. Sayce, "Thomas Ashby (1874–1931)," *PBA* 17 (1931): 515–541; Ian A. Richmond, *DNB*, 1931–1940; *WWW*, 1929–1940; *TL* (May 18, 1931), (May 20, 1931), (May 21, 1931), (May 23, 1931).

BERNARD ASHMOLE

b: June 22, 1894. Ilford, England.
d: February 25, 1988. Peebles, Scotland.

EDUCATION

Hertford College, Oxford Univ., 1923 (B. Litt.).

APPOINTMENTS AND AWARDS

Oxford Univ.: Craven Scholarship (1920); Ashmolean Museum, Oxford: Asst. Curator of Coins (1923); British School at Rome: Director (1925–28); Univ. of London: Yates Professor of Archaeology (1928–48); British Museum: Keeper, Greek and Roman Department (1939–56); Oxford Univ.: Lincoln Professor of Classical Archaeology and Art (1956–61); Univ. of Aberdeen: Geddes-Harrower Professor of Greek Art and Archaeology (1961–63); Yale Univ.: Visiting Professor (1964). Hon. Member: Archaeological Institute of America (1940). Fellow: King's College, London. Hon. Fellow: Hertford and Lincoln Colleges, Oxford, and University College, London; Archaeological Society of Athens (1978). Hon. Degree: LL.D., Univ. of Aberdeen. Awards: C.B.E. (Commander of the British Empire, 1957); Kenyon Medal, British Academy (1979).

PUBLICATIONS

"Locri Epizephyrii and the Ludovisi Throne," *JHS*, 1922; "Hygieia on the Acropolis and Palatine," *BSR* 10 (1927); *Catalogue of the Ancient Sculptures at Ince Blundell*, Oxford: The Clarendon Press, 1929; *Greek Sculpture and Painting to the End of the Hellenistic Period* (with J. D. BEAZLEY), Cambridge:

Cambridge University Press (1932), 1966; "Late Archaic and Early Classical Greek Sculpture in Sicily and South Italy," *PBA* 20, 1934; *Forgeries of Ancient Sculpture: Creation and Detection*, Oxford: Blackwell, 1962; *The Classical Ideal in Greek Sculpture*, Cincinnati: University of Cincinnati Press, 1964; *Art of the Ancient World* (with H. Groenewegen-Frankfort), New York: New American Library, 1967; *Olympia: The Sculptures of the Temple of Zeus* (with N. Yalouris and A. Frantz), London: Phaidon Press, 1967.

Bernard Ashmole's[1] contribution to the field of archaeology lay in his expertise in Greek sculpture (especially archaic) and in his ability as a teacher. He was a keen observer of sculptural technique and because of this was often consulted to verify the authenticity of various pieces of ancient Greek art. He wrote several important articles in this regard (some listed above) and was one of the main advisors to J. Paul Getty when the latter was putting together the collection now housed in the Getty Museum in Malibu, California.

He was a widely respected teacher and presented a number of lecture series including the Rhind Lectures (1957), the J. L. Myres Memorial Lecture at Oxford (1961), the Louise Taft Semple Lectures (1964), and the Wrightsman Lectures (1967).

Ashmole was a skilled photographer whose talent was employed by his friend RHYS CARPENTER to illustrate the latter's *The Sculpture of the Nike Temple Parapet* published in 1929.

His professors at Oxford included PERCY GARDNER and J. D. BEAZLEY.

SOURCES

John Boardman, "Bernard Ashmole, 1894–1988," *AJA* 93 (1989): 135–136; Martin Robertson, "Bernard Ashmole 1894–1988," *PBA* 75 (1989): 313–328; *TL* (February 26, 1988).

NOTE

1. Ashmole was indirectly descended from Elias Ashmole, the founder of the Ashmolean Museum at Oxford University.

(SIR) J(OHN) D(AVIDSON) BEAZLEY

b: September 13, 1885. Glasgow, Scotland.
d: May 6, 1970. Oxford, England.

EDUCATION

Balliol College, Oxford University, 1905.

APPOINTMENTS AND AWARDS

Christ Church, Oxford: Lecturer (1907), Student and Tutor, (1908–25); Oxford: Lincoln and Merton Professor of Classical Archaeology (1925–56); Univ. of California, Berkeley: Sather Professor (1949). Fellow: British Academy (1927). Hon. Fellow: Balliol and Lincoln Colleges, Oxford Univ.; Metropolitan Museum of Art, New York. Hon. Student: Christ Church, Oxford Univ.; Hon. Student of the British School at Athens. Hon. Degrees: D.Litt, Lincoln College, Oxford Univ. (1956); other hon. degrees conferred by the universities of Cambridge, Glasgow, Durham, Reading, Paris, Lyons, Thessaloniki, and Marburg. Award: Kenyon Medal, British Academy (1957).

PUBLICATIONS

Herodotus at the Zoo (1907), 1911, 1968; *Attic Red-Figured Vases in American Museums*, Cambridge, Mass.: Harvard University Press, 1918; *The Lewes House Collection of Ancient Gems*, Oxford: The Clarendon Press, 1920; *Attische Vasenmaler des rotfigurigen Stils*, Tübingen: Mohr, 1925; *Corpus Vasorum Antiquorum, Oxford* 1–2, Oxford: The Clarendon Press, 1927–31 (Vol. 2 with HUMFRY PAYNE); *Greek Vases in Poland*, Oxford: The Clarendon Press, 1928; *Der Berliner Maler* (1930), Mainz: Verlag P. von Zabern, 1974; *Der Pan-Maler* (1931),

31

Mainz: Verlag P. von Zabern, rev. ed. 1944, reprinted 1974; *Attic Vase-Paintings in the Museum of Fine Arts*, (Part 1, with L. D. Caskey; Part 2, Part 3) Oxford: Oxford University Press, 1931, 1954, 1963; *Greek Sculpture and Painting to the End of the Hellenistic Period* (with BERNARD ASHMOLE), Cambridge: Cambridge University Press, 1932; *Der Kleophrades-Maler* (1933), Mainz: Verlag P. von Zabern, rev. ed. 1944, reprinted 1948 ; *Campana Fragments in Florence*, Oxford: Oxford University Press, 1933; *Attic White Lekythoi*, Oxford: Oxford University Press, 1938; *Attic Red-Figure Vase-Painters*, Oxford: The Clarendon Press, 1942, 2d. ed. 1963; *Potter and Painter in Ancient Athens*, London: G. Cumberledge, 1944; *Etruscan Vase-Painting* (1947), New York: Hacker Art Books, 1976; *The Development of Attic Black-Figure*, 1951 (Sather Lectures), University of California Press, rev. ed. 1986; *Attic Black-Figure Vase-Painters* (1956), New York: Hacker Art Books, 1978; *The Berlin Painter*, Mainz: Verlag P. von Zabern (1965), reprinted 1974; *Paralipomena: Additions to Attic Black-Figure Vase-Painters and to Attic Red-Figure Vase-Painters*, Oxford: The Clarendon Press, 1971 (posthumously published with help of D. von Bothmer and M. Robertson).

J. D. Beazley is universally recognized as a major figure in Classical scholarship for having revolutionized the study of Greek vase-painting. His monumental treatises in which individual painters of Greek vases are identified for the first time are based upon observations of style. Through the close study of commonly occurring physical details such as ears, eyes, and hands, decorative details such as borders, and to a lesser extent vase shapes, he was able initially to identify from ten thousand vases the styles of one hundred fifty individuals of the red-figure technique (1925, above). This was expanded upon in his 1942 publication to four hundred fifty painters and in its second, enlarged edition, to seven hundred named painters. Unlike his predecessors Beazley was not content to study only the masters of the field but concentrated on less gifted artists as well, thereby broadening our knowledge of vase-painting in general.

Beazley's methodology was greatly influenced by the work of Giovanni Morelli who studied the various styles of ears, eyes, and hands in order to identify specific Italian painters, and it was Beazley himself who credited the pioneering work done by ADOLF FURTWÅNGLER who had previously established a systematic approach to the study of ancient vase painting.

Among his students were HUMFRY PAYNE, BERNARD ASHMOLE, T. J. Dunbabin and Dietrich von Bothmer. Beazley was knighted in 1949.

SOURCES

Bernard Ashmole, "Sir John Beazley, 1885–1970," *PBA* 56 (1970): 443–461; Martin Robertson, *DNB* 1961–1970; *WWW* 1961–1970; *TL* (May 7, 1970).

J(AMES) THEODORE BENT

b: March 30, 1852. Baildon House, Near Leeds, England.
d: May 5, 1897. London, England.

EDUCATION

Repton School, England.
Wadham College, Oxford University, 1875 (B.A.).

PUBLICATIONS

A Freak of Freedom, or the Republic of San Marino (1879), New York: Kennikat Press, 1970; *Genoa: How the Republic Rose and Fell*, London: C. K. Paul and Co., 1881; *Life of Giuseppe Garibaldi*, London: Longmans, Green, and Co. (1881), reprinted 1882; "Researches among the Cyclades," *JHS* 5 (1884): 42–59; *The Cyclades, or Life among the Insular Greeks* (1885), Chicago: Argonaut, 1966; "What St. John saw on Patmos," *The Nineteenth Century* 24 (1888): 813–821; "Explorations in Cilicia Tracheia," *Journal of the Royal Geographic Society* 8 (1890): 445–463; *The Ruined Cities of Mashonaland* (1892), Freeport, N.Y.: Books for Libraries Press, 1971; *The Sacred City of the Ethiopians* (1893), Michigan: Scholarly Press, 1971; *Early Voyages and Travels in the Levant, with an Introduction giving a History of the Levant Company of Turkey Merchants* (editor) (1893), New York: B. Franklin, 1964; "The Hadramut: a journey in southern Arabia," *The Nineteenth Century* 36 (1894): 419–437; *Southern Arabia, Soudan and Sakotra* (1900, posthumously published by Mrs. Theodore Bent), Reading, U.K.: Garnet Publishers, 1994.

Bent was the first archaeologist active in the Cycladic Islands. In light of the fact that this area in general does not possess the finer ruins of the Greek mainland there has been relatively little archaeological investigation of it; indeed, there was very little interest even in antiquity. Consequently, Bent's major publication (1885, above) still provides one of the best detailed references to the area, its people, and its ruins.

Bent spent three years traveling throughout the Greek Islands studying the local people, their customs, and traditions; he also carried out a substantial amount of excavation work including the copying of ancient inscriptions. He was a meticulous excavator for his day, taking careful measurements of where artifacts were found and making detailed drawings of the sites and excavations.

He also traveled to the coast of Asia Minor (visiting Cilicia) and in 1889 visited the Bahrein Islands (the Persian Gulf) where he did more excavation work believing that here he had located an ancient Phoenician site. He then heard of some remarkable archaeological remains at Zimbabwe in Africa and in 1891 went there to carry out a thorough study of the region, eventually erroneously concluding that these ruins were related to the Phoenician site he had previously excavated in the Bahrein area (see RANDALL-MACIVER).

He next set off for Abyssinia in search of more "Phoenician" ruins and then spent the remainder of his life exploring the southern Arabian peninsula. His wife, Mabel, accompanied him on all of his travels and took all photographs.

From his excursions in the Greek Islands Bent brought back a great number of Cycladic grave goods including many Cycladic "idols" which were purchased by the British Museum and today form a large part of that institution's Cycladic collection.

SOURCES

Bent, *Aegean Islands: The Cyclades, or Life among the Insular Greeks* (new and enlarged edition, edited by Oikonomides), 1966; *DNB*, Vol. 22 Supplement; Weber, *Voyages and Travels . . .* , 1952; Barber, *The Cyclades in the Bronze Age*, 1987.

MARGARETE BIEBER

b: July 31, 1879.
Schoenau, West Prussia (present-day Poland).
d: February 25, 1978. New Canaan, Connecticut.

EDUCATION

Berlin University, 1904.
Bonn University, 1907 (Ph.D.).

APPOINTMENTS AND AWARDS

Dept. of Archaeology, Justus-Lieg Univ., Giessen (Germany): Lecturer (1919–32), Associate Professor and Director (1932–33); Sommerville College, Oxford (1933); Barnard College (1934); Columbia University (1935–48). Member: American Academy of Arts and Sciences.

PUBLICATIONS

Das Dresdener Schauspielerrief, Bonn: F. Cohen, 1907; *Die antiken Skulpturen und Bronzen des Konigl*, Marburg: N. G. Elwertsche Verlag, 1915; *Die Denkmäler zum Theaterwesen im Altertum*, Berlin and Liepzig: Vereinigung wissenschaftlicher verleger, 1920; *Griechische Kleidung*, Berlin and Liepzig: Walter de Gruyter and Co., 1928; *Entwicklungsgeschichte der griechischen Tracht* (1934), Berlin: Mann, 1966; *The History of the Greek and Roman Theater* (1939), 2d. ed. Princeton, N.J.: Princeton University Press, 1961; *Laocoön: The Influence of the Group since Its Rediscovery* (1942), 2d. ed. Detroit: Wayne State University Press, 1966; *German Readings in the History and Theory of Fine Arts*, Ann Arbor, Mich.: Edwards Bros., 1946; *The Sculpture of the Hellenistic Age*, New York: Columbia University Press (1955), rev. ed. 1961; *German Readings: A Survey of Greek and*

Roman Art (1958), 1968; *The Greek and Roman Portraits of Alexander the Great*, Chicago: Argonaut, 1964; *The Statue of Cybele in the J. Paul Getty Museum*, 1968; *Graeco-Roman Copies*, 1973; *Copies of Greek and Roman Art*, 1975; *The History of Greek, Etruscan and Roman Clothing*, 1975; *Ancient Copies: Contributions to the History of Greek and Roman Art*, New York: New York University Press, 1977.

Born the second of four children to a West Prussian industrialist, Margarete Bieber was the first female to attend the Helene Lange Gymnasium in Berlin. She went on to become one of the few women studying at the University of Berlin and later the University of Bonn. After leaving Nazi Germany in 1933 she went to England and a year later moved to the United States.

She authored definitive works in four areas of study: the Greek and Roman theater, Hellenistic sculpture, ancient dress, and Roman copies of Greek art. Her lifetime interest in the latter culminated in her last publication, *Ancient Copies . . .* (1977, above) in which she emphasized that Roman reproductions of Greek originals were essentially Roman works and carried the stamp of that civilization.

In addition to the major works listed above Bieber contributed more than three hundred articles to various professional journals. In 1974 she was awarded the Gold Medal for Distinguished Archaeological Achievement by the Archaeological Institute of America.

SOURCES

James B. Pritchard, *Archaeology* (April, 1975): 74–75; *CA* 19–20R; *CANRS*, Vol. 2; *DAS*, Vol. 1, 1974; *NYT* (May 22, 1971), (February 28, 1978); *IWWE*, 1975.

CARL W(ILLIAM) BLEGEN

b: January 27, 1887. Minneapolis, Minnesota.
d: August 24, 1971. Athens, Greece.

EDUCATION

Augsburg Seminary, 1904 (B.A.).
University of Minnesota, 1907 (B.A.).
Yale University, 1908 (B.A.), 1920 (Ph.D.).
American School of Classical Studies at Athens, 1910–13.

APPOINTMENTS AND AWARDS

Univ. of Cincinnati: Professor of Archaeology (1927–50), Chairman, Department of Classics (1950–57), Professor Emeritus (beg. 1957); American School of Classical Studies at Athens [ASCSA]: Secretary (1913–20), Assistant Director (1920–26), Acting Director (1926–27), Director (1948–49). Hon. degrees: Universities of Oslo (1951), Oxford (1957), Cincinnati (1958), Athens (1963), Cambridge (1963), and Hebrew Union College (1963). Fellow: American Academy of Arts and Sciences. Corresponding Fellow: British Academy. Member: American Philosophical Society (1941). Hon. Member: Archaeological Society of Athens; Norwegian Academy; Swedish Royal Academy; Society for the Promotion of Hellenic Studies. Award: Gold Medal, Archaeological Institute of America (1965).

EXCAVATIONS

Corinth; Locris; Korakou, 1915–16; Colophon, Asia Minor; Mycenae, 1920–23 (with A. J. B. WACE); Zygouries, 1921–22; Nemea, 1924–27; Phlius, 1924; Prosymna, 1925–28; Troy, 1932–38; Epano Englianos (Pylos), 1939–52.

PUBLICATIONS

"The Pre-Mycenaean Pottery of the Mainland," (with A. J. B. WACE) *BSA* 22 (1916–18): 175–189; *Korakou: A Prehistoric Settlement near Corinth*, Boston, New York: American School of Classical Studies at Athens, 1921; *Zygouries: A Prehistoric Settlement in the Valley of Cleonae*, Cambridge, Mass.: Harvard University Press, 1928; "The Coming of the Greeks, II, The Geographical Distribution of Prehistoric Remains in Greece," (with J. B. Haley) *AJA* 32 (1928): 146–154; *Acrocorinth* (with R. STILLWELL, et al.), 1930; *Prosymna: The Helladic Settlement* (with Elizabeth Pierce Blegen), Cambridge: Cambridge University Press, 1937; *The Mycenaean Age: The Trojan War, the Dorian Invasion, and Other Problems*, Cincinnati: University of Cincinnati, 1962; *Troy: Excavations Conducted by the University of Cincinnati, 1932–1938* (with collaboration of J. L. CASKEY and Marion Rawson), Volumes 1–4, Princeton, N.J.: Princeton University Press, 1950–58; *Troy and the Trojans*, New York: Praeger, 1963; *The Palace of Nestor*, Volumes 1–3, Princeton, N.J.: Princeton University Press, 1966–73.

Carl W. Blegen is regarded as one of the foremost American archaeologists, and his discovery of hundreds of Linear B tablets on the Greek mainland helped rewrite the history of prehistoric Greece.

At the American School of Classical Studies at Athens Blegen came under the influence of its then director, BERT HODGE HILL. It was Hill who was largely responsible for introducing the young Blegen to the latest excavation techniques and for teaching him a scientific approach which was not widely practiced at that time.

Blegen carried out his first archaeological fieldwork at Locris and Corinth and soon focused his attention on the relatively little known subject of pre-Classical mainland Greece. This area of study has been opened up by the work of HEINRICH SCHLIEMANN, and a context for the chronology of the Bronze Age Aegean had been set by Sir ARTHUR EVANS'S division of the Bronze Age on Crete into Early, Middle and Late Minoan; yet little work had been done to establish a time frame for the Greek mainland, and it was to this subject that Blegen turned his attention when he dug at Korakou near Corinth.

Korakou was a relatively small settlement but was ideal for this study since it had been inhabited throughout the Bronze Age.

From Blegen's work at Korakou, A.J.B. WACE's earlier work in Thessaly, and from the British School's work at Phylakopi, Blegen (in collaboration with Wace) was able to establish a chronology for the Greek mainland which was termed Early, Middle, and Late Helladic (see *BSA*, 1918, above).

Blegen and Wace's findings negated Evans's theory that Mycenae was merely an outpost of Cretan civilization. Their focus on the development of mainland Greece in the Bronze Age culminated in their view that though Mycenaean culture was heavily influenced by Minoan Crete, it had already possessed a distinct character of its own which in turn shone through any Cretan attributes. In his publication on Korakou, Blegen concluded that Mycenaean pottery had, in fact, dominated the Mediterranean area by the end of the Bronze Age.

Blegen led a reexamination of the site at Troy in northwest Asia Minor which had been discovered by Schliemann in the previous century. The latter, who had initially been unscientific in his approach to the stratigraphy at the site, had later brought in the German architect WILHELM DÖRPFELD to assist him. Despite the work of Dörpfeld, Blegen felt that much of the site needed to be reexamined and a new stratigraphy, which retained Schliemann's and Dörpfeld's nine main levels but which added many subphases, was set forth in his publications on Troy (above). In addition, he identified Troy level VIIa as the Troy of Homer's *Iliad*. Dörpfeld had believed it to be level VI but Blegen found evidence that Troy VI had succumbed to an earthquake, not human attack, while Troy VIIa had been destroyed by a great conflagration.

In 1939 he began a dig at Epano Englianos in the western Peloponnese, a site which was to have enormous ramifications regarding our knowledge of the history of prehistoric Greece. On the first day of excavations a trench was dug and a large deposit of Linear B tablets uncovered—the only such tablets found at that time on the Greek mainland. This discovery would lead directly to MICHAEL VENTRIS'S decipherment of Linear B in 1952 and to the recognition that this script was an early form of Greek. These findings rewrote the history books on prehistoric Greece and subsequently led to an understanding of the development of events on Crete when Minoan civilization came to an abrupt end. Blegen's work at Epano Englianos continued, and he eventually uncovered a complete Mycenaean palace at the site which has become known as Pylos.[1]

SOURCES

J. L. Caskey, "Carl William Blegen (1887–1971)" *APSY* (1972): 121–25; Lord, *History of the American School* . . . , 1947; "Bibliography of Carl William Blegen," *Hesperia* 35 (1966): 287–294; McDonald, *The Discovery of Homeric Greece*, 1967; Leekley and Noyes, *AESG*, 1975; Fitton, *The Discovery of the Greek Bronze Age*, 1995; J. Dexter, "Troy's Trek from Fable to Fact," *Horizons* 15 (May 1986): 12–14 (Univ. of Cincinnati Alumni Assoc.); Correspondence with the Classics Library, Univ. of Cincinnati; *WWWA*; *NYT* (August 26, 1971); *TL* (August 26, 1971).

NOTE

1. Pylos was the home of Nestor in Homer's *Iliad*.

AXEL BOËTHIUS

b: July 18, 1889. Sweden.
d: May 7, 1969. Rome, Italy.

EDUCATION

University of Uppsala, 1918 (Ph.D.).

APPOINTMENTS AND AWARDS

University of Uppsala: Lecturer, Classical Archaeology and Ancient History (1919–25); Swedish Institute of Classical Studies in Rome: Director (1926–35, 1952–53, 1955–57); Univ. of Göteborg: Professor of Classical Archaeology and Ancient History (1934–55), Vice-Chancellor (1946–51). Member: American Philosophical Society (1955); British Academy. Awards: Jubilee Medal of Pompeii (1948); Gold Medal, "Cultori di Roma" (1958).

EXCAVATIONS

Mycenae, 1921–24 (under A. J. B. WACE); Ardea (Latium); San Giovenale.

PUBLICATIONS

Die Pythaïs: Studien zur Geschichte der Verbindungen zwischen Athen und Delphi, 1918 (published dissertation); *The Golden House of Nero: Some Aspects of Roman Architecture*, Ann Arbor, Mich.: University of Michigan Press, 1960 (Jerome Lectures); *Etruscan Culture, Land and People* (contributor), New York: Columbia University Press, 1962; *Etruscan and Roman Architecture*, (Part 1), Harmondsworth: Penguin

Books, 1970 (published posthumously with J. WARD-PERKINS, later published under Boëthius as *Etruscan and Early Roman Architecture* (revised by R. Ling and T. Rasmussen), New York: Penguin Books, 1978.

Axel Boëthius is considered among the foremost of Swedish archaeologists and was a leading authority on early Roman architecture. He was also an expert on the topography of the Campagna (the area lying southeast of Rome) and of the ancient city of Rome itself.

In his best known work (1970, above) he authored a detailed account of the development of Roman architecture from its roots down to the Early Roman period, focusing first on the influence of Etruscan culture and then on that of Greece and the gradual Hellenization of Roman architecture that occurred during the early Roman period of expansion.

Boëthius was the first director of the Swedish Institute in Rome and as such played a major part in its initial organization. It was during his tenure as director that he first began to acquire his vast knowledge of ancient Rome and its surrounding areas.

SOURCES

Arvid Andrén, "Axel Boëthius (1889–1969)," *APSY* (1970): 114–18; Boëthius, *Etruscan and Early Roman Architecture*, 1978; Sture Brunnsåker, "Classical Archaeology and Ancient History," *Uppsala University: 500 Years; History, Art and Philosophy*, 1976: 19–33; *TL* (May 10, 1969).

RICHARD C(ARR) BOSANQUET

b: June 7, 1871. London, England.
d: April 21, 1935. Newcastle, England.

EDUCATION

Eton School (King's Scholar).
Trinity College, Cambridge University, 1892 (B.A.), 1894.
British School at Athens, 1892–97.

APPOINTMENTS AND AWARDS

Craven Student (1895–97); British School at Athens: Assistant Director (1899), Director (1900–06); Director of Cretan Exploration Fund; University of Liverpool: Professor of Classical Archaeology (1906–20).

EXCAVATIONS

Phylakopi, 1896–99; Housesteads (Borcovicium), 1898; Praisos, Crete, 1901–02; Palaikastro, Crete, 1902–05; Laconia, 1905–06.

PUBLICATIONS

Borcovicium, 1904; "Phylakopi," *JHS*, Supplement No. 4, 1904 (contributor); "The Roman Camp at Housesteads," *Archaeologia Aeliana* 25 (1904); *The Unpublished Objects from the Palaikastro Excavations, 1902–1906* (with R. M. DAWKINS), London: Macmillan and Co., 1923.

Bosanquet spent many years in Greece first as a student and then as director of the British School at Athens. He was among the early pioneers of Mediterranean archaeology and carried out excavations at several key sites including Palaikastro on Crete. As director of the British School at Athens he oversaw the publications of the excavations at Phylakopi on the island of Melos. With its three distinct levels of occupation dating through the Early, Middle, and Late Cycladic periods, Phylakopi has proved to be one of the most important excavations ever carried out in the Cyclades. Of the exemplary work performed at this site, CARL BLEGEN commented, "(It was) the first really serious effort to understand stratification, the first really good excavation in Greece."[1]

After returning to England he focused his attention on the archaeology of Roman Britain and was regarded as an authority in this field.

SOURCES

E. S. Bosanquet, *DNB*, 1931–40; Leekley and Noyes, *AEGI*, 1975; Waterhouse, *British School at Athens*, 1986; *WWW*, 1929–40; *TL* (April 23, 1935), (April 24, 1935), (April 27, 1935).

NOTE

1. Waterhouse, *British School at Athens*, pp. 100, 104.

OSCAR (THEODORE) BRONEER

b: December 28, 1894. Bakebo, Sweden.
d: February 22, 1992. Corinth, Greece.

EDUCATION

Augustana College, Illinois, 1922 (B.A.).
University of California, Berkeley, 1923 (M.A.), 1931 (Ph.D.).

APPOINTMENTS AND AWARDS

American School of Classical Studies at Athens: Instructor, Professor of Archaeology (beg. 1927); Univ. of Chicago: Professor of Archaeology and Classical Languages and Literature (1948–60); American School of Classical Studies at Athens: Acting Director (1940–52); Princeton Institute for Advanced Study. Award: Gold Medal, Archaeological Institute of America (1969).

EXCAVATIONS

Corinth, beg. 1925; Athenian acropolis beg. 1930s; Amphipolis (joint ASCSA and French School at Athens project), 1938–41; Isthmia, 1952–60 (Director).

PUBLICATIONS

Corinth, Vol. 3: Part 1, Acrocorinth, Cambridge, Mass.: Harvard University Press, 1930; *Corinth, Vol. 4: Part 2, Terracotta Lamps*, Cambridge, Mass.: Harvard University Press, 1930; *Corinth, Vol. 10: The Odeum*, Cambridge, Mass.: Harvard University Press, 1932; *Corinth, Vol. 1: Part 4, The South Stoa and its Successors*, Cambridge, Mass.: Harvard University Press, 1954;

46

(Other excavation reports on Corinth appear in *AJA* including the years 1926, 1928, 1933, 1935); *The Lion Monument at Amphipolis*, Cambridge, Mass.: Harvard University Press, 1941; *Ancient Corinth, A Guide to the Excavations*, American School of Classical Studies at Athens, 4th. ed. 1947; "The Cyclopaean Wall on the Isthmus of Corinth and its Bearing on Late Bronze Age Chronology," *Hesperia* 35 (1966): 346–362; *Isthmia, Volume 1: Temple of Poseidon*, Princeton, N.J.: Princeton University Press, 1971, *Isthmia, Volume 2: Topography and Architecture*, Princeton, N.J.: Princeton University Press, 1973, and *Volume 3: The Lamps*, Princeton, N.J.: Princeton University Press, 1977.

Born into a farming family in Sweden, Oscar Broneer emigrated to the United States at the age of nineteen. He attended preparatory school at night and earned his B.A. degree before going on to complete graduate work at the University of California at Berkeley. His major work was carried out at Corinth, Isthmia, and on the acropolis at Athens.

Among Broneer's more spectacular discoveries during his long and accomplished career was locating the buildings on the site of the ancient panhellenic Isthmian Games. Other excavators had explored the area before him and had declared it devoid of any interest. Broneer reinvestigated the area and uncovered two stadia, a Roman shrine, and earlier monumental buildings.

During his excavations on the acropolis at Athens he was to find a crater by Exekias and the celebrated pedimental head of Herakles, and in 1938 he discovered the Mycenaean well which, from pottery finds, suggests that it was first constructed at the end of the thirteenth century B.C.E. This would support Herodotus's contention that Athens felt threatened by the possibility of a Dorian invasion from the north at this time, and Broneer's discovery suggests that the inhabitants of Athens built the well in order to maintain their water supply during the expected siege.

SOURCES

Elizabeth Gebhard, "Oscar Theodore Broneer, 1894–1992," *AJA* 96 (1992): 543–546; "The Bibliography of Oscar Theodore Broneer," *Hesperia* 43, 4 (1974): 392–400; *AJA* 74 (1970): 184 (AIA Gold Medal Award); Correspondence with the University of California, Berkeley; Lord, *History of the American School . . .* , 1947; *NYT* (February 2, 1992).

Rhys Carpenter

b: August 5, 1889. Cotuit, Massachussetts.
d: January 2, 1980. Devon, Pennsylvania.

EDUCATION

Columbia University, 1909 (B.A.), 1914 (M.A.), 1916 (Ph.D.).

Rhodes Scholar, Balliol College, Oxford University 1909–11.

American School of Classical Studies at Athens, 1912–13.

APPOINTMENTS AND AWARDS

Dept. of Classical Archaeology, Bryn Mawr College, Pennsylvania: Instructor (1913–15), Associate (1915–16), Assoc. Professor (1916–18), Professor (1918–55), Professor Emeritus (1955); American Academy at Rome: Annual Professor (1926–27); American School of Classical Studies at Athens: Director (1927–32, 1946–48); Classical School, American Academy in Rome: Professor-in-Charge (1939–40); Univ. of California: Sather Professor (1944–45); Cambridge Univ.: J. H. Gray Lectures (1965). Member: Pontifical Roman Academy of Archaeology; Greek Archaeological Society; German Archaeological Institute; American Philosophical Society. Award: Gold Medal, Archaeological Institute of America (1969).

PUBLICATIONS

The Tragedy of Etarre, New York: Sturgis and Walton, 1912; *The Sun Thief and other Poems*, Oxford: Oxford University Press, 1920; *The Aesthetic Basis of Greek Art of the Fifth and Fourth Centuries* B.C. (1921), Bloomington, Ind.: Indiana University Press, rev. ed. 1959; *The Greeks in Spain* (1925), New York: AMS Press, 1971; *The Sculptures of the Nike Temple Parapet* (1929), Maryland: McGrath Publishing Co., 1971; "New Material for the West Pediment of the Parthenon," *Hesperia* 1 (1932): 1–30; "The Lost Statues of the East Pediment of the Parthenon," *Hesperia* 2 (1933): 1–88; "The Antiquity of the Greek Alphabet," *AJA* 37 (1933): 8–29; *The Humanistic Value of Archaeology* (1933), Westport, Conn.: Greenwood Press, 1971; *The Defenses of Acrocorinth and the Lower Town* (with Antoine Bon and contributions by A. W. Parsons) Cambridge, Mass.: Harvard University Press, 1936; "The Greek Alphabet Again," *AJA* 42 (1938): 58–69; *Folk Tale, Fiction and Saga in the Homeric Epics*, Berkeley, Calif.: University of California Press (1946), (Sather Classical Lectures), 1956; *Greek Sculpture: A Critical Review*, Chicago: University of Chicago Press, 1960; *Greek Art: A Study of the Formal Evolution of Style*, University of Pennsylvania Press, 1962; *Art and Archaeology* (with J. S. Ackerman), New Jersey: Prentice-Hall, 1963; *Beyond the Pillars of Herakles: The Classical World Seen Through the Eyes of Its Discoverers*, New York: Delacorte Press, 1966; *Discontinuity in Greek Civilization*, Cambridge: Cambridge University Press, 1966 (J. H. Gray Lectures, 1965); *The Architects of the Parthenon*, Harmondsworth: Penguin Books, 1970.

Rhys Carpenter's contribution to the field of Mediterranean archaeology was profound and wide-ranging. His many interests included ancient sculpture, history, archaeology, and language.

His originality of thought helped shape our picture of ancient history. Until his work, it was assumed that the transition from Bronze Age Minoan-Mycenaean culture to the Greece of Pericles, the Parthenon, and Plato had been a steady and gradual one and that the Dorian invasions had caused only a blip in the continuity of Greek civilization. It was widely accepted that the Dorians had moved into mainland Greece c. 1100 B.C.E. (bringing with them the Iron Age), that the Phoenician alphabet was introduced just slightly later (the tenth or ninth century B.C.E.), and that the culture had remained at a fairly sophisticated level until its final flowering in the fifth century B.C.E. Scholars were aided in the formulation of this erroneous scenario by the fact that the ancient Greeks themselves had had no tradition of their country ever having experienced a period of prolonged cultural deprivation between the Homeric Age and the Classical period.

However, after having spent some time in Greece as director of the American School, Carpenter noticed something very important; that though there is pottery dating from the Dorian invasions (Sub-Mycenaean through Geometric) there is no writing on any of it, while writing on later pottery is common. It was Carpenter's conclusion that Greek culture had become nonliterate after the fall of the Mycenaeans (c. 1200 B.C.E. down to c. 700 B.C.E.) that prompted scholars to note the gravity and the great length of Greece's Dark Age; Greece had indeed experienced an extended period of cultural deprivation that began c. 1100 and did not end until nearly 700 B.C.E.

Carpenter came to some provocative conclusions about other key issues in ancient history. For instance, he did not believe that the Dorian invasions brought about the end of the Mycenaean culture. Instead, in *Discontinuity in Greek Culture* (1966) he posited the idea that the Mycenaean culture was brought to an end by disastrous climactic changes which produced drought and famine throughout the area. He accounted for the destruction of the palaces by suggesting that the local peasantry had stormed them in a desperate effort to obtain food and water. In this scenario, the Dorian invasions did not occur until sometime later, just before the reappearance of literacy, trade, and the arts. Although not accepted generally, this theory is tempting as it accounts for the extreme length of Greece's Dark Age.

Carpenter also revolutionized the approach to ancient sculpture. Previously the focus of scholars had been to identify ancient sculptors (known from literary sources) with extant works. The problem was that there was no established method for doing this and as a result, there was no reliable basis for allocating a specific piece of sculpture to one artist as opposed to another. Carpenter formulated a more intelligent approach, that of studying the style and technique of the artist. In this way, taking into account the similarities (and dissimilarities) of different works, one may reasonably link a number of sculptures to the hands of one artist, even if the name of that artist is not known. The advantage of using this approach is that much more is learned about ancient sculpture and its development even if a famous name cannot be reliably attached to it. In his 1929 publication (above) Carpenter examined the relief sculptures which adorn the parapet of the Athena Nike temple on the acropolis in Athens. With his emphasis on examining the style and technique of the works he was able to identify with confidence six sculptors as having produced these reliefs.

Carpenter also founded the Department of Classical Archaeology at Bryn Mawr College which at that time was the only institution in the United States to offer an undergraduate degree in this discipline.

SOURCES

Machteld J. Mellink, "Rhys Carpenter," *AJA* 84 (1980): 260; Dow, *A Century of Humane Archaeology*, 1979; "Bibliography of Rhys Carpenter," *Hesperia* 38 (1969): 123–32; *AJA* 74 (1970): 186 (AIA Gold Medal Award); Martin Robinson, *CR* 17 (1967): 338–39; *Greece and Rome* 14 (1967): 98; *AJA* 37 (1933): 8–29; *AJA* 42 (1938): 58–69, 125; *JHS* 50 (1930): 338; Harold N. Fowler, *Art and Archaeology* 31 (1931): 192; Carpenter, *Discontinuity in Greek Culture*, 1966; *NYT* (January 1, 1980); *TL* (January 7, 1980).

J(OHN) L(ANGDON) CASKEY

b: December 7, 1908. Boston, Massachusetts.
d: December 4, 1981. Cincinnati, Ohio.

EDUCATION

Choate School.
Yale University, 1931 (B.A.).
University of Cincinnati, 1939 (Ph.D.).

APPOINTMENTS AND AWARDS

Univ. of Cincinnati: Instructor in Classics (1939–42), Chair, Department of Classics (1959–72), Professor of Classics (to 1979), Professor Emeritus (1979); American School of Classical Studies at Athens: Assistant Director (1948–49), Director (1949–59). Member: American Philosophical Society (1967). Awards: Order of the Phoenix (Greece); Gold Medal, Archaeological Institute of America (1980).

EXCAVATIONS

Troy, 1932–38 (under CARL W. BLEGEN); Lerna, 1952–58; Keos (beg. 1960).

PUBLICATIONS

Excavation reports on Lerna appeared in *Hesperia* Vols. 23–27 (1954–60); "The House of the Tiles at Lerna—an Early Bronze Age Palace," *Archaeology* 8 (1955): 116ff.; "The Early Helladic Period in the Argolid," *Hesperia* 29 (1960): 285ff.; "Greece, Crete and the Aegean Islands in the Early Bronze Age," *Cambridge Ancient History*, Vol. 1 (1964): Chap. 26; *Greece and the Aegean Islands in the Middle Bronze Age* (Vol. 2, Chap. 4), Cambridge: Cambridge University Press, 1966; "Investigations in Keos" "Part 1: Excavations and Explorations, 1961–1970," *Hesperia* 40 (1971): 359–96, "Part 2: A Conspectus of the Pottery," *Hesperia* 41 (1972): 357–401; "The Early Bronze Age at Ayia Irini in Keos," *Archaeology* 23 (1970): 339ff.; "Marble Figurines from Ayia Irini in Keos," *Hesperia* 40 (1971): 113ff; *The End of the Early Bronze Age in the Aegean* (edited by Gerald Cadogan), Leiden: E. J. Brill, 1986; *The Temple of Ayia Irini,* by Miriam Ervin Caskey (with the collaboration of John L. Caskey), Princeton, N.J.: American School of Classical Studies at Athens, 1986; *Lerna in the Argolid: A Short Guide* (with E. T. Blackburn), Athens: American School of Classical Studies at Athens, rev. ed. 1997.

J. L. Caskey is best known for his work at the Bronze Age sites of Lerna in the Peloponnese and Ayia Irini on the island of Keos.

Caskey was born into a distinctly archaeological background; he was the son of Lacey D. Caskey, curator of Classical antiquities at the Boston Museum of Fine Arts, his godfather was BERT HODGE HILL, and CARL W. BLEGEN was a close friend of the family. Some of his earliest excavation work was at Troy where he became one of Blegen's most trusted assistants and where he received much advice from the then elderly WILHELM DÖRPFELD, who was a frequent visitor to the site.

As director of the American School of Classical Studies at Athens, Caskey initiated and headed the excavations at Lerna. The excavations illuminated our understanding of prehistoric Greece and its early development (this fortified site was settled as early as 6,000 B.C.E., during the Neolithic period). Caskey's work led to a recognition of the monumentality of Early Helladic II architecture and of the level of sophistication of the period's art and trading practices. Furthermore, it was learned from the excavations at this site that the first Greeks had arrived in the area at a much earlier time (Early Helladic III) than had previously been assumed.

On Keos, Caskey gathered copious information regarding trade, travel, and cultural contact between the island itself, Minoan Crete, and the Greek mainland. This provided much needed information on the links between the three cultures. He also discovered large terracotta statues (some life-size) at the site, which added a new dimension to our knowledge of Aegean cult practices.

SOURCES

Machteld Mellink, "John Langdon Caskey (1908–1981)," *APSY* (1982): 454–459; Machteld Mellink, "John Langdon Caskey (1908–1981)," *AJA* 86 (1982): 317; Leekley and Noyes, *AEGI*, 1975; Renfrew, *The Emergence of Civilization*, 1972; *NYT* (December 8, 1981).

STANLEY CASSON

b: May 7, 1889. England.
d: April 17, 1944.[1]

EDUCATION

Merchant Taylors School.
Lincoln College, St. John's College (Senior Scholar, 1912)
Oxford University.
British School at Athens, 1913.

APPOINTMENTS AND AWARDS

British School at Athens: Assistant Director (1919–22);
Oxford Univ.: Reader, Classical Archaeology (1927), Junior
Proctor (1928); Bristol University: Special Lecturer in Art
(1931); Bowdoin College, Maine: Visiting Professor (1933–34).
Fellow: New College, Oxford Univ. (1920). Awards: Conington
Prize (1924); Greek Order of the Redeemer.

EXCAVATIONS

Macedonia; Thrace; Constantinople, 1928–29.

PUBLICATIONS

Catalogue of the Acropolis Museum, Vol. 2, 1922 (editor and
major contributor); *Essays in Aegean Archaeology Presented to Sir
Arthur Evans in Honour of His 75th Birthday* (editor), Oxford: The
Clarendon Press, 1927; *Macedonia, Thrace and Illyria: their rela-
tion to Greece from the earliest times down to the time of Philip, son of
Amyntas* (1926), Westport, Conn.: Greenwood Press, 1971; *Some
Modern Sculptors* (1928), Freeport, N.Y.: Books for Libraries
Press, 1967; *20th Century Sculpture* (1930); *Technique of Early*

Greek Sculpture (1933), New York: Hacker Art Books, 1970; *Artists at Work*, 1933 (editor); *Greece and the Aegean* (by ERNEST ARTHUR GARDNER, chapter on Constantinople by S. Casson), London: G. G. Harrap and Co., Ltd., 1933; *Progress of Archaeology*, London: G. Bell and Sons, Ltd., 1934; *Steady Drummer*, London: G. Bell and Sons, Ltd., 1935; *Progress and Catastrophe*, 1937; *Ancient Cyprus: Its Art and Archaeology* (1937), Westport, Conn.: Greenwood Press, 1970; *Murder by Burial*, 1938; *Ancient Greece*, Oxford: The Clarendon Press, 1939; *The Discovery of Man*, New York: Harper and Brothers, 1939; *Greece and Britain*, London: Collins, 1942; *Greece Against the Axis*, Washington, D.C.: American Council on Public Affairs, 1943.

Casson received the Conington Prize for his book *Macedonia, Thrace and Illyria* (1928, above), a work which was the product of his excavations made just prior to, during, and after World War One. He combined the existing data with his own work in order to provide a comprehensive study of the history and archaeological landscape of the area.

He is also noted for his pioneering work on the techniques and tools used by ancient Greek sculptors, and his 1933 publication (above) was the first book in English written on this topic. Casson's survey begins with a study of the sculptural techniques of Minoan artisans and ends with the sculptors of the Classical period. It was especially well-received for its original contribution to our knowledge of the production of sculpture in the Bronze Age.

Stanley Casson's interests were far ranging: he published books on topics as diverse as modern sculpture and the philosophy of history (above). He was killed in action during World War Two.

SOURCES

J. L. Myres, "Stanley Casson: 1889–1944," *BSA* 41 (1946): 1–4; *WWW*, 1941–1950; E. A. Gardner, *JHS* (1926): 291; G. M. A. Richter, *AJA* (1933): 637–38; Walter R. Agard, *CJ*, 28 (1933): 624–28; *JHS* (1933): 306–308; *TL* (April 24, 1944).

NOTE

1. Professor Casson was killed in action during World War Two. The place of his death was not reported.

(Emmanuele Pietro Pauolo Maria) Luigi Palma di Cesnola

b: June 28, 1832. Rivarolo, Italy.
d: November 21, 1904. New York, New York.

EDUCATION

Royal Military School, Turin, Italy, 1845–1848.

APPOINTMENTS AND AWARDS

Italian military: Lieutenant; 4th New York Cavalry Regiment: Colonel (1862–64); American Consul, Larnaka, Cyprus, 1865–76 (concurrently Russian Consul); Metropolitan Museum of Art, New York: Secretary (1877–79), Director (1879–1904). Hon. Degrees: Columbia University; Princeton University.

PUBLICATIONS

Cyprus: Its Ancient Cities, Tombs and Temples (1877), (rev. American ed. 1878), Nicosia: Star Graphics, 1991 (reprint edition with a foreword by Stuart Swiny); *A Descriptive Atlas of the Cesnola Collection of Cypriot Antiquities in the Metropolitan Museum of Art, New York* (3 vols.), Boston: J. R. Osgood, 1885–1903.

Few figures in Classical archaeology have been surrounded by as much controversy as has Luigi Palma di Cesnola. On the one hand he put the island of Cyprus on the archaeological map and provided the Metropolitan Museum of Art in New York with the nucleus of its world calibre collection of ancient art. On the other hand, he was soundly criticized for his excavation techniques, inaccurate reporting of excavations, and was even accused of knowingly pasting together wrong parts of various statues in the course of their restoration, in addition to being suspected of having applied false patinas to bronzes in the Metropolitan Museum's collection.

Cesnola was born into an aristocratic (but poor) family in the Piedmont district of Italy, entered the military at the age of thirteen, and migrated to the United States at the age of twenty-four. In New York he enlisted in the Union Army, served with distinction, and went to Cyprus as U.S. consul in 1865. He found that the position of consul left him with time on his hands, and he soon became interested in the island's ubiquitous antiquities. The collecting and selling of ancient artifacts had just become popular, and Cesnola saw that there was profit to be made in their acquisition and disposal. He soon began a campaign of excavation throughout the island, digging up and hoarding as much ancient material as he could find.

Once he had amassed a large quantity of artifacts he contacted major museums throughout the world to see if there was any interest in buying the collection. After negotiating a major deal with the new Metropolitan Museum of Art in New York for most of his hoard, he returned to Cyprus (still as American consul) and took up renewed excavations at a fevered pace. It was during this last campaign that Cesnola acquired his most controversial find, the "Treasure of Curium." The find at Curium, consisting of hundreds of objects of gold, silver, and bronze, constituted his richest find on the island; Cesnola claimed that he had discovered the objects in a royal tomb that had been dug under a temple. His claims were immediately and vehemently criticized, since it was obvious that the artifacts dated to different time periods and were of differing provenance. Nonetheless, the Metropolitan Museum purchased this second collection from him at a cost of $60,000 (the same amount that was paid for the first collection) and appointed him secretary, and then first director, of the museum. He was to hold the post for the next twenty-five years, until his death.

Cesnola's published account (1877) of his excavations on Cyprus was generally labeled as being a flagrant lie and he was criticized for his lack of personal involvement in much of the excavations carried out in his name. In his book he stated that he had spent several months digging at Palaeopaphos but it was discovered that he had spent just one day at the site and had left the entire excavation work to hired locals. Despite the controversy which surrounds his career, Cesnola can be credited with a number of things: first, from the beginning, he was determined to keep the artifacts intact and to sell them as collections rather than selling them singly or in small groups (which would have proved more lucrative); although the excavations themselves (due to Cesnola's methods) were useless regarding stratigraphy or provenance, at least the collections could be studied as a whole for form, style, decoration, and general observations regarding the character of Cypriot pottery. Secondly, his acquisition of so much ancient material on Cyprus resulted in scholars recognizing that Cyprus had played a major role in the history of the ancient Mediterranean. His exploits led to the scientific work of individuals like JOHN L. MYRES and later, EINAR GJERSTAD. Finally, and probably most pertinently, Cesnola was very much a man of his time; during his day, archaeology was not yet a science and was conceived of as being very much an occupation of plunder and pillage. HEINRICH SCHLIEMANN (whom Cesnola admired enormously) had originally searched for Troy, to some degree, in pursuit of gold and fame. Cesnola's wish to gain wealth, rather than knowledge, from his excavations was the norm for the mid-nineteenth-century archaeologist.

SOURCES

McFadden, *The Glitter and the Gold*, 1971; Tomkins, *Merchants and Masterpieces*, 1970; Goring, *A Mischievous Pastime: Digging in Cyprus in the Nineteenth Century*, 1988; Howe, *A History of the Metropolitan Museum of Art*, 1974; Myres, *A Handbook of the Cesnola Collection of Antiquities from Cyprus*, 1914; Fitton, *The Discovery of the Greek Bronze Age*, 1995; Hibbard, *The Metropolitan Museum of Art*, 1980; Cesnola, *Cyprus: Its Cities, Tombs and Temples* (1878), reprint, 1991; *NYT* (November 22, 1904).

RICHARD CHANDLER

b: 1738. Elson, Hampshire, England.
d: February 9, 1810. Tilehurst, England.

EDUCATION

Winchester School.
Queen's College and Magdalen College, Oxford, 1759
(B.A), 1773 (B.D.), 1773 (D.D.).

APPOINTMENTS AND AWARDS

Oxford Univ: Fellow (1770, Magdalen College), Senior
Proctor (beg. 1772); Clergyman, East Worldham and West
Tisted (1779–1800), Tylehurst, Hampshire (1800–1810).

PUBLICATIONS

Elegiaca Graeca, 1759 (published anonymously); *Marmora
Oxoniensia* (two volumes), Oxford: The Clarendon Press, 1763;
*Ionian Antiquities; or, Ruins of Magnificent and Famous Buildings
in Ionia* (with N. REVETT) (1769), London: W. Bulmer and
W. Nicol, 1821; *Inscriptiones antiquae, pleraeque nondum editae,
in Asia Minore et Graecia, presertim Athenis, collected (cum appen-
dice)*, Oxford: The Clarendon Press, 1774; *Travels in Asia Minor:
or, an Account of a Tour made at the Expense of the Society of Dilettanti*, Oxford: The Clarendon Press, 1775; *Travels in Greece; or,
an Account of a Tour made at the Expense of the Society of Dilettanti*, 1776; *The History of Ilium including the adjacent Country,
and the opposite coast of the Chersonesus of Thrace*, London:
Nichols and Son, 1802; *The Life of W. Waynflete, Bishop of Winchester*, London: White and Cochran, 1811 (published posthumously, edited by C. Lambert); *Travels in Asia Minor and Greece*

(with corrections and remarks by NICHOLAS REVET).
Oxford: The Clarendon Press, 1825.

Chandler's works were considered to be the most important descriptions of Greece and Asia Minor available in the eighteenth century, and he was regarded as having greatly improved upon the works of WHELER, Chardis, and Spon.

Following his well received publication (1763, above) on the Oxford and Arundel Marbles, Chandler was commissioned by the Society of Dilettanti to lead an expedition to Asia Minor and Greece. The express purpose of the expedition was to make drawings of architectural objects and other ornaments and to make precise copies of all inscriptions found. A diary was also required so as to document every minute detail of the journey.

Chandler's group, which was comprised of Chandler (as leader and treasurer), NICHOLAS REVETT, a well-respected architect, and a young painter named William Pars, left England in June of 1764. The three spent a little more than a year in Asia Minor and much of this time they were headquartered at Smyrna (modern Izmir). Among other sites they visited were Chios, Priene, Ephesus, Troas, Hierapolis, Miletus, Sardis, and Didyma. The second half of the expedition was taken up by a trip to Greece where they spent some time in Athens; they also traveled to Olympia, Aegina, and Nemea among other sites. At Athens, Chandler expressed concern for the fate of the many ancient artifacts which lay strewn over the acropolis following the explosion of 1687 (see GEORGE WHELER) and he was able to purchase two pieces of the Parthenon frieze which he found situated above house doorways in the town.

Upon his return to London Chandler published four major works based on the expedition. His publication of the inscriptions made these available to scholars in the West for the first time, and in several instances Chandler's work is the only record of inscriptions which have long since disappeared. The publication of his diaries (1775 and 1776) proved to be very popular and these were later issued in one volume English and three volume French editions.

Chandler's detailed descriptions of the places that he visited are still widely used by scholars of ancient topography.

SOURCES

Chandler, *Travels in Asia Minor and Greece*, 1825; Clay, editor, *Richard Chandler: Travels in Asia Minor*, 1971; Clarke, *Greek Studies in England, 1700–1830*, 1945; Michaelis, *Ancient Marbles in Great Britain*, 1882; *DNB*, Vol. 3, 1908; Miller, *Greece Through the Ages*, 1972; *Gentleman's Magazine* 80 (1810): 188; *CBD*, 1962.

V(ERE) GORDON CHILDE

b: April 14, 1892. Sydney, Australia.
d: October 20, 1957. Blue Mountains, Australia.

EDUCATION

Queen's College, Oxford University, 1914 (B.Litt.).

APPOINTMENTS AND AWARDS

Royal Anthropological Institute: Librarian (1922–27); Univ. of Edinburgh: Abercromby Professor (1927–46); Univ. of London: University Professor of European Archaeology, Director of the Institute of Archaeology (1946–56).

EXCAVATIONS

Skara Brae, Orkney, Scotland.

PUBLICATIONS

How Labor Governs (1923), Cambridge: Cambridge University Press, 1964; *Dawn of European Civilization* (1925), London: Routledge and Paul, 1957, 6th rev. ed.; *The Aryans: A Study of Indo-European Origins (*1926), New York: Kennikat Press, 1970; *The Most Ancient East: The Oriental Prelude to European Prehistory*, London, 1928; *The Danube in Prehistory* (1929), New York: AMS Press, 1976; *The Bronze Age* (1930), New York: Biblo and Tannen, 1963; *Skara Brae: A Pictish Village in Orkney* (with T. H. Bryce and D. M. S. Watson), London: Kegan Paul, Trench, Trubner and Co., Ltd., 1931; *New Light on The Most Ancient East* (1934), London: Kegan Paul, Trench, Trubner and Co., 1952; *The Prehistory of Scotland*, London: Kegan Paul,

Trench, Trubner and Co., 1935; *Man Makes Himself* (1936), New York: New American Library, 1983; *Prehistoric Communities of the British Isles* (1940), New York: B. Blum, 1972; *What Happened in History*, Harmondsworth: Penguin Books, 1943; *The Story of Tools*, London: Cobbett Publishing Co., Ltd., 1944; *Progress and Archaeology* (1945), Westport, Conn.: Greenwood Press, 1971; *Scotland Before the Scots: being The Rhind Lectures for 1944*, 1946; *History*, 1947; *Social Evolution*, New York: H. Schuman, 1951; *Piecing Together the Past: The Interpretation of Archaeological Data*, London: Routledge and Paul, 1956; *A Short Introduction to Archaeology*, London: F. Muller, 1956; *Society and Knowledge* (1956), Westport, Conn.: Greenwood Press, 1973; *Prehistory of European Society*, Harmondsworth: Penguin Books, 1958 (published posthumously); "Retrospect" *Antiquity* 32 (1958): 69–74 (published posthumously).

Although he did not himself carry out major archaeological excavations, V. Gordon Childe succeeded in systematizing the mass of already existing (but disparate) archaeological data of prehistoric Europe and provided a model for a cultural-historical approach to prehistory which changed the field of prehistoric archaeology forever.

Prior to Childe, periods of history had been divided into a three-fold chronology (Stone Age, Bronze Age, and Iron Age, with subdivisions of Palaeolithic, Mesolithic, and Neolithic), and it was believed that this division was absolutely sequential (always moving forward toward the next stage of development) and that features of one period were universal to all peoples within that period and geographic location. For instance, if one looked at Greece in the Neolithic period, one would find that all people living in Greece at that time would display the same cultural traits and level of technological development, and that the culture would naturally be progressing toward the next stage of development. Childe's research pointed to the fact that in prehistoric Europe one could find a Bronze Age culture existing next to a Neolithic culture and that it was even possible that the Neolithic culture had regressed from a Bronze Age level of development. No longer were "ages" to be the focus of study, but rather cultural groups within geographic areas; and rather than assuming that all cultures developed in a linear progression he pointed to the reality of cultural regression. Childe suggested that terms such as "Neolithic" and "Palaeolithic" be used to connote technological—rather than chronological—development and that cultures should be studied and named according to cultural traits, sequences, and stratigraphical occurrences, rather like FLINDERS PETRIE'S method of sequence dating pottery. Bound up in Childe's theory were concepts such as cultural revolution, issues of cultural diffusion, social evolution, and social and economic theories, and their roles in cultural development; all ideas that are current in cultural theory today and which form the framework of all archaeological investigation.

The overall goal of Childe's studies had been to demonstrate that prehistoric Europe had received its impetus in its initial development from the more advanced cultures of the ancient Near East, specifically Mesopotamia. Although this theory was largely disproved through radiocarbon-14 dating during the 1950s, the basic components of his theory produced a new focus and a new vocabulary for prehistoric archaeology.

He published his ideas for the edification of both scholars and lay people. The latter works in particular proved to have universal appeal; they have been translated into many languages including Italian, German, French, Dutch, Russian, and Chinese.

Childe was born in Sydney, Australia into a strict and religious family; he left Australia in 1914 when he took up a graduate scholarship in Classics at Queen's College, Oxford where he eventually studied under ARTHUR EVANS and J. L. MYRES. He died in a fall while on a rare visit to his native Australia.

SOURCES

Stuart Piggott, "Vere Gordon Childe 1892–1957," *PBA* 44 (1958): 305–12; "Retrospect," *Antiquity* 32 (1958): 69–74, "The Dawn; and an Epilogue," 75–79; *The Danube in Prehistory* (Preface, 1929 ed.); "Bibliography of the Publications of Professor V. Gordon Childe," *PPS* 21 (1956): 295–304; Harris, editor, *The Archaeology of V. Gordon Childe*, 1994; Christopher Chippendale " 'Social Archaeology' in the Nineteenth Century: Is It Right to Look for Modern Ideas in Old Places?" in Christenson, editor, *Tracing Archaeology's Past*, 1989; Daniel and Renfrew, *The Idea of Prehistory*, 1988, 2d. ed.; Daniel, *A Hundred and Fifty Years of Archaeology*, 1975, 2d. ed.; Stiebing Jr., *Uncovering the Past*, 1993; Renfrew, *The Emergence of Civilisation*, 1972; *TL* (October 21, 1957); *NYT* (October 20, 1957).

E(DWARD) D(ANIEL) CLARKE

b: June 5, 1769. Willingdon, Sussex, England.
d: March 9, 1822. London, England.

EDUCATION

Tonbridge Grammer School, England.
Jesus College, Cambridge Univ., 1790 (B.A.), 1794 (M.A.).

APPOINTMENTS AND AWARDS

Various private tutorships; Cambridge Univ.: Fellow, Jesus College (1798), Senior Tutor (1805), Lecturer (1807), Professor of Mineralogy (1808–21); Rector: Harlton, England (1805–22), and Yeldham, Essex (1809–22) (held simultaneously). Hon. Degree: LL.D., Cambridge Univ. (1803).

PUBLICATIONS

Testimony of different Authors respecting the Colossal statue of Ceres, placed in the vestibule of the Public Library at Cambridge, with an account of its removal from Eleusis, Nov. 22, 1801, 1803; *The Tomb of Alexander, a dissertation on the Sarcophagus, brought from Alexandria, and now in the British Museum*, Cambridge: Cambridge University Press, 1805; *A Methodological Distribution of the Mineral Kingdom*, 1807; *Description of the Greek Marbles brought from the shores of the Euxine, Archipelago, and Mediterranean, and deposited in the vestibule of the University Library, Cambridge*, Cambridge: Cambridge University Press, 1809; *Travels in various Countries of Europe, Asia, and Africa*, 6 vols., London: T. Cadell and W. Davies, 1816–24 (Volume 6 was completed by Rev. Robert Walpole); "Observations on the Lituus of the Antient Romans," *Archaeologia* 19 (1821);

66

Numerous publications on mineralogy (for a more detailed bibliography of these see *DNB*, Vol. 4: 423–424).

Clarke was a late-eighteenth/early-nineteenth-century traveler and antiquary as well as a pioneer in the field of mineralogy. He traveled extensively throughout Italy, Greece, Cyprus, North Africa, and Asia Minor and provided detailed descriptions of sites in Greece including Athens, Mycenae (particularly the Lion Gate), Eleusis, Nemea, and Epidaurus. Apart from his topographical descriptions, his works today are considered to be rather superficial in terms of archaeological scholarship, though they were extremely popular at the time of their publication and contributed greatly to the West's growing interest in the antiquities of the Mediterranean area.

Typical of Clarke's superficiality is his criticism of the removal of the sculptures from the Parthenon by Lord Elgin. Clarke happened to witness the removal of a metope which had been insufficiently secured, causing the block to fall to the ground and break into hundreds of pieces. At the same time, he decried the removal of some of the pedimental statuary, saying that they could not be fully appreciated once removed from the locations for which their artist-creators had intended them. This sensitivity to the preservation and treatment of ancient artifacts could be better appreciated and understood if Clarke himself had not shipped back from the Mediterranean some seventy-six cases of ancient fragments including the two-ton so-called "Ceres" statue from Eleusis. For the procurement of this statue from reticent Greek natives he earned the nickname, "Eleusinian Clarke" and this very statue of "Ceres" has subsequently been identified as one of a pair of caryatids from a later (Roman) propylaea.

During his travels Clarke collected more than one hundred volumes of manuscripts (including ones of Plato, Lycurgus and Dinarchus) which were later sold to the British Museum and to Oxford University. His collection of ancient Greek silver and bronze coins was also eventually acquired by the British Museum, and many of the pieces of sculpture and architectural fragments that he brought back to Britain were presented to Cambridge University.

SOURCES

DNB, Vol. 4; Edwards, *Lives of the Founders of the British Museum* (1870) reprint, 1969; Miller, *Greece Through the Ages*, 1972; Weber, *Voyages and Travels*, 1952; Michaelis, *Ancient Marbles in Great Britain*, 1882; Clarke, *Greek Studies in England 1700–1830*, 1945; *The Gentleman's Magazine* 92, Part 1 (1822): 274–76.

C(HARLES) R(OBERT) COCKERELL

b: April 28, 1788. London, England.
d: September 17, 1863. London, England.

EDUCATION

Westminister School, London.
Apprentice in the architectural firm of his father, Samuel
Pepys Cockerell, 1804–09.

APPOINTMENTS AND AWARDS

Oxford Univ.: Professor of Architecture (1840–57), Professor Emeritus (1857); Royal Academy; Royal Institute of British Architects: President (1860–61); Architect to the Bank of England, St. Paul's Cathedral, London. Hon. Degree: D.C.L., Oxford Univ. (1845). Member: Society of Dilettanti (1858); Academies of Munich, Berlin and Berne; Archaeological Society of Athens; American Institute of Architecture; Foreign Associate, Academie des Beaux-Arts de France.

EXCAVATIONS

Aegina, 1811; Bassae, 1812.

PUBLICATIONS

Congettura del Signor Cockerell sopra la Famiglia di Niobe, 1816 (a sketch with notes); *Le Statue della Favola di Niobe dell' Imp. e.R. Galleria di Firenze situate nella primitiva loro disposizione da C.R.C.,* Pisa: N. Capurro, 1821; "The Temple of Jupiter Olympeus at Argrigentum," *Antiquities of Athens and other places in Greece, Sicily . . . , supplementary to the Antiquities of Athens by*

Stuart and Revett, 1830; *Ancient Sculptures in Lincoln Cathedral*, 1848; *Iconography of the West Front of Wells Cathedral, with an Appendix on the Sculptures of other Mediaeval Churches in England*, London: J. H. Parker, 1851; *The Temples of Jupiter Panhellenius at Aegina, and of Apollo Epicurius at Bassae near Phigaleia in Arcadia*, London: J. Weale, 1860; *Travels in southern Europe and the Levant, 1810–1817: The Journal of C. R. Cockerell, R.A.*, London: Longmans, Green and Co., 1903 (edited by his son Samuel Pepys Cockerell).

At the age of twenty-two, C. R. Cockerell set out for Cadiz, Malta, and Constantinople to deliver official dispatches to various sectors of the British fleet. While in Constantinople he met the poet Byron and another young Englishman, John Foster. He and Foster became friends and traveled extensively together in the Mediterranean area.

Cockerell was to become one of Britain's most famous architects and at this time had a special fascination with the architecture of ancient Greece. He visited sites throughout Greece with the express purpose of measuring and drawing as many architectural remains as he could find in order to increase the West's knowledge of Classical architecture. He first visited the island of Delos and carried out a small excavation there but found little of interest. He and Foster then moved on to Athens where they met two German archaeologists, J. Linkh and Haller von Hallerstein. The four became friends and decided to team up and travel to Aegina where there was a small Doric temple which, though well-known (it was first recorded by an English traveler in 1675), had not yet been excavated.

The four began their excavation of the temple (later identified by ADOLF FURTWÄNGLER as the Temple of Aphaia) in 1811 and, just three feet below the surface, found a large number of finely sculpted marble statues from the temple's pediments. The problem that faced the four was how to divide the findings between Britain and Germany, as each thought that they should go to his respective country for further study. It was decided that it would be wrong to divide the figures up, and so an auction was arranged as being the fairest alternative. Unfortunately for Cockerell, through a series of mishaps and misunderstandings, the British representative found himself in Malta with the sculptures where they were being held for safe-keeping, while they were in fact being auctioned at Zante. They were purchased by a representative of Crown Prince Louis of Bavaria and today are housed at the Glyptothek Museum in Munich. The group has proved to be one of the most important sculptural finds in Classical archaeology and spans the transitional period between Archaic and Early Classical.

The four next traveled to the Peloponnese and made an important discovery at the Temple of Apollo at Bassae in Arcadia. Here Cockerell himself serendipitously uncovered part of the inner frieze of the temple, but due to time and permit constraints the team was unable to excavate the rest of the frieze which was then covered up for safekeeping until the following year. Cockerell then had to leave for Sicily where he studied and drew the ruined temples at Selinus, Segesta, and Agrigentum; it was at the Olympieium at Agrigentum that he demonstrated his genius for being able to intelligently reconstruct ancient buildings on paper. While he was in Sicily, his friends resumed their work at Bassae and organized what is the earliest large-scale excavation, staying at the site for three months and utilizing some eighty workmen. During this time the whole of the "Phygalean frieze" was uncovered and, after it was obtained at auction for the sum of £19,000, was installed in its present home at the British Museum.

Cockerell then returned to Athens to study more of its ancient architecture and it was at this time that he discovered through careful measurement the use of entasis in the Greek column; entasis had been noted in the Roman column as far back as the Renaissance but had been missed in the Greek because of its more subtle treatment. He next moved to Italy where he lived for two more years (visiting Naples, Rome, Florence, and Pompeii) and returned to Britain in 1817 to begin his very successful career as an architect. He made contributions to a number of buildings in Britain including the completion of the Fitzwilliam Museum at Cambridge University. He also designed the Taylorian and Randolph Buildings at Oxford University and worked on the restoration of St. Paul's Cathedral in London where his remains were interred on September 24, 1863 near those of Sir Christopher Wren.

SOURCES

Clarke, *Greek Studies in England*, 1945; Cust, *History of the Society of Dilettanti*, 1914; Edwards, *Lives of the Founders of the*

British Museum (1870), reprint, 1969; Michaelis, *Ancient Marbles in Great Britain*, 1882; Michaelis, *A Century of Archaeological Discoveries*, 1908; Miller, *Greece Through the Ages*, 1972; *DNB, Pre–1900*; Ohly, Dieter, *The Munich Glyptothek: Greek and Roman Sculpture*, Munich: Verlag C. H. Beck, 1974; Leekely and Noyes, *AEGI*, 1975; *TL* (September 24, 1863).

ERNST CURTIUS

b: September 2, 1814. Lübeck, Germany.
d: November 7, 1896. Berlin, Germany.

EDUCATION

Göttingen University, 1835.
University of Bonn.
University of Berlin.
University of Halle, 1841 (Ph.D.).

APPOINTMENTS AND AWARDS

Univ. of Berlin: Extraordinary Professor (1844–67); Tutor to Crown Prince Frederich III (1844–67); Göttingen Univ.: Professor of Classical Philology (1855–67); Univ. of Berlin: Professor of History of the Fine Arts (beg. 1868).

EXCAVATIONS

Naxos; The Pnyx (Athens), 1862; Pergamon, 1871 (with F. Adler); Olympia, 1875–81.

PUBLICATIONS

Die Acropolis von Athen, 1844; *Naxos*, 1846; *Peloponnesos, eine historisch-geographische Beschreibung der Halbinsel* (2 vols.), Gotha: J. Perthes, 1851–52; *Olympia*, 1852; *Die Ionier vor der ionischen Wanderung*, 1855; *The History of Greece* (3 vols., 1857, 1861, 1867), New York: C. Scribner's Sons, 1892; *Olympia: Die Ergenbnisse der vom deutschen Reich veranstalteten Ausgrabung* (with Friedrich Adler), (5 vols., 1890–97), Amsterdam: A. M. Hakkert, 1966.

Ernst Curtius carried out a lengthy excavation of one of antiquity's most famous sites, Olympia, and in the process gained the reputation of providing a model for future archaeological method and publication. His career also influenced the character (and success) of archaeological research in foreign lands, particularly in Greece.

Curtius first visited the site of Olympia at the age of twenty-four, but it was not until 1874 that he was sent to Greece by the German government (with the enthusiastic support of the Emperor Wilhelm I) to negotiate the German Institute's excavation of the site. The agreement which ensued with the Greek government was to have major ramifications for the future of archaeological research in that country and in others; up to that time it had been usual for individuals to dig in countries like Greece and to carry off spoils to the excavator's native country for display in its museums or for private sale. In contrast, according to the agreement worked out between Curtius and the Greek government, Germany agreed to carry out the excavations (at a total cost of $200,000) purely for research purposes; all artifacts were to remain in the possession of Greece (except in the case of duplicates) while German scholars would be allowed to publish the finds and conclusions regarding the excavation. This new and enlightened approach to archaeology in foreign lands was masterminded by Curtius and no doubt later led to the successful founding of other foreign schools of archaeology in Athens (the French School being the only one resident in Athens at the time).

In addition to uncovering the plan of the site, Curtius's excavation at Olympia made other major discoveries including the Late Classical sculpture "Hermes and Dionysus" by Praxiteles and the Early Classical pedimental sculptures from the Temple of Zeus. Olympia was the first site at which reconstruction was attempted *in situ*.

Throughout the excavation Curtius stressed the need to take careful account of the archaeological context of finds (a new idea at the time), and it was at this excavation that one of Curtius's most famous students, WILHELM DÖRPFELD, learned his trade.

SOURCES

Heinz Kähler, *NDB* 3 (1957): 446–47; Leekley and Noyes, *AESG*, 1976; Daniel, *A Hundred and Fifty Years of Archaeology*, 1975; Cleator, *Archaeology in the Making*, 1976; Fitton, *The Discovery of the Greek Bronze Age*, 1995; Miller, *Greece Through the Ages*, 1972; Gardiner, *Olympia: Its History and Remains*, 1973; *TL* (July 13, 1896).

RICHARD M(CGILLIVRAY) DAWKINS

b: October 24, 1871. Surrey, England.
d: May 4, 1955. Oxford, England.

EDUCATION

Emmanuel College, Cambridge, 1901 (B.A.).

APPOINTMENTS AND AWARDS

British School at Athens: Director (1906–14); Oxford Univ.: Byewater and Sotheby Chair of Byzantine and Modern Greek Language and Literature (1919–39). Hon. Degrees: Oxford Univ.; Univ. of Athens; Univ. of Salonica.

EXCAVATIONS

Palaikastro, Crete, 1904–05 (Director); Artemis Orthia, Sparta, 1906–10 (Director); Phylakopi, Melos, 1910 (Director); Short campaigns on Crete 1913, 1914 (Kamares Cave, Plati, and Lasithi).

PUBLICATIONS

"The Modern Carnival in Thrace," *JHS* 26 (1906): 191–206; "Excavations at Phylakopi in Melos," (with J. Droop) *BSA* 17 (1910–11): 1–22; *Modern Greek in Asia Minor*, Cambridge: Cambridge University Press, 1916; "The Sanctuary of Artemis Orthia at Sparta," (co-contributor) *JHS*, Supplement No. 5, 1929; *Chronicle of Makhairas*, 1932 (2 vols.); *Monks of Athos*, London: G. Allen and Unwin, 1936; *Forty-five Stories from the Dodekanese* (editor and translator) (1950), New York: Arno Press, 1980; *Modern Greek Folk-Tales* (1953), Westport, Conn.: Greenwood Press, 1974; *More Greek Folk-Tales* (1955), Westport, Conn.: Greenwood Press, 1974.

Dawkins excavated one of the earliest major finds of the Archaic period, the Sanctuary of Artemis Orthia, a site which elucidated Sparta's position during that era. It is widely regarded that his painstaking work on the stratigraphy of the site helped set the standard for modern excavation. He considered himself to be first and foremost a linguist with a deep interest in modern Greek dialects and Greek folklore, especially as they survived in Asia Minor.

SOURCES

R. J. H. Jenkins, "Richard McGillivray Dawkins 1871–1955," *PBA* 41 (1955): 373–88; Waterhouse, *British School at Athens*, 1986; Leekley and Noyes, *AEGI*, 1975.

GEORGE DENNIS

b: July 21, 1814. London, England.
d: November 15, 1898. London, England.

EDUCATION

Charterhouse School, England.

APPOINTMENTS AND AWARDS

Private Secretary to Governor, British Guiana (1849–51); Inspector of Schools, British Guiana (1851–62); Receiver-General and Govt. Secretary, British Guiana (1862–63); British Vice Consul, Bengazi (Tripoli, 1863); British Surveyor (Cyrenaica [1865–66], Asia Minor [1867]); Consul, Crete (1869); British Consul, Palermo (Sicily, 1870–79); British Consul, Smyrna (1879–88). Hon. Degree: D.C.L., Oxford Univ. (1885). Member: British and American Archaeological Society of Rome, Vice President (1891–96).

EXCAVATIONS

Terranova, Sicily, 1863; Girgenti, Sicily, 1863; Berenice, 1864; Cyrene, Teucheira and Ptolemais, 1868; Sardis, 1888; Gela; Cosa.

Etruscan sites: Tarquinia, Viterbo, Orvieto, Veii, Castel d'Asso, Sutri, Cerveteri, Todi, Perugia, Volterra, Vetulonia, Sovana, Cortona, Florence, Vulci.

PUBLICATIONS

A Summer in Andalucia (2 vols.), London: R. Bentley, 1839 (published anonymously); *The Cid*, 1845; "On an Etruscan

City, recently discovered, and probably the Vetulonia of antiquity," *Classical Museum*, 1845; *Cities and Cemeteries of Etruria* (2 vols.) (1848), Princeton, N.J.: Princeton University Press, 1985 (abridged edition); *Handbook for Travelers in Sicily* (1864), London: J. Murray, 1892; "On recent excavations in the Greek cemeteries of the Cyrenaica," *TRSL* 9, 2d. series (1870): 135–182; "Two archaic Greek sarcophagi recently discovered in the necropolis of Clazomenae," *JHS* 4 (1883): 1–22; "Ancient Greek Art in the parts of Libia about Cyrene," *JBAASR* 2 (No. 5) (1895): 227–242.

Though both he and his work were (and continue to be) largely ignored by his fellow countrymen, George Dennis earned great recognition and respect among antiquarians throughout the rest of Europe with his ground-breaking opus, *The Cities and Cemeteries of Etruria*.

Dennis went to Etruria in 1842 at the age of twenty-eight and had originally intended to write a travel companion for visitors to the area; however, with its scholarly approach and painstakingly detailed descriptions and illustrations, the book was recognized as one of the foremost archaeological publications of its day. This work is still regarded by Etruscan scholars as the fundamental reference on the topography and archaeology of Etruscan sites, especially since many of the remains that Dennis described have since been lost.

Dennis also dug at the early Lydian necropolis of Bin Tepé and the Temple of Artemis at Sardis.

SOURCES

Rhodes, *Dennis of Etruria*, 1973; Pallottino, *The Etruscans*, 1975, 2d. ed.; Edwards, *Lives of the Founders of the British Museum* (1870), reprint, 1969; Michaelis, *A Century of Archaeological Discoveries*, 1908; *Athenaeum* (London), 1898; *Edinburgh Review* (July, 1849): 107–32 (Review of *Cities and Cemeteries of Etruria*); Butler *Sardis*, Vol. 1 (1922), reprint, 1969; MacKendrick, *The Mute Stones Speak: The Story of Archaeology in Italy*, 1960; *TL* (November 17, 1898).

VINCENT (ROBIN D'ARBA) DESBOROUGH

b: July 19, 1914. Tunbridge Wells, England.
d: July 24, 1978. Dordogne, France.

EDUCATION

New College, Oxford University, 1936 (B.A.), 1939 (B.Litt.).

APPOINTMENTS AND AWARDS

British School at Athens: Asst. Director (1947–48); Univ. of Manchester: Asst. Lecturer, Lecturer, Senior Lecturer, Reader (1948–68); New College, Oxford Univ.: Senior Research Fellow (beg. 1968). Fellow: British Academy (1966); Society of Antiquaries.

EXCAVATIONS

Knossos (assisted T. J. Dunbabin); Karphi, Crete (with J. PENDLEBURY); Aetos, Ithaca.

PUBLICATIONS

Protogeometric Pottery, Oxford: The Clarendon Press, 1952; *The Last of the Mycenaeans and their Successors*, Oxford: The Clarendon Press, 1964; *The Greek Dark Ages*, London: Benn, 1972; "What is Protogeometric?" *BSA* 43 (1948): 260–272; "Mycenaeans in Cyprus in the 11th Century B.C." *Acts of the International Archaeological Symposium 'The Mycenaeans in the Eastern Mediterranean'* (Nicosia, 1973): 79–87.

Desborough's supervisor for the B.Litt. at Oxford was Sir JOHN MYRES, and it was under Myres's influence that he became interested in the study of the period of history which lay between the fall of Bronze Age Mycenaean Greece and the subsequent Archaic Period. Myres believed that a chronology for the "Dark Age" could be reconstructed from later literary sources while Desborough eventually sought this information in the field of archaeology.

At this time very little was known of this period and because it was thought of as a culturally "dark" age, very few scholars were interested in studying it. Vincent Desborough wrote three major works which served to bring this period into the light of day.

Material for examination of this period had been lacking but the German excavation of the Athenian Kerameikos in the 1930s provided Desborough with a pottery sequence which ran the length of the Dark Age. Careful study of this material and the little found elsewhere in Greece led him to conclude that the Protogeometric pottery style had originated in Athens and that it was Athens itself that influenced the style of pottery production in other areas of Greece. These ideas were expressed in his publication of 1952 (above).

For his next project, Desborough carried out an extensive study of the state of sites throughout Greece at the time of (and immediately following) the collapse of Mycenaean culture (see 1964, above). For this work he surveyed areas as far afield as Cyprus and Kephallenia in order to examine the effect of those who had fled mainland Greece from what Desborough supposed to be an invasion from the north.

Among the areas reexamined by Desborough in the last of his three major publications was Cyprus and its role in the development of Greece c.1100 B.C.E. Cyprus had become home to many refugees of the Mycenaean collapse and had maintained some prosperity. Having studied Cyprus in the light of more recent excavations, he came to the conclusion that this island had played a rather important role in influencing the Attic Protogeometric style as well as having introduced iron-working into Greece at this time.

SOURCES

J. N. Coldstream and C. A. Rodewald, "Vincent Robin D'Arba Desborough 1914–1978," *PBA* 66 (1980): 439–53; H. W. Catling, "Vincent Robin d'Arba Desborough MA, B.Litt, FBA, FSA, 1914–1978," *RDAC* (1979): 7–11; H. W. Catling, Vincent Robin d'Arba Desborough," *BSAAnnR*, 1977–1978 Session: 21–22; Waterhouse, *British School at Athens . . .* , 1986; Leekley and Noyes, *AEGI*, 1975; *TL* (August 1, 1978).

PORPHYRIOS DIKAIOS

b: August 16, 1904. Nicosia, Cyprus.
d: August 23, 1971. Heidelberg, Germany.

EDUCATION

Pankyprion Gymnasium, Nicosia, 1915–21.
University of Athens, British School at Athens, 1924–25.
University of Liverpool, 1925–26.
University of Paris, 1926–29 (Ph.D.).

APPOINTMENTS AND AWARDS

Dept. of Antiquities, Cyprus: Assistant Curator (1929–31), Curator, Cyprus Museum (1931–60), Acting Director (1939–45), Director (1960–63); Bryn Mawr College: Visiting Professor (1964); Brandeis Univ.: Professor (1965–66); Univ. of Heidelberg: Professor of Archaeology (beg. 1966). Fellow: Society of Antiquaries, London (1940). Hon. Degrees: Univ. of Nancy (1954); Oxford Univ. (1964). Member: Institute for Advanced Study, Princeton Univ. (1963–65).

EXCAVATIONS

Vounous-Bellapais, 1931–32; Kourion-Kaloriziki; Khirikitia, 1936–39; Sotira, 1951, 1952, 1954, 1956; Enkomi, 1948–58; Salamis, 1958; Pyla-Kokkinokremos.

PUBLICATIONS

The Excavations at Erini, 1937; "The Excavation at Vounous-Bellapais in Cyprus, 1931–32," *Archaeologia* 88 (1938): 1–174; *A Guide to the Cyprus Museum* (1947), Nicosia:

83

Republic of Cyprus, Dept. of Antiquities, 1961; *Khirokitia: Final Report on the Excavations of a Neolithic Settlement in Cyprus on behalf of the Department of Antiquities, 1936–1946*, London: Oxford University Press, 1953; *Sotira*, Philadelphia: University Museum, 1961; *Swedish Cyprus Expedition*, Vol. 4. 1A: "The Stone Age and the Early Bronze Age in Cyprus," 1962: 1–204; *Enkomi: Excavations 1948–1958* (3 vols.), Mainz: Ph. Von Zabern, 1968–71.

Porphyrios Dikaios was one of the most noted Cypriot archaeologists and the first Cypriot to become director of the Department of Antiquities on Cyprus. He focused upon the prehistoric period of the island's history, building upon the work of JOHN L. MYRES and EINAR GJERSTAD.

At Khirokitia he unearthed the first plan of a Neolithic town in the eastern Mediterranean area, uncovering some forty-seven dwellings (of *tholos* type). The large size of the area excavated allowed a comprehensive picture of the different aspects of life in Neolithic Cyprus to come to light for the first time, including its architecture, economy and its relationship to its Near Eastern neighbors. Through a careful study of the various phases at Khirokitia, Dikaios was able to provide the earliest cultural sequence on the island. He concluded that the Stone Age on Cyprus existed c. 3700 B.C.E., a date which was confirmed some years later by radiocarbon-14 studies.

Dikaios's excavation report on the Late Cypriot (Late Bronze Age) site of Enkomi is regarded as a model among excavation publications. In these volumes he traces the history of the site from its earliest level (c. 1700–1600 B.C.E.) through various invasions by Mycenaean Greeks who were fleeing the Greek mainland; the narration continues down to c. 600 B.C.E. Throughout the publication Dikaios displays meticulous scholarship, providing descriptions, illustrations, and carefully drawn conclusions.

As curator of the Cypriot Museum for twenty nine years, Dikaios played a major role in developing and strengthening the Cypriot Archaeological Service.

SOURCES

K. Nikolaou, "ΠΟΡΦΥΡΙΟΣ ΔΙΚΑΙΟΣ: 1904–1971," *RDAC* (1973): 226–29; Paul Åström, editor, "Who's Who in Cypriote

Archaeology: Biographical and Bibliographical Notes," *SIMA* 23, 1971; Karageorghis, Vassos, et al., *Studies Presented in the Memory of Porphyrios Dikaios*, 1979; Dikaios, *Enkomi, Excavations 1948–1958*, Vol. 1, 1968; ΚΥΠΡΙΑΚΑ ΣΠΟΥΔΑΙ Tomos ΛΑ (1967): iv-vii (Bibliography to 1967); Saul S. Weinberg, *AJA* 61 (1957): 96–98; Porphyrios Dikaios, "Excavations and Historical Background: Enkomi in Cyprus," *JHisS* 1 (1967): 41ff.; Gjerstad, *Ages and Days on Cyprus*, 1980; R. S. Merrillees, "Einar Gjerstad: Reflections on the Past and the Present," *Medelhavsmuseet* 9 (1994): 45–53; Saul S. Weinberg, *Archaeology* 25 (1972): 236–238; Karageorghis, *Cyprus: From the Stone Age to the Romans*, 1982; Meyers, *OEANE*, 1996.

WILLIAM BELL DINSMOOR

b: July 28, 1886. Windham, New Hampshire.
d: July 2, 1973. Athens, Greece.

EDUCATION

Harvard College, 1906 (B.Sc.).

APPOINTMENTS AND AWARDS

American School of Classical Studies at Athens: Fellow (1908–12), Architect (1912–19), Professor of Architecture (1924–28), Visiting Professor (1947); Columbia Univ.: School of Architecture (1920, Avery Library [1920–26]); Bryn Mawr College: Visiting Lecturer (1926); Columbia Univ.: Executive Director, Dept. of Fine Arts (1933–55), Professor of Archaeology (1935–55); Archaeological Institute of America: President (1930–45). Member: German Archaeological Institute; American Philosophical Society (1933, Vice President [1944– 47]). Award: Gold Medal, Archaeological Institute of America (1969).

PUBLICATIONS

The Architecture of Ancient Greece: An Account of Its Historic Development, Being the First Part of the Architecture of Greece and Rome, by William J. Anderson and R. Phené (revised and rewritten by Dinsmoor), London: B. T. Batsford, 1927; "The Nike Parapet Once More," *AJA* 34 (1930): 281–295; *The Archons of Athens in the Hellenistic Age* (1931), Amsterdam: A. M. Hakkert, 1966; "The Date of the Older Parthenon," *AJA* 38 (1934): 408–448; *The Athenian Archon List in the Light of Recent Discoveries* (1939), Westport, Conn.: Greenwood Press, 1974; *Observations on the Hephaisteion*, Baltimore: American

School of Classical Studies at Athens, 1941; "The Hekatompedon on the Athenian Acropolis," *AJA* 51 (1947): 109–151; *The Architecture of Ancient Greece* (1950), New York: W. W. Norton, 1975; "The Departments of Fine Arts and Archaeology," *A History of the Faculty of Philosophy, Columbia University*, 1957: 251–269.

William Bell Dinsmoor was an expert in ancient Greek architecture, particularly in reference to the buildings of the Classical period found on and around the acropolis at Athens.

Much of Dinsmoor's work was published in scholarly articles but he did produce two significant books. In his best known publication (1950, above) Dinsmoor traced the history and development of Greek architecture from the Bronze Age through the Hellenistic period; this manual is still regarded as the most complete and authoritative work on the subject.

His 1931 publication (above) constituted a major contribution to our knowledge of Athenian chronology and came about after his chance discovery of a third century B.C.E. inscription in front of the Propylaea at Athens. In this five hundred page work Dinsmoor provided a chronological list of the annual magistrates (*archons*) of Athens during the Hellenistic period. This work helped enormously in the study of thousands of inscriptions which were being unearthed in the excavation of the Athenian Agora.

He solved a number of problems regarding the original design of the Athenian Propylaia and had intended to publish a major work on this subject; unfortunately this project was never completed. For many years he concentrated his scholarly activities on working out the histories of the Erechtheum and the Parthenon, and these findings were published in a series of articles dating mainly to the 1930s (see above).

Dinsmoor was presented with a unique opportunity to test his theories regarding the building techniques employed in the construction of the Athenian Parthenon when he was asked to assist the city of Nashville, Tennessee in constructing a concrete replica of the building (a wooden replica of the temple had been erected at the site in 1896 as part of the state's centennial celebrations). Dinsmoor was the design consultant for the project which took eleven years to complete (1920–1931); the original, in Pentellic marble, had been completed in fifteen years.

Dinsmoor was interested in many aspects of ancient architecture including its financing and the identifiable traits of individual architects. The latter interest led him to the identification of one individual (whom he called the "Theseum Architect") as having designed four temples that were contemporary with the Parthenon. He based these identifications upon similarities among these four buildings in terms of their plans, proportions, and moldings.

As president of the Archaeological Institute of America, Dinsmoor played a major role in the protection of ancient artifacts and archaeological remains in Europe and the Far East during World War Two, and in 1943 President Roosevelt appointed him to the American Commission for the Protection and Salvage of Artistic and Historic Monuments in War Areas.

SOURCES

Homer A. Thompson, "William Bell Dinsmoor (1886–1973)," *APSY* (1974): 156–63; *Archaeology* 26 (1973): 308; *AJA* 74 (1970): 185 (AIA Gold Medal Award); Lord, *History of the American School . . .* , 1947; Dow, *A Century of Humane Archaeology*, 1979; Correspondence with the Dept. of Art History and Archaeology, Columbia Univ.; *WWA* 21, 1940–41; *NYT* (July 3, 1973).

EDWARD DODWELL

b: 1767. England.
d: May 13, 1832. Rome, Italy.

EDUCATION

Trinity College, Cambridge University, 1800 (B.A.).

PUBLICATIONS

Alcuni Bassi rilievi della Grecia descritti e pubblicati in viii tavole, 1812; *A Classical and Topographical Tour through Greece, during the years 1801, 1805, and 1806* (2 vols.), London: Rodwell and Martin, 1819 (German translation published in 1821–22); *Views in Greece, from drawings by E. Dodwell* (2 vols.), London: Rodwell and Martin, 1821; *Views and Descriptions of Cyclopian or Pelasgic Remains in Greece and Italy . . . from drawings by E. Dodwell*, London: A. Richter, 1834 (published with French text, 1834).

Edward Dodwell was one of the most widely traveled of the nineteenth-century visitors to Greece, seeing Athens, Sounion, Delphi, Aegina, Mycenae, Tiryns, Epidauros, Olympia, Thessaly, Thebes, and Orchomenos. Of particular value are the four hundred finely detailed sketches that he made of these ancient sites.

He excavated burials at Corinth and in Attica, unearthing a number of pottery remains. Dodwell, who was a conscientious and intelligent excavator for his time, kept notes detailing where a specific object had been found and actually measured out a number of the sites. He also bought ancient artifacts from residents in Greece which, together with those unearthed by his own hand, formed a collection of 143 vases and 115 bronzes. His collection of vases was purchased by the Glyptothek Museum in Munich.

SOURCES

DNB, Vol. 5; Miller, *Greece Through the Ages*, 1972; Clarke, *Greek Studies in England, 1700–1830*, 1945; Weber, *Voyages and Travels* . . . , 1952; Cook, *Greek Painted Pottery*, 1960; *Gentleman's Magazine* 102 (1832): 649.

EDITH (HAYWARD) HALL DOHAN

b: December 31, 1877. New Haven,[1] Connecticut.
d: July 14, 1943. Philadelphia, Pennsylvania.

EDUCATION

Smith College, 1899 (B.A.).
American School of Classical Studies at Athens, 1903-05.
Bryn Mawr College, 1908 (Ph.D.).

APPOINTMENTS AND AWARDS

Mt. Holyoke College: Instructor (1908–12); Mediterranean Section, University Museum, Univ. of Pennsylvania: Asst. Curator (1912–15), Associate Curator (1920–42), Curator (1942–43); Bryn Mawr College: Lecturer (1923–24, 1926–27, 1929–30); *American Journal of Archaeology:* Book Review Editor (1932–43).

EXCAVATIONS

Gournia, Crete, 1904 (under HARRIET BOYD HAWES); Sphoungaras, 1910; Vrokastro, 1910, 1912 (Director).

PUBLICATIONS

The Decorative Art of Crete in the Bronze Age, Philadelphia: J. C. Winston, 1907; *Gournia, Vasiliki and Other Prehistoric Sites on the Isthmus of Hierapetra, Crete: Excavations of the Wells-Houston-Cramp Expeditions, 1901, 1903, 1904* (Edith H. Hall et al.), Philadelphia: The American Exploration Society, 1908; *Excavations in Eastern Crete: Sphoungaras* (contributor), Philadelphia University Museum, 1912; "The Cretan Expedition," *MusJ* 3 (3) (1912):

39–44; "The Greco-Roman Section" *MusJ* 4 (4) (1913): 117–167; *Excavations in Eastern Crete: Vrokastro*, Philadelphia: University Museum, 1914; *Italic Tomb-Groups in the University Museum*, Univ. of Pennsylvania Press, 1942.

Edith Hall Dohan followed closely in the footsteps of HARRIET BOYD HAWES by being one of the first women archaeologists to be allowed to carry out a major excavation in the Mediterranean area. Her most important excavation was the sub-Minoan site of Vrokastro, Crete, and in her exploration of Sphoungaras she was the first person to excavate a Minoan cemetery.

Part way through her career she turned from the study of prehistoric Greece to a new interest, the Etruscan period in Italy. The University Museum at the University of Pennsylvania possessed a large number of uncataloged, seventh century B.C.E. Etruscan tomb groups which had been procured for the museum by A. L. Frothingham in the late 1890s. Dohan painstakingly cataloged this large collection (twenty nine tombs in all), and in 1942 published an important work on this then little-known subject. Her daughter, Katherine Elizabeth, married the English classicist Denys Page.

SOURCES

G. M. A. Richter and M. H. Swindler, "Edith Hall Dohan," *AJA* 47 (1943): 466; Dorothy Burr Thompson, *NAW*; Paul Jacobsthal, *JHS* 33 (1943): 97–100; G. M. A. Hanfmann, *AJA* 48 (1944): 114–16.

NOTE

1. Dr. Dohan's birthplace is given as Woodstock, Connecticut in *AJA* 47 (1943): 466.

WILHELM DÖRPFELD

b: December 26, 1853. Barmen, Germany.
d: April 26, 1940. Leukas, Greece.

EDUCATION

Academy of Architecture, Berlin, 1876.

APPOINTMENTS AND AWARDS

German Archaeological Institute: Director, Athens (1887–1912). Hon. Member: Prussian Academy of Science.

EXCAVATIONS

Olympia, 1877–81; Troy, 1882–94; Tiryns, 1884–85; Orchomenos; Crete; Athens (1886–95); Pergamon; Pylos; Leukas.

PUBLICATIONS

Troja: Results of the Latest Researches (contributor) (1884), Bronx, N.Y.: B. Blom, 1967; *Tiryns* (with H. Schliemann), New York: C. Scribner's Sons, 1885 (French edition: *Tirynthe*, Paris: C. Reinwald, 1885); *Das griechische Theater* (1896), Aalen: Scientia Verlag, 1966; *Die südliche Städten von Pergamon*, Berlin: K. Akadamie der Wissenschaften, 1901; *Troja and Ilion* (contributor), Athens: Beck and Barth, 1902; *Die Arbeit zu Pergamon, Die Bauwerke*, 1902–11; *Homer Odyssee*, Munich: Buchenau and Reichert, 1924; *Die Heimkehr des Odysseus*, 1925; *Alt-Ithaka* (1927), Osnabrück: Zeller, 1965; *Strabo und die Küste von Pergamon*, 1928; *Alt-Olympia* (1935), Osnabrück: Zeller, 1966; *Alt-Athen und seine Agora* (1939), Osnabrück: Zeller, 1968.

Wilhelm Dörpfeld is considered one of the giants in Classical archaeology. Among his many accomplishments can be listed the discovery of the pre-Classical Parthenon (the Hekatompedon) on the acropolis in Athens and his 1896 publication (above) which constituted the first study of Greek theater construction ever undertaken; but it is for his immense contributions to our knowledge of the Greek Bronze Age that he is best remembered.

After receiving his education in architecture at Berlin, Dörpfeld applied the same scientific approach to archaeology during his first excavation work at Olympia, where German archaeologists (like ERNST CURTIUS) had begun to realize the importance of strata, rather than depth, in reconstructing the ancient past.

In 1881 HEINRICH SCHLIEMANN, the famous excavator of Troy and Mycenae, visited Olympia and was so impressed by the young Dörpfeld's work that he was eventually able to persuade the latter to assist him with his work at Troy. Schliemann had come under much criticism for his unscientific approach to archaeological excavation and it seems that he accepted this criticism to a degree and sought to rectify it. Indeed, it has been said (by ARTHUR EVANS, among others) that Wilhelm Dörpfeld was "Schliemann's greatest discovery of all." Dörpfeld clarified the stratification of the site, systematized the data, and put the work on a firm scientific basis for the first time. He assisted Schliemann at other sites including Mycenae where he was able to correct a number of Schliemann's erroneous conclusions including his theory that the Shaft Graves held only one-time burials. Although he was not present at the time of Schliemann's excavation of the graves, Dörpfeld was able, from Schliemann's detailed notes, to reconstruct the original configuration of the shafts and to show that multiple burials would have been quite a simple procedure.

He and Schliemann began excavations at Tiryns in 1884; the site proved to be of great importance because of its extensive Bronze Age palace remains, the first to be discovered (TSOUNTAS had not yet unearthed the more meager remains of the palace at the top of the citadel at Mycenae). Indeed, according to one author[1] Dörpfeld can be credited with having saved the great Cyclopean walls of Tiryns; Schliemann had arrived at the site some time before him and had thought that the off-white debris between the great pieces of stone was mortar. Knowing that Greeks did not use mortar, Schliemann had determined that the walls were Roman and that they must come down in order to uncover the "true" Homeric palace below. Dörpfeld arrived just in time, and recognized that the "mortar" was in fact the remains of marble slabs that had decomposed, partly due to a conflagration.

Throughout his work Dörpfeld took pains to draw parallels between the artifacts and buildings mentioned in the Homeric epics and those that were now being uncovered. At Troy he concluded that the civilization that had occupied Level VI was the same as that of Homer's *Iliad*. It was not until the work of CARL W. BLEGEN that it was shown that Dörpfeld's calculations were off, but only slightly. Blegen was able to show that Troy VI had been destroyed not by human hands but by an earthquake and that the palace of Homer's Priam and Hecuba had in fact occupied the next building level, Troy VIIa.

Dörpfeld continued his interest in establishing the verisimilitude of Homer's epics to the end of his life. He died at his home on the Greek island of Leukas which he believed was the "Ithaca" of Homer's *Odyssey*.

SOURCES

"Wilhelm Dörpfeld," *AJA* (1940): 360; Frazer, *Pausanias's Description of Greece*, reprint, 1965; Schuchhardt, *Schliemann's Discoveries of the Ancient World* (1891), reprint, 1979; Michaelis, *A Century of Archaeological Discoveries*, 1908; *NDB*, Vol. 4; Leekley and Noyes, *AESG* 1976; McDonald, *The Discovery of Homeric Greece*, 1967; Fitton, *The Discovery of the Greek Bronze Age*, 1995; Daniel, *One Hundred and Fifty Years of Archaeology*, 1975, 2d. ed.; Cleator, *Archaeology in the Making*, 1976; *CB* (1940): 255; *NYT* (April 27, 1940); *TL* (April 30, 1940), (May 1, 1940).

NOTE

1. Michaelis, *A Century of Archaeological Discoveries*.

STERLING DOW

b: November 19, 1903. Portland, Maine.
d: January 9, 1995. Cambridge, Massachussetts.

EDUCATION

Kennebunk High School, Maine.
Phillips Exeter Academy.
Harvard University, 1925 (B.A.), 1928 (M.A.), 1936 (Ph.D.).
Trinity College, Cambridge University (Fiske Scholar), 1926.

APPOINTMENTS AND AWARDS

Harvard University: Tutor, Instructor (1936–41), Assoc. Professor (1941–46), Professor of History and Greek (1946–49), John E. Hudson Professor of Archaeology (1949–70), Professor Emeritus (1970); Boston College: Distinguished Professor of Greek Civilization and History (1970–77); Vassar College: Blegen Distinguished Professor of Classics (1978); Archaeological Institute of America: President (1946–48); Sather Professor of Classical Literature (1964); Annual Professor of the American School of Classical Studies in Athens (1966–67). Fellow: Guggenheim Fellow (1934–35, 1959–60, 1966–67). Hon. Member: Deutshes Archaologisches Institute, Berlin; Hon. Life Member and Honorable American Secretary, Society for the Promotion of Hellenic Studies; Honorable American Secretary, Society for the Promotion of Roman Studies. Hon. Degree: LL.D., Univ. of California, Berkeley.

PUBLICATIONS

Prytaneis: A Study of the Inscriptions Honoring the Athenian Councillors, Hesperia Suppl. 1, 1937; "Homer: The Epics and Their Period," *AJA* 52 (1948): 1–198, Ibid. 54 (1950): 161–222; "Minoan Writing," *AJA* 58 (1954): 77–129; *Fifty Years of Sathers: The Sather Professorship of Classical Literature in the University of California, Berkeley, 1913/4–1963/4,* Berkeley, Calif.: University of California Press, 1965; *A Sacred Calendar of Eleusis* (with R. F. Healey), Cambridge, Mass.: Harvard University Press, 1965; *A Century of Humane Archaeology,* New York: The Institute, 1979.

Sterling Dow's major field of interest was epigraphical studies but he also made significant contributions in the areas of ancient history and archaeology.

One of his most important works, on the *prytaneis* of ancient Athens, was the fruit born of years of careful study of Athenian inscriptions (see *Hesperia*, 1937, above). While carrying out research in this area he also discovered the *kleroterion*, an ancient Athenian mechanical device which was used to allocate offices to Athenian citizens at random rather than by electing individuals to office. This discovery led to an enhanced understanding of the character of Athenian democracy.

While working on inscriptions at the American School of Classical Studies at Athens during the 1930s, Dow perfected the process of making squeezes; this was a major advance since it resulted in a much clearer reading of ancient inscriptions than had previously been possible.

His studies led him to anticipate that Linear B was an early form of Greek years before the work of MICHAEL VENTRIS; regarding the Dark Age that occurred after the fall of Mycenae, he believed that Greece had tumbled into a state of cultural decline because the roots of civilization (that is, literacy, arts, and crafts) had been focused in the palaces and in turn were destroyed with them, leaving the country desolate.

Sterling Dow was a cofounder of the popular magazine published by the Archaeological Institute of America called *Archaeology* (first published in 1948), and was the author of more than 150 articles and reviews.

SOURCES

Boegehold, et al., *Studies Presented to Sterling Dow on His Eightieth Birthday*, 1984; Emily Vermeule, "Sterling Dow, 1903–1995," *AJA* 99 (1995): 729–30; *CANE* (1995): 14; Alan L. Boegehold, "Sterling Dow 1903–1995," *AIA Newsletter*, Vol. 10, No. 3, (Spring 1995): 13, 15; Dow, *A Century of Humane Archaeology*, 1979; *NYT* (January 14, 1995).

LORD ELGIN
(THOMAS BRUCE,
SEVENTH EARL OF ELGIN AND
ELEVENTH EARL OF KINCARDINE)

b: July 20, 1766. Elgin, Scotland.
d: November 14, 1841. Paris, France.

EDUCATION

Harrow School, England.
Westminster School, London.
St. Andrew's University.

APPOINTMENTS AND AWARDS

British Army: Ensign (1785), Major-General (1809), Lieutenant-General (1814), General (1837); Envoy Extraordinary: Vienna (1791), Berlin (1795); Ambassador, Constantinople (1799).

Controversy has surrounded the Elgin Marbles from the day they were removed from the acropolis in Athens. Lord Elgin was appointed ambassador to Constantinople in July of 1799. He had a deep interest in Classical architecture and was determined from the beginning to use this post to further his knowledge. He had hoped to take artists and modelers with him to draw, paint, and take casts of the buildings and inscriptions that he would see in Greece, which at this time was under Turkish control. Initially, he had no intention of bringing any sculpture back to London and, after failing to secure British government financial backing he decided to take all of the expenses for the drawing and modeling project upon himself.

Having arrived in Constantinople and familiarized himself with the situation in Greece, he became distressed by what he perceived as shoddy treatment of the ancient Greek monuments by the Turkish government. He applied for permission to draw and cast the various ancient remains but eventually obtained a *firman* which not only allowed him to draw and cast pieces, but also to remove any pieces which were unattached to buildings. While he was in Constantinople, Elgin's main appointee at the acropolis was the Italian artist, Giovanni Battista Lusieri, who had been introduced to Elgin by Sir WILLIAM HAMILTON. Lusieri was especially upset by the treatment of the ancient remains and decided to violate the last part of the *firman* by removing the attached pieces as well. The collection that he amassed has since become known as the "Elgin Marbles" and is comprised mainly of pieces from the Parthenon, including the Ionic and Doric friezes and the pediments, sculpted slabs from the Athena Nike temple, a caryatid from the Erechtheum, and various pieces which had been previously collected by Elgin from other parts of Greece.

The fragments were packed into a number of ships which departed Athens in 1803. One of these ships sunk at the mouth of the harbor at Kythera, and it took three years for Elgin to retrieve this particular shipment from a depth of twelve fathoms.

Upon his arrival in London, Elgin was so roundly criticized for his actions that he decided to ameliorate his critics by placing the sculptures on public display, first at his own residence and then at Burlington House. Elgin further defended his actions by revealing that although the original meaning of the *firman* had been violated, the Turkish government had signed release papers for all of the pieces which he had shipped to London.

In 1816 a select committee of the British House of Commons recommended the purchase (for £30,000) of the Elgin Marbles in order that they be presented to the nation. During the same set of hearings it was concluded that Elgin's conduct in Athens had been acceptable and that he was within the law in claiming ownership of the ancient works.

The Elgin Marbles went on display at the British Museum for the first time in 1816.

SOURCES

Edwards, *Lives of the Founders of the British Museum* (1870), reprint, 1969; *DNB*, Vol. 4, 1908; Cook, *The Elgin Marbles*, 1984; St. Clair, *Lord Elgin and the Marbles*, 1967; Miller, *Greece Through the Ages*, 1972; *TL* (November 22, 1841), (December 7, 1841).

KENAN T(EVFIK) ERIM

b: February 13, 1929. Istanbul, Turkey.
d: November 3, 1990. Ankara, Turkey.

EDUCATION

New York University, 1953 (A.B.).
Princeton University, 1958 (Ph.D.).

APPOINTMENTS AND AWARDS

New York University: Asst. Professor (1958–71), Professor
(beg. 1971). Awards: Liberty Medal of New York City (1986);
Order of Merit of the Republic of Italy (1987).

EXCAVATIONS

Sicily (as a student); Aphrodisias, Turkey (Director), 1961.

PUBLICATIONS

"Morgantina," *AJA* 62 (1958): 79–90; "The School of
Aphrodisias," *Archaeology* 20.1 (1967): 18–27; "Aphrodisias,
Awakened City of Ancient Art," *National Geographic* 141, 6
(1972): 766–791; "The 'Acropolis' of Aphrodisias: Investiga-
tions of the Theater and the Prehistoric Mounds, 1966–1967,"
NGSRR (1973): 89–112; *Aphrodisias, City of Venus Aphrodite*,
New York: Facts on File, 1986; *Aphrodisias Papers*, Ann Arbor,
Mich.: University of Michigan Press, 1990.

Erim was born in Turkey and grew up in Geneva, Switzerland. His family moved to New York in the 1950s.
His career as a scholar began auspiciously with the publi-

cation of an important article (1958, above) which established the location of the ancient Sicilian city of Morgantina at present-day Serra Orlando. His argument was based upon examination of the "Hispanorum" issue of coins and relevant written references to the city of Morgantina.

Erim's most noted achievement, however, was the work he carried out at the site of Aphrodisias in southwestern Turkey. There he worked for thirty-one years, and during that time uncovered the ancient Roman city, fine examples of marble sculpture and reliefs, epigraphy, coins, and monumental architecture including a theater that could accommodate ten thousand and a large stadium which could seat forty thousand.

Although he excavated the site for more than thirty years, Erim produced only one major publication on it—a fact which evoked much criticism and caused him to lose valuable funding. He did, however, enlist a number of scholars to aid him in his work, and they have generated several well researched and informative publications.

SOURCES

G. W. Bowersock, "Kenan Tevfik Erim, 1929–1990," *AJA* 95 (1991): 281–283; Stillwell, editor, *PECS*, 1976; *NYT* (November 5, 1990).

(Sir) Arthur J(ohn) Evans

b: July 8, 1851. Hemel Hempstead, England.
d: July 11, 1941. Oxford, England.

EDUCATION

Harrow School, 1870.
Brasenose College, Oxford University, 1874 (B.A.).
Göttingen University, 1875.

APPOINTMENTS AND AWARDS

Ashmolean Museum: Keeper (1884–1908), Honorary Keeper (beg. 1908); Society for the Promotion of Hellenic Studies: President (1911); Society of Antiquaries: President (1914). Hon. Degrees: Ph.D., Univ. of Berlin (1910); D.Litt., Univ. of Cambridge (1924).

EXCAVATIONS

Canali, near Ragusa, 1877; Frilford, England, 1885; Aylesford, Kent, 1887; (Preliminary investigations) Knossos, Psychro and Goulas, Crete, 1895; Papoura and Psychro, 1896; Knossos, 1900–05, 1909, 1922–26, 1931, 1935.

PUBLICATIONS

Through Bosnia and the Herzegovina on foot, during the insurrection, August and September 1875, with an historical review of Bosnia (1876), New York: Arno Press, 1971; *Illyrian Letters: a revised selection of correspondence from the Illyrian provinces of Bosnia, Herzegovina, Montenegro, Albania, Dalmatia, Croatia and Slavonia, addressed to the Manchester Guardian during the year*

1877, London: Longmans, Green and Co., 1878; *The 'Horsemen' of Tarentum*, 1889; *Syracusan 'Medallions' and their Engravers*, 1891; *Catalogue of the Greek Vases in the Ashmolean Museum*, Oxford: The Clarendon Press, 1893; *The History of Sicily from Earliest Times* by E. A. Freeman (Vol. 4 edited from posthumous MSS with supplements and notes by A. J. Evans), Oxford: The Clarendon Press, 1891–1894; *Cretan Pictographs and Prae-Phoenician script, with an account of a sepulchral deposit at Hagios Onuphrios near Phaistos in its relation to primitive Cretan and Aegean culture*, 1895; *Further Discoveries of Cretan and Aegean Script with Libyan and Proto-Egyptian Comparisons*, 1898; *The Mycenaean Tree and Pillar Cult and its Mediterranean Relations*, London: Macmillan and Co., 1901; *The Prehistoric Tombs of Knossos: I. The Cemetery of Zafer Papoura, with a comparative note on a Chamber tomb at Milatos; II. The Royal Tomb of Isopata*, 1906; *Essai de classification des époques de la civilisation minoénne; résumé d'un discours fait au Congrès d'Archeologie a Athènes, 1905*, 1906; *Anthropology and the Classics: Six Lectures Delivered Before the University of Oxford* (1908), New York: Barnes and Noble, 1967 (edited by R. R. Marett); *Scripta Minoa: The Written Documents of Minoan Crete with special reference to the Archives of Knossos, I. The Hieroglyphic and Primitive Linear Classes* (2 vols.), Oxford: The Clarendon Press, 1909; *The Tomb of the Double Axes and Associated Group, and the Pillar Rooms and Ritual Vessels of he Little Palace at Knossos*, 1914; *The Palace of Minos. A Comparative Account of the Successive Stages of the Early Cretan Civilization as Illustrated by the Discoveries at Knossos, Vols. 1–4* (1921–35), New York: Biblo and Tannen, 1964 (reprint edition, 4 vols.); *Palace of Minos, Index Volume* by Joan Evans,[1] 1936; *'The Ring of Nestor': A Glimpse into the Minoan After-world, and a Sepulchral Treasure of Gold Signet-rings and Bead-seals from Thisbé, Boeotia*, London: Macmillan and Co., 1925; *Holland and the Dutch. Handbook for the British Contingent, Boy Scouts . . . at Vogelenzang, near Haarlem*, 1937; Posthumous publications: *Scripta Minoa, Volume II*, edited by Sir JOHN MYRES, 1952; *Inscriptions in the Minoan Linear Script of Class A* (third volume of *Scripta Minoa*) edited by W. C. Brice with notes of Arthur Evans and Sir John Myres, 1961.

With his discovery of the Minoan culture of Bronze Age Crete, Arthur Evans joined HEINRICH SCHLIEMANN as one of the "founding fathers" of Mediterranean archaeology.

Evans was the son of the renowned British archaeologist Sir John Evans. After extensive travel in the Balkans in 1877 he became Balkan correspondent of the *Manchester Guardian*. His journalism career ended in 1882 with his arrest and imprisonment by Austrian authorities upon charges of complicity in the Crivoscian insurrection in South Dalmatia. He was released after six weeks imprisonment and returned to Britain to seek a new career.

Evans was appointed keeper of the Ashmolean Museum at Oxford University in 1884. The museum at this time was without specific purpose since many of its exhibits had recently been transferred to other buildings within the university. Evans determined to make the Ashmolean a world-class museum of archaeology and achieved this goal by quickly procuring a large private collection of Classical and medieval art. He went on to greatly expand the Egyptian, Greek, and Roman collections, and with his own finds established what is considered to be the best collection of Minoan artifacts outside of Crete.

Evans's major contribution, however, was in the area of Mediterranean archaeology, specifically in the prehistoric period of Crete. He became interested in the pictographs which were then being discovered among the finds of the Mycenaean civilization of mainland Greece. He went to Crete in a bid to find more examples of these pictographs which he believed to be a form of ancient script. In 1900, after the liberation of Crete from Turkish domination, he purchased the site of Knossos and began excavations. Work was concentrated in the first six seasons (1900–1905) though Evans continued intermittent excavation work at the site through 1935. Evans was assisted in his work by DUNCAN MACKENZIE, JOHN PENDLEBURY, and Richard W. Hutchinson.

At Knossos Evans uncovered what has proved to be an older and richer Bronze Age civilization than that of the Mycenaean mainland. Through his meticulous work and record-keeping, in 1905 he was able to propose a nine-period chronological division for Bronze Age Crete. This chronology was based on his classification of three forms of an ancient script (hieroglyphic, Linear A, and Linear B) and on pottery styles, and it was this compendium which provided a framework for the further study of Mediterranean prehistoric archaeology.

Evans was correct in most of his thinking, save one major point: he held, despite the mounting evidence against it, that Minoan Crete had dominated the Greek mainland beginning c. 1600 B.C.E. and that it had continued its rule until the destruction of the Minoan palaces c. 1400 B.C.E. This theory, which Evans held until his death, was eventually refuted by the discovery of large amounts of Linear B tablets at Pylos (see CARL W. BLEGEN and MICHAEL VENTRIS) and by pottery analysis carried out by ARNE FURUMARK.

SOURCES

J. L. Myres, "Sir Arthur Evans 1851–1941," *PBA* 27 (1942): 323–57; J. L. Myres, *DNB*, Supplement 1941–50; Harden, *Sir Arthur Evans: A Memoir* 1983, 2d. ed.; *ONFRS* 3, No. 10 (December 1941): 941–968; *AJA* 22 (1942): 69–73; Joan Evans, *Time and Chance: the Story of Arthur Evans and his Forebears*, 1943; McDonald, *Discovery of Homeric Greece*, 1967; Fitton, *Discovery of the Greek Bronze Age*, 1995; Daniel, *A Hundred and Fifty Years of Archaeology*, 1975, 2d. ed.

NOTE

1. Joan Evans was a half-sister to Arthur Evans.

(SIR) CHARLES FELLOWS

b: August, 1799. Nottingham, England.
d: November 8, 1860. London, England.

PUBLICATIONS

A Narrative of an Ascent to the Summit of Mont Blanc, London: T. Davison, 1827; *A Journal written during an Excursion in Asia Minor,* London: J. Murray, 1839; *An Account of Discoveries in Lycia, being a Journal kept during a second Excursion in Asia Minor,* London: J. Murray, 1841; *The Xanthian Marbles, their Acquisition and Transmission to England,* London: J. Murray, 1843; *Lycia, Caria, Lydia, illustrated by G. Scharf, with descriptive letterpress by C. Fellows,* Part 1, 1847 (No additional parts were published.); *An Account of the Ionic Trophy Monument excavated at Xanthus,* London: J. Murray, 1848; *Travels and Researches in Asia Minor, more particularly in the Province of Lycia* (1852), Hildesheim: Georg Olms Verlag, 1975; *Coins of ancient Lycia before the Reign of Alexander, with an Essay on the relative Dates of Lycian Monuments in the British Museum* (1855), Chicago: Obol International, 1976.

Charles Fellows is one of the most renowned of the nineteenth-century travelers. An adventurous man, in 1827 he became the thirteenth successful climber of Mont Blanc and much of his youth was spent traveling throughout Britain. After the death of his mother, he traveled and lived in Italy and Greece and in 1837 began a tour of Asia Minor, arriving in Smyrna in 1838. Here he noticed that the architecture and buildings of the modern city had been fused with ancient architectural pieces such as columns and carved entablature; architectural fragments had been reused for tombstones, and in one instance he recorded a still brilliantly colorful Roman mosaic that had been incorporated into a wall that surrounded a cornfield just outside the city.

Spurred by the sight of these ancient remains, Fellows determined to go deeper into Asia Minor (where no European had set foot) in search of ancient monuments which he hoped had not been despoiled as others had been.

He journeyed through Phrygia, Pamphylia, Pisidia, and into Lycia, and then went on to discover Xanthus, the ancient capital of Lycia. Fellows, an accomplished artist, sketched a number of the ruins and copied various inscriptions. Upon his return to Britain he wrote *A Journal written during an Excursion in Asia Minor* (1839). The journal and its illustrations created such interest that the trustees of the British Museum asked the Turkish sultan for permission for Fellows to embark upon another trip to Lycia, this time at their behest, and to be allowed to bring back fragments of ancient art and architecture. Permission for the trip was granted but the request regarding the removal of art was denied. While on this trip in 1839–40, Fellows led an expedition during which ten more ancient cities were discovered.

After having arrived home in England, the British Museum was at last able to secure permission to bring back pieces of ancient art and architecture, and so Fellows made his third trip to Lycia in 1841. After some initial difficulty, a great amount of ancient art was packed into seventy-eight crates and eventually shipped back to London. A fourth expedition was carried out in 1844 during which another twenty-seven crates were packed and exported.

Fellows's acquisition of the Lycian fragments was not without criticism; his 1843 publication (above) was a pamphlet issued in response to this rebuke. In 1845 he was knighted by the queen with special recognition regarding the acquisition of the sculptures from Xanthus.

Fellows's expeditions added greatly to the West's knowledge and appreciation of both Lycian and late Hellenic art and architecture. Among the ancient remains that he brought back to Britain were the Nereid Monument and the reliefs from the Harpy Tomb which are now in the British Museum.

SOURCES

DNB, Vol. 6, 1917; *Gentleman's Magazine* (January 1861): 103–104; Edwards, *Lives of the Founders of the British Museum* (1870), reprint, 1969; Fellows, *Travels and Researches in Asia Minor, more particularly in the Province of Lycia*, 1852; *CBD*, 1962; *TL* (November 10, 1860).

ADOLF (MICHAEL) FURTWÄNGLER

b. June 30, 1853. Freiburg, Brisgau, Germany.
d. October 12, 1907. Athens, Greece.

EDUCATION

University of Freiburg.
University of Munich, 1876 (Ph.D.).

APPOINTMENTS AND AWARDS

Univ. of Bonn (1879–80); Royal Museum, Berlin: Assistant
(beg. 1880); Glyptothek Museum, Munich: Director (under
ERNST CURTIUS); Univ. of Munich: Professor of Classical
Archaeology (beg. 1894). Member: Bavarian Academy.

EXCAVATIONS

Olympia (Director, 1878); Aegina, 1901; Orchomenos,
1903–05; Amyklai, 1904.

PUBLICATIONS

Eros in der Vasenmalerei, Munich: T. Ackermann, 1874;
Pliny and His Sources Concerning Ancient Art, 1877; *Mycenaean
Painted Pottery* (with GEORG LOESCHCKE), 1879; *Die
Bronzefunde aus Olympia und deren Kunstgeschichtliche Bedeu-
tung*, 1879; *The Gold Finds of Vetterfelde*, 1883; *Mykenische Vasen*
(with Georg Loeschcke), Berlin: A. Asher and Co., 1866; *The
Vases in the Antiquarium of the Royal Museum of Berlin*, 1885;
Die Sammlung Sabouroff: kunst-denkmaäler aus griechenland,
Berlin: A. Asher and Co., 1883–87; *Olympia, Results of the Exca-
vation*, Vol. 4, 1890; *Meisterwerke der griechischen Plastik* (1893)

(English edition: *Masterpieces of Greek Sculpture* [1895]), Chicago: Argonaut Publishers, 1964; *Copying Statues in Antiquity*, 1896; *Catalogue of Vases in the Old Pinakothek, Munich*, 1896; *Intermezzi, and Historical Studies*, 1896; *Art Gems in the Berlin Museum*, 1896; *Collection Sornzee*, 1897; *Original Antiquities in Venice*, 1898; *Die Antiken Gemmen: Geschichte der Steinschneide-Kunst im klassischen Altertum* (3 vols.), Leipzig, Berlin: Gesecke and Devrient, 1900; *Catalogue of the Glyptothek, Munich*, 1900; *Aegina, das Heiligtum der Aphaia* (with Thiersch and Fiechter) (2 vols.), Munich: G. Franz'schen verlags, 1906.

Adolf Furtwängler is a monumental figure in the history of ancient art and Classical archaeology, and is credited with having laid the foundation for the explosive growth of basic knowledge in these areas which occurred in the first quarter of the twentieth century through the work of Furtwängler's successors including CARL W. BLEGEN and A. J. B. WACE.

Furtwängler called attention to the importance of taking note of the recurrence of similar vase patterns and the strata in which they occurred; thus he was the first to recognize that pottery could be used as a basis for the chronological dating of ancient sites. Up to this time pottery had generally been considered by excavators to be the least interesting and least informative of ancient artifacts; sherds were routinely discarded without much consideration. Although it is true that he only considered painted pottery to be of importance, his work nonetheless helped change the whole focus of this field of study (see also GEORG LOESCHCKE).

In their 1886 joint publication (above), the two published an account of painted Mycenaean vases and sherds. This was important not only with regard to dating but also because, in effect, they had produced the first Corpus—something that has proved to be indispensable to all subsequent researchers in the field.

Furtwängler was a pioneer in the practice of attributing specific pottery to specific artists. In spite of the fact that he made a number of errors, he was able to separate out many groups successfully. This was no small feat when one considers the mass of unorganized data with which he was confronted at that time, and J. D. BEAZLEY was among those who never failed to state his indebtedness to the foundation laid by Dr. Furtwängler.

Another of his major works was his publication on Greek sculpture (1893, above). In this sensitive work he discussed the sculpture of specific artists (including Pheidias, Praxitiles, and so on) and focused especially upon the apparent differences in the character of the sculptors as shown by their works. In his *Die antiken Gemmen* (above) he included a well-conceived survey of art in Italy from the Archaic through Augustan periods in addition to having created a new field of study, the history of ancient gems.

SOURCES

Salomon Reinach, "Adolf Furtwängler," *RA* 10 (1907): 326–27; *NDB*, 5, 1961; *AA* (1906): 458; Edmund von Mach, "Adolf Furtwängler," *Records of the Past* 6 (1907): 317–18; Johannes Sieveking, "Adolf Furtwängler," *BJDN*, 1909; Cook, *Greek Painted Pottery*, 1972; Brendel, *Prolegomena to the Study of Roman Art*, 1979; Michaelis, *A Century of Archaeological Discoveries*, 1908; Leekley and Noyes, *AESG*, 1976; Leekley and Noyes, *AEGI*, 1975; Leekley and Efstratiou, *AECNG*, 1980; *Glyptothek*, 1974; de Grummond, *EHCA*, 1996; Matz, *Art of Crete and Early Greece*, 1962; McDonald, *The Discovery of Homeric Greece*, 1967; Daniel, *A Hundred and Fifty Years of Archaeology*, 1975, 2d. ed.; Albright, *From the Stone Age to Christianity*, 1957, 2d. ed.; *NYT* (February 11, 1895); *TL* (October 15, 1907).

ARNE FURUMARK

b: September 26, 1903. Oslo, Sweden.
d: October 8, 1982. Uppsala, Sweden.

EDUCATION

Uppsala University.

APPOINTMENTS AND AWARDS

Uppsala Univ.: Professor in Classical Archaeology and Ancient History (1952–70).

EXCAVATIONS

Sinda, Cyprus; San Giovenale, Italy.

PUBLICATIONS

Mycenaean Pottery, 1. Analysis and classification, 1941; *Mycenaean Pottery, 2. Chronology*, 1941 (published simultaneously, reprinted 1972); *Mycenaean Pottery, 3. The Plates* (Åström, et al., editors, published posthumously, 1992), Stockholm: Svenska Institutet I Athen, 1972–92; "The Mycenaean IIIC pottery and its relation to Cypriote fabrics," *OpArch* 3 (1944): 194–265; *Det äldsta Italien*, Uppsala: J. A. Lindblad, 1947; "The Settlement at Ialysos and Aegean Prehistory c. 1550–1400 B.C.," *OpArch* 6 (1950): 150–271; "Ägäische Texte in griechischer Sprache, 1," *Eranos* 51 (1953): 103–120; "Ägäische Texte in griechischer Sprache, 2" *Eranos* 52 (1954): 18–60; *Redan de gamla grekerna*, 1961; *Hellener och barbarians*, 1962; "The excavation at Sinda: Some historical results," *OpAth* (1965); "Thera catastrophe: Consequences for European civilization," in C.

Doumas, editor, *Thera and the Aegean world. Papers presented at the Second International Scientific Congress, Santorini, Greece, August 1978*, 1978: 667–674.

Arne Furumark produced one of the most important works on the pottery of Bronze Age Greece. His 1941 *Mycenaean Pottery* is a landmark two-volume[1] work which deals with the classification, analysis, and chronology of Mycenaean pottery, and is the definitive reference on the subject.

In this work Furumark is careful to show that those who argued for the mainland roots of Mycenaean pottery were correct (see BLEGEN, WACE), but that one must also allow that Minoan pottery styles and decoration had a profound influence on the development of Greek mainland pottery. To aid in this understanding he does not use the term "Helladic" (as coined by Blegen and Wace) to refer to mainland pottery, but instead uses the term "Mycenaean" believing that "Helladic" connotes a strong sense of an isolated development. Since Furumark's work, the two terms have become almost interchangeable.

As important as his classification, analysis, and chronology are the ramifications of this publication: Furumark's work provided a final refutation of ARTHUR EVANS'S theory that the pottery produced on the Greek mainland from c. 1550–1100 B.C.E. was merely a product of Minoan colonies. Furumark was able to demonstrate that although Minoan influence is clearly seen in many Mycenaean wares, some Mycenaean pottery shapes and decoration from Mycenae's early period were retained at Mycenaean centers through the Late Bronze Age III period, unaffected by Minoan contact. Conversely, some of the more sophisticated Mycenaean shapes (such as stemmed cups [*kylix*]) were adopted and produced on Crete.

Prior to Furumark's work, it had been assumed that the Mycenaean civilization on the Greek mainland had experienced a complete collapse (presumably due to the Dorian invasions) around the twelfth century B.C.E. and that there had been a cultural break before the next pottery period, the proto-Geometric. However, his analysis showed that proto-Geometric pottery is truly a continuation of Mycenaean pottery production, though obviously in a much reduced and degenerated form.

A list of subsequent amendments to Furumark's classifications is provided in Paul Åström's introduction to volume 3 of *Mycenaean Pottery*, 1992.

SOURCES

Robin Hägg, "The Published Writings of Arne Furumark," *OpAth* 8 (1968): 213–17; Robin Hägg, "The Published Writings of Arne Furumark Published Between 1968 and 1984," *OpAth* 15 (1984): 17; McDonald, *The Discovery of Homeric Greece*, 1967; Sture, Brunnsåker, "Classical Archaeology and Ancient History," *Uppsala University. 500 Years: History, Art and Philosophy*, 1976: 19–33; Furumark, *Mycenaean Pottery 3. Plates*, 1992; John Franklin Daniel, *AJA* 47 (1943): 252–54; Dikaios, *Enkomi: Excavations 1948–1958*, Vol. 1, 1968; MacKendrick, *The Greek Stones Speak*, 1981, 2d. ed.

NOTE

1. A third volume (plates) was posthumously published in 1992. See "Publications," above.

ERNEST A(RTHUR) GARDNER

b: March 16, 1862. London, England.
d: November 27, 1939. Maidenhead, England.

Education
City of London School.
Gonville and Caius College, Cambridge University, 1884.

APPOINTMENTS AND AWARDS

Cambridge Univ.: Fellow, Gonville and Caius College (1885–94) (Craven University Student [1887–90]); British School at Athens: Director (1887–95); University of London: Yates Professor of Archaeology (1896–1929), Emeritus Professor of Archaeology (1929 [retained lectureship to 1933]); *Journal of Hellenic Studies*: Joint Editor (1897–1932); Society for the Promotion of Hellenic Studies: President (1929–32). Hon. Fellow: Gonville and Caius College, Cambridge (1926). Hon. Degree: Litt.D., Trinity College, Dublin. Award: Greek Order of the Redeemer.

EXCAVATIONS

Naucratis, 1885–86; Paphos, 1888; Polis tis Chrysochou, 1889; Megalopolis, 1890–91.

PUBLICATIONS

Naukratis, Vol. 1 (co-contributor) (1886), *Naukratis, Vol. 2* (1888), Chicago: Ares Publishers, 1992 (2 vols.); *Handbook of Greek Sculpture* (1915, 2d. ed.), London: Macmillan and Co., 1920; *Catalogue of Vases in the Fitzwilliam Museum*, 1897; *Ancient Athens* (1902), New York: Haskell House Publishers,

1968; *Introduction to Greek Epigraphy* (with F. S. Roberts), Cambridge: Cambridge University Press, 1905; *Six Greek Sculptors* (1910), Freeport, N.Y.: Books for Libraries Press, 1967; *Religion and Art in Ancient Greece* (1910), New York: Kennikat Press, 1969; *The Art of Greece* (1925), New York: Cooper Square Publishers, 1975; *Poet and Artist in Greece*, 1933; *Greece and the Aegean* (with a chapter on Constantinople by S. CASSON), New York: R.M. McBride, 1933.

Ernest Gardner accompanied FLINDERS PETRIE to the site of Naukratis as his assistant, but became the dig's director soon afterward. He made several important discoveries at the site including a seventh century B.C.E. Temple of Aphrodite; thus his work at Naukratis established important early connections between Greece and Egypt by demonstrating that a Greek colony had been founded there as early as the mid-seventh century B.C.E.

Gardner's 1896–97 publication on Greek sculpture, though an important work at the time, betrays an overly idealistic view toward Greek art. He was a critic of contemporary art, disliking its focus on the individuality of the artist. He felt that the Greek artist had achieved a balance between the individual and the traditional values of the polis; like other scholars of his day he found in the appreciation of Greek sculpture, in particular, a way for contemporary society to come together against what he considered to be the chaos of the age, brought about by the rise of individualism.

He was the first student to attend the British School at Athens and became its second director in 1887. As such he played an important role in the school's development into a world-class center for research in Classical archaeology. Students such as J. G. Frazer and JOHN L. MYRES were admitted to the school during his tenure. When he was appointed Yates Professor of Archaeology at the University of London he again used his organizational skills to the full and established its Department of Classical Archaeology. He was a younger brother of PERCY GARDNER.

SOURCES

Waterhouse, *British School at Athens . . .* , 1986; Jocelyn M. C. Toynbee and H. D. A. Major, *DNB*, 1931–40; Turner, *The Greek*

Heritage in Victorian Britain, 1981; *JHS* 10 (1889): 283–84; Leekley and Noyes, *AESG*, 1976; *WWWEEA*, 1931–49, Vol. 2; Dawson and Uphill, *Who Was Who in Egyptian Archaeology*, 1972; *TL* (November 29, 1939).

PERCY GARDNER

b: November 24, 1846. London, England.
d: July 17, 1937. England.

EDUCATION

Christ's College, Cambridge, 1869.

APPOINTMENTS AND AWARDS

British Museum: Department of Coins (1871–87); Cambridge Univ.: Disney Professor of Archaeology (1880–87); Oxford Univ.: Chair of Classical Archaeology, (1887–1925), Professor Emeritus (1925); *Journal of Hellenic Studies*: Editor (1880–96). Fellow: British Academy (1903). Hon. Fellow: Christ's College, Oxford Univ. (1897). Corresponding Member: Prussian Academy; Göttingen Academy of Sciences; French Institute.

PUBLICATIONS

Catalogue of Greek Coins: Italy (1873), *Sicily* (with BARCLAY HEAD and Stuart Poole) (1876), *Thrace* (with Barclay Head) (1877); *The Coins of the Greek and Scythic Kings of Bactria and India in the British Museum* (1886), Chicago: Argonaut, 1966; *Catalog of Greek Coins: Thessaly to Aetolia* (1883), Bologna: A Forni, 1963 (edited by Reginald Stuart Poole); *Catalogue of Greek Coins: Peloponnesus (excluding Corinth)* (1887) Bologna: A. Forni, 1963; *Parthian Coinage*, 1877; *Catalogue of Coins of the Seleucid Kings of Syria* (1878) Bologna: A. Forni, 1963; *Macedonian and Greek Coins of the Seleucidae*, London: J. R. Smith, 1878; *Samos and Samian Coins*, 1882; *Types of Greek Coins: An Archaeological Essay*, Cambridge: Cambridge University Press, 1883; *Numismatic Commentary on Pausanias* (with Friedrich Imhoff-Blumer), 1885–86; *Greek and Scythic Kings of Bactria and India*, 1886; *New Chapters in Greek History*, London: J. Murray, 1892; *Sculptured Tombs of Hellas* (1896), Washington: McGrath Pub. Co., 1973; *Oxford at the Cross-roads*, London: A. and C. Black, 1903; *The Gold Coinage of Asia Before Alexander the Great*, Oxford: Oxford University Press, 1908; *History of Ancient Coinage, 700–300 B.C.* (1918), Chicago: Ares Publishers, 1974; *A Grammar of Greek Art*, London: Macmillan and Co., 1905; *Principles of Greek Art*, New York: The Macmillan Company, 1914; *Greek Art and Architecture: Their Legacy to Us*, Oxford: Oxford University Press, 1922; *New Chapters in Greek Art* (1926), New York: AMS Press, 1971; *Principles of Christian Art*, London: J. Murray, 1928; *The Coinage of Parthia by Percy Gardner with an Introduction and Supplementary Catalog of a Recent Hoard* by Joel L. Malter, San Diego, Calif.: Malter-Westerfeld Publishing Co., 1968. Theological titles include: *Faith and Conduct*, 1887; *Exploration Evangelica*, 1899; *The Growth of Christianity*, London: A. and C. Black, 1907; *The Religious Experience of St. Paul*, London: Williams and Norgate, 1911; *Modernism and the English Church*, 1926; *Interpretation of Religious Experience*, 1931.

Elder brother of ERNEST A. GARDNER, Percy Gardner was employed by the British Museum's Department of Coins having had no experience in numismatics or Classical archaeology. However, it quickly became apparent that Gardner had found his niche. He worked with other colleagues to begin the *Catalogue of Greek Coins* series which was to become a major reference work on the subject of ancient numismatics. He was sole contributor for the volumes *Thrace*, *Thessaly to Aetolia*, and *Peloponnesus*.

His other major contribution was in the acceptance of Classical archaeology as a legitimate discipline for study. When he took the chair in Classical archaeology at Oxford in 1887 he found that the field was not considered by many to be a very serious subject. It is widely felt that it was solely due to the determined and diligent work of Percy Gardner that Classical archaeology was eventually given credibility and support by the university. Some of his pupils at Oxford included J. L. MYERS, J. D. BEAZLEY, and STANLEY CASSON.

SOURCES

George Hill, "Percy Gardner 1846–1937," *PBA* 23 (1937): 459–69; *TL* (July 19, 1937).

(Sir) William Gell

b: 1777. Derbyshire, England.
d: February 4, 1836. Naples, Italy.

EDUCATION

Jesus College, Cambridge University.
Emanuel College, Cambridge University, 1798 (B.A.),
1804 (M.A.).

APPOINTMENTS AND AWARDS

Fellow: Society of Antiquaries; Royal Society. Member:
Society of Dilettanti (1897); Royal Academy of Berlin; Institute of France.

PUBLICATIONS

Topography of Troy and its Vicinity, 1804; *The Geography and
Antiquities of Ithaca*, London: Longman, Hurst, Rees, and Orme,
1807; *The Itinerary of Greece with a Commentary on Pausanias and
Strabo, and an account of the monuments of antiquity at present existing
in that country*, 1810 (1827, 2d. ed.); *Itinerary of the Morea being a
particular description of that Peninsula with a map of the routes*,
London: Rodwell and Martin, 1817; *The Itinerary of Greece: Containing One Hundred Routes in Attica, Boeotia, Phocis, Locris, and
Thessaly*, London: Rodwell and Martin, 1819; *Narrative of a
Journey in the Morea*, London: Longman, Hurst, Rees, Orme, and
Browne, 1823; *Pompeiana: or Observations upon the Topography, Edifices and Ornaments of Pompeii* (with J. P. Gandy), 1817–19; *Attica*,
1817; *Pompeiana: the Topography, Ornaments* (2 vols.), 1832; *Rome
and Its Environs from a Trigonometrical Survey*, London: Saunders
and Otley, 1834; *Pompeii: Its Destruction and Re-discovery, with*

engravings and Descriptions of the Art and Architecture of Its Inhabitants (with J. P. Gandy), New York: R. Worthington, 1880.

William Gell is known chiefly for his useful topographical descriptions of Mediterranean lands and for his finely-detailed sketches of ancient sites and artifacts. He traveled extensively through Spain, Italy, Syria, Dalmatia, the Ionian Islands, Greece, and western Asia Minor.

In 1801 he visited the Troad in search of the site of ancient Troy and erroneously determined that it had occupied the town of Bounabashi. Being a prominent member of the influential Society of Dilettanti he was commissioned by that group to lead an expedition to Greece and Asia Minor; the journey began in 1812 with a visit to Eleusis where he directed some important excavations during which the Propylaea and the Temple of Artemis were discovered and cleared. They traveled on to Asia Minor visiting a number of key sites including the Temple of Hera at Samos, the Temple of Apollo at Didyma, Aphrodisias, Cnidus, Halicarnassus, and Antiphellus in Lycia. The trip ended in Attica with excavations at the Temple of Nemesis at Rhamnous and visits to Sounion and Thorikos; they returned to London in 1813.

Gell left Britain in 1820, moving permanently to Italy where he acted as resident plenipotentiary for the Society of Dilettanti, keeping it apprised of archaeological activities in and around Rome. The ruins of Pompeii were of special interest to him and he produced a number of popular publications on the site and its antiquities.

Gell was a gifted artist and during his career amassed more than eight hundred drawings made during his travels; these were acquired by the British Museum in 1852.

SOURCES

DNB, Vol. 7; Cust, *History of the Society of Dilettanti*, 1914; *Athenaeum* (London), (March 19, 1836): 209; *The Gentleman's Magazine* 5 (1836): 665–66; Clarke, *Greek Studies in England, 1700–1830*, 1945; Mylonas, *Eleusis and the Eleusinian Mysteries*, 1961; Miller, *Greece Through the Ages*, 1972.

EINAR (NILSON) GJERSTAD

b: October 30, 1897. Orebro, Sweden.
d: January 8, 1988. Sweden.

EDUCATION

University of Uppsala, 1922 (M.A.), 1926 (Ph.D.).

APPOINTMENTS AND AWARDS

Univ. of Uppsala: Senior Lecturer, Classical Archaeology
and Ancient History (1926–34); Swedish Cyprus Expedition:
Director (1927–31); Swedish Institute of Classical Studies in
Rome: Director (1935–40); Univ. of Lund: Professor of Clas-
sical Archaeology and Ancient History (1939–56); Royal
Society of Lund: Secretary (1945–53), Chairman (1967–69).
Hon. Member: Society of Cypriote Studies; Archaeological
Institute of America. Award: Order of the Phoenix (Greece).

EXCAVATIONS

Asine, Greece, 1922 (under A. W. PERSSON); Alambra,
Kalopsidha, Ayios Sozomenos, Cyprus, 1923–24, 1927–31;
Palestrina, Italy, 1940; Rome, 1939, 1949, 1953–54, 1959.

PUBLICATIONS

Studies in Prehistoric Cyprus, Uppsala, Sweden: Uppsala
University, 1926; *The Swedish Cyprus Expedition*, Vols. 1–4,
Stockholm: The Swedish Cyprus Expedition, 1934–72, editor;
"The Colonization of Cyprus in Greek Legend," *OpArch* 3
(1944): 107–23; "Decorated Metal Bowls from Cyprus,"
OpArch 4 (1946): 1–18; "Four Kings," (Ibid.): 21–24; *Early*

Rome, Vols. 1–4, Lund: C. W. K. Gleerup, 1953–73; *Legends and Facts of Early Roman History*, Lund: Gleerup, 1962; *Greek Geometric and Archaic Pottery Found in Cyprus* (with Yves Calvert et al.), Stockholm: Svenska Institutet I Athen, 1977; *Les Origines de la République romaine*, Andoeuvres-Genéve: Foundation Hardt pour l'étude de l'Antiquité classique, 1967; "Ages and Days in Cyprus," *SIMA-PB* 12, 1980 (originally published in Swedish as *Sekler och Dagar*, 1933); *Det äldsta Rom*, Stockholm: Norstedt, 1972; "The origin and chronology of the Early Bronze Age in Cyprus," *RDAC*, 1980; Aström, Gjerstad, et al., "Fantastic Years on Cyprus: The Swedish Cyprus Expedition and Its Members," *SIMA-PB* 79, 1994.

A student of AXEL W. PERSSON, Gjerstad is best known for having directed the Swedish Cyprus Expedition, cited by one scholar as being one of the most fruitful foreign archaeological expeditions ever to have been carried out on the island.[1]

During this four year expedition (1927–31), Gjerstad (assisted by ERIK SJÖQVIST, Alfred Westholm, and John Lindros) excavated more than twenty sites and uncovered remains which dated from the Neolithic (the first Neolithic finds on the island) to the Late Roman period. One of the major finds of the expedition was the fifth century B.C.E. Palace of Vouni, the only extant palace of the Classical period.

Gjerstad was the first to propose the theory that the culture of Early Bronze Age Cyprus had originated in Anatolia. He believed that immigrants had come into Cyprus and had mingled peaceably with Cyprus's indigenous population. Although his hypothesis has been widely accepted, today it still finds a small number of detractors. In his doctoral thesis published in 1926, Gjerstad established a typology of Cypriot pottery (based in large part on the work of J. L. MYRES and MAX OHNE-FALSCH-RICHTER) and subsequently presented a cultural sequence for prehistoric Cyprus which, like ARTHUR EVANS'S chronological division for Minoan Crete, consisted of three main divisions, each containing three subdivisions.

After spending twenty-five years on the excavations of Cyprus, Gjerstad spent the following twenty-five years of his career in Italy and, after having carried out excavations near the Equus Domitianus in the Forum Romanum in Rome, created a major sensation when he announced that the traditional founding date of Rome (753 B.C.E. derived from the ancient historian Livy) had to be moved down to c. 575 B.C.E. He received much criticism for this theory but remained adamant that the archaeological data were more reliable than the ancient texts. Recent excavations have set the date of Rome's foundation back to at least c. 625 B.C.E.

Gjerstad, whose excavations and discoveries are so well documented, was noted for his careful, scientific, and unbiased approach to scholarship, and for the timely publication of his findings.

SOURCES

Åström et al., "The Fantastic Years on Cyprus: The Swedish Cyprus Expedition and Its Members," *SIMA-PB*, 79 (1994); "The Swedish Cyprus Expedition: The Living Past," *Medelhavsmusett* 9, E. Rystedt, editor (1994); Karageorghis, Vassos et al., "Cypriot Antiquities in the Medelhavsmuseet, Stockholm," *Medelhavsmuseet* 2 (1977): 7–10; H. W. Catling, *Antiquity* 57 (1983): 71–72; *WWWorld*, 1974–76; Gjerstad, *Studies in Prehistoric Cyprus*, 1926; Karageorghis, *Cyprus: From the Stone Age to the Romans*, 1982; *NYT* (March 30, 1950).

NOTE

1. H. W. Catling, *Antiquity* 57 (1983): 71–72.

HETTY GOLDMAN

b: December 19, 1881. New York, New York.
d: May 4, 1972. Princeton, New Jersey.

EDUCATION

Bryn Mawr College, 1903 (B.A.).
Radcliffe College, 1910 (M.A.), 1916 (Ph.D.).
American School of Classical Studies at Athens, 1910–12.

APPOINTMENTS AND AWARDS

Princeton Univ.: Professor, Institute for Advanced Study
(1936–56). Award: Gold Medal, Archaeological Institute of
America (1966).

EXCAVATIONS

Halae, central Greece, 1911–12, 1921, 1923, 1931, and
1935 (Codirector with A. L. Walker-Kosmopoulos); Colophon,
1922 (Director); Eutresis, 1924–27 (Director); Tarsus, Cilicia,
1934–39 (Director).

PUBLICATIONS

Excavations at Eutresis in Boeotia, Cambridge, Mass.: Harvard University Press, 1931; *Excavations at Gözlü Kule, Tarsus*
(3 vols.), Princeton, N.J.: Princeton University Press, 1950,
1956 and 1963.

The first female professor to teach at Princeton's Institute
for Advanced Study, Hetty Goldman focused on the prehistoric period of Greek history and was particularly interested in

understanding the relationship between Anatolia and early Greece. From her work at Eutresis she recorded the various stages of human development in mainland prehistoric Greece, and at her excavations in Tarsus she uncovered inscribed tablets, seals, and seal impressions which documented the relations between Tarsus and the Hittite kings of central Anatolia.

Her careful and objective observation of archaeological data led her to be considered one of the foremost scholars in this area of study. Among her many students were CARL W. BLEGEN and the epigraphist BENJAMIN D. MERITT.

SOURCES

M. J. Mellink, *NAW*, Vol. 4, 1980; Weinberg, editor, *The Aegean and the Near East: Studies Presented to Hetty Goldman*, 1956; Patricia S. Wren, "Remembering 'Aunt Hetty,' Excavations at Halae—Then and Now," *AIA Newsletter* 10, no. 4 (1995): 1ff; Leekley and Efstratiou, *AECNG*, 1980; *Archaeology* (April, 1967): 83; *NYT* (May 6, 1972).

VIRGINIA R(ANDOLPH) GRACE

b: 1901. New York, New York.
d: May 22, 1994. Athens, Greece.

EDUCATION

Brearley School, New York, New York.
Bryn Mawr College, 1922 (B.A.), 1934 (Ph.D.).
American School of Classical Studies at Athens, 1927–28.

APPOINTMENTS AND AWARDS

Fellow: Athenian Agora Excavations (1932–39, 1949–94). Visiting Member: Institute for Advanced Study, Princeton Univ. (1945). Award: Gold Medal, Archaeological Institute of America (1989).

EXCAVATIONS

Pergamon, 1931; Halae (central Greece), 1931–32; Lapithos, Cyprus; Tarsus, Asia Minor, 1935 (under HETTY GOLDMAN); Kourion, Cyprus, 1940s.

PUBLICATIONS

"Stamped Amphora Handles found in 1931–32," *Hesperia* 3 (1934): 197–310; "The Stamped Amphora Handles," in Hetty Goldman, editor, *Tarsus I, Excavations at Gözlü Kule* 1950: 135–148; "Samian Amphoras," *Hesperia* 40 (1971): 52–95; "Revisions in Early Hellenistic Chronology," *AM* (1974): 193–203; *Amphoras and the Ancient Wine Trade* (*Excavations of the Athenian Agora* series, Picture Book No. 6), 1961 (1979, 2d ed.).

Virginia Grace's studies have had an immense impact on our knowledge of ancient trading practices and on the chronology of the Hellenistic period. How she achieved these diverse ends is the story of an individual who possessed extraordinary foresight and a capacity for perseverance in the study of minutiae, the minutiae in this case being the cataloging of thousands of stamped amphora handles.

Amphoras were routinely stamped on their handles with information regarding their place and date of manufacture. Grace realized that by carefully studying these stamps she could build up a detailed picture of ancient trade and its practices. She began this work in 1931 and cataloged tens of thousands of stamped amphora handles from many different sources including Rhodes, Knidos, Thasos, Delos, Sinope, and the Athenian Agora (she cataloged twenty-five thousand pieces from the latter site alone).

The ramifications of this work have been widespread; her lists of magistrates (stamped on the handles) led to a rewriting of the chronology of the Hellenistic period. We have also learned something of the standard measurements used in ancient trade and of the development of amphora styles from her descriptions of their various shapes. However, the greatest reward for her painstaking work (which spanned sixty years) has been the detailed picture that we have gained of the structure and practices of ancient sea trade in the Mediterranean area.

SOURCES

Carolyn G. Koehler, "Virginia Randolph Grace, 1901–1994," *AJA* 100 (1996): 153–55; Doreen Spitzer, "A Fond Farewell," *ASCSA Newsletter* (Fall 1994): 2; *Hesperia* 51 (1982): 365–67 (full bibliography); *NYT* (June 16, 1994).

J(AMES) WALTER GRAHAM

b: August 5, 1906. Liverpool, Nova Scotia, Canada.
d: August 22, 1991. Canada.

EDUCATION

Acadia University, 1927 (B.A.), 1928 (M.A.).
Johns Hopkins University, 1933 (Ph.D.).

APPOINTMENTS AND AWARDS

Acadia Univ.: Instructor in Latin (1928–29); Johns Hopkins
Univ.: Res. Asst. (1933–35); Univ. of Missouri: Asst. Professor of
Archaeology (1935–47); Dept. of Fine Art, Univ. of Toronto: Asst.
Professor of Art and Archaeology (1947–60), Professor (1960–72);
Royal Ontario Museum: Curator, Dept. of Greek and Roman
Antiquities (beg. 1947); American School of Classical Studies at
Athens: Visiting Professor (1959). Fellow: American School of
Classical Studies at Athens (1930–31). Member: Canadian Classical Association; Society for the Promotion of Hellenic Studies.

EXCAVATIONS

Olynthus, 1931, 1934; Athens, 1965 (vicinity of Agora).

PUBLICATIONS

Domestic Architecture in Classical Greece, Baltimore, Md.:
The Johns Hopkins Press, 1938; *Olynthus, Part 8* (*The Hellenic
House*) (with D. M. ROBINSON), 1938; "The Phaistos 'Piano
Nobile,' " *AJA* 60 (1956): 151–157; "The Central Court as the
Minoan Bull-Ring," *AJA* 61 (1957): 255–262; "The Residential
Quarter of the Minoan Palace," *AJA* 63 (1959): 47–52; "The

Minoan unit of length and Minoan palace planning," *AJA* 64 (1960): 335–41, and in *Proceedings of the Second International Cretological Congress* (1967): 157–165; "The Minoan Banquet Hall," *AJA* 65 (1961): 165–172; *Palaces of Crete* (1972), Princeton, N.J.: Princeton University Press, 1987 (rev. ed.).

Graham's contributions lie in the areas of Greek domestic architecture and in Cretan palace construction. His excavations yielded major progress in our understanding of the domestic architecture of ancient Greece, and he authored our most comprehensive work on Minoan palace construction in Bronze Age Crete.

In his Olynthus publication[1] he was able to establish a typology for Greek domestic architecture and although ostensibly an excavation report, it is to this day regarded as the premier reference work for domestic architecture dating from the late fifth century down to the early fourth century B.C.E.

In his 1962 publication on Minoan palaces he gave detailed descriptions of these buildings and of Minoan builders' methods. He presented several theories regarding the form of the upper stories of the palaces and developed several hypotheses regarding the use of various areas, including the central court. Although on initial inspection the palaces would seem to have developed in a haphazard fashion, careful measurement of the remains of these structures established that they were the product of meticulous planning based upon a standard measurement of 30.3 cm (the Minoan foot).

SOURCES

Joseph W. Shaw, "James Walter Graham, 1906–1991," *AJA* 96 (1992): 325–26; Frederick E. Winter, "James Walter Graham," *Fine Art News* (April/May, 1992): 1–2 (Dept. of Fine Art, University of Toronto); *DAS* 4th. ed.; Renfrew, *The Emergence of Civilization*, 1972; *CR* 77 (1963): 335–37; Lucy T. Shoe, *AJA* 43 (1939): 707–08; M. S. F. Hood, *AJA* 68 (1964): 309–10; Correspondence with the Dept. of Fine Art, University of Toronto.

NOTE

1. Although David M. Robinson is listed as joint author on this publication, it is primarily Graham's work (Shaw, *AJA* 96 [1992]:325).

FEDERICO HALBHERR

b: February 15, 1857. Rovereto, Italy.
d: July 17, 1930. Rome, Italy.

EDUCATION

University of Rome, 1880.
University of Florence.
University of Berlin.

APPOINTMENTS AND AWARDS

Univ. of Rome: Professor of Greek Epigraphy (beg. 1889).

EXCAVATIONS

Gortyn, 1884–85 (with Comparetti), 1893–94 (with Taramelli); Erganos, 1894; Ayia Triadha beg. 1904; Idaian Cave, 1885; Psychro (Dictaean Cave), 1886; Phaistos, 1894, 1900-09; Cyrenaica, 1910; Tripolitania, 1911.

PUBLICATIONS

"Researches in Crete," *Antiquity* (1893): 110–112; "Cretan Expedition XI, Three Cretan Necropoleis: Report on the researches of Erganos, Panglina and Courtes," *AJA* (1901): 259–293. The excavation reports for the palace at Phaistos were published as *Il Palazzo Minoico de Festos* by L. Pernier and L. Banti, 1935–51 (2 vols.).

Sir ARTHUR EVANS referred to Federico Halbherr as the "Patriarch of Cretan excavation."[1] As founder and director of the Italian Archaeological Mission to Crete he played a pivotal role in the development of Cretan archaeology and oversaw excavations at two key Cretan sites, Phaistos and Gortyn.

Schooled as an epigrapher, Halbherr originally journeyed to Crete in 1884 (at the behest of his teacher, Domenico Comparetti) in order to find ancient inscriptions. At the time, archaeological inscriptions were quickly becoming regarded as a reliable new source for gaining knowledge of ancient law and history. Within a month of his arrival on the island, he had discovered one of the most significant epigraphical finds of Classical archaeology, the "Great Inscription" of Gortyn. This long inscription dates to the fifth century B.C.E. and provides us with a great deal of information regarding Cretan civilization from the seventh century B.C.E. on. With this early discovery, Halbherr was instrumental in generating worldwide interest in the archaeology of Crete.

In 1894 Halbherr was shown some ancient artifacts that had been taken from a tomb near the Mesara Plain. The finds indicated to Halbherr that a settlement must have existed close to these tombs, and he determined to begin excavation in the area as soon as possible. Unfortunately, the political conditions on Crete at that time were in flux, and so he could not begin until 1900. What Halbherr was to uncover was Phaistos, the second largest of the Bronze Age Minoan palaces on Crete. This site was of particular importance because it allowed archaeologists to see clearly the form of the buildings during the First Palatial Period and much of it had not been altered by subsequent construction (which was not the case at Knossos).

In addition, Halbherr played a major role in securing the site of Knossos for excavation by ARTHUR EVANS.

SOURCES

Di Vita, *Ancient Crete: A Hundred Years of Italian Archaeology (1884–1984)*, 1985; *AJA* (1930): 64; Ugo Antonielli, "Federico Halbherr," *Bullettino di paletnologia italiana*, (1930): 151–53; Evans, *The Palace of Minos*, Vol. 4, Part 1; Higgins, *The Archaeology of Minoan Crete*, 1973; Michaelis, *A Century of Archaeological Discoveries*, 1908; Leekley and Noyes, *AEGI*, 1975; Graham, *The Palaces of Minoan Crete*, 1961.

NOTE

1. Evans, *The Palace of Minos*, Vol. 4, Part 1 (1935): ix.

H(ARRY) R(EGINALD) (HOLLAND) HALL

b: September 30, 1873. London, England.
d: October 13, 1930. London, England.

EDUCATION

Merchant Taylor's School, 1891.
St. John's College, Oxford University, 1895 (B.A.), 1897 (M.A.).

APPOINTMENTS AND AWARDS

Dept. of Egyptian and Assyrian Antiquities, British Museum: Assistant (to E. Wallis Budge, 1896), Asst. Keeper (1919–24), Keeper (1924–30); Palestine Exploration Fund: Chairman (1922); Society of Antiquaries: Vice President (1929). Fellow: Society of Antiquaries (1911); British Academy (1926). Hon. Fellow: St. John's College, Oxford Univ. (1929). Hon. Degree: D.Litt., Oxford Univ. Member: Society for the Promotion of Hellenic Studies; Royal Asiatic Society. Award: M.B.E. (Member of the British Empire [for wartime services]).

EXCAVATIONS

Dair-al-Bahari, 1903–07; Abydos, 1910, 1925; Director, Ur, Tell al-Ubaid, Abu Shaharain (British Museum excavations), 1919.

PUBLICATIONS

The Oldest Civilization of Greece, London: D. Nutt, 1901; *Coptic and Greek Texts of the Christian Period in the British Museum*, London: Board of Trustees of the British Museum, 1905; *Egypt and Western Asia in the Light of Recent Discoveries* (with L. W. King), 1907; *The Eleventh Dynasty Temple at Deir el Bahari* (with E. Naville and others) (3 vols.), London: Egypt Exploration Fund, 1907–13; *Hieroglyphic Texts from Egyptian Stelae in the British Museum*, Vols. 2–7, 1912–25; *Ancient History of the Near East from the Earliest Times to the Battle of Salamis*, (1913), London: Methuen, 1960 (11th ed.); *The Civilization of Greece in the Bronze Age* (1923), New York: Cooper Square Publishers, 1970 (Rhind Lectures); *Ur Excavations* (with C. L. Woolley), Oxford: Oxford University Press, 1927; *A Season's Work at Ur*, London: Methuen and Co., 1930.

Although he was considered the preeminent authority on the art of ancient Egypt and Mesopotamia, H. R. Hall's interests encompassed the whole of the Near East including Egypt, Asia Minor, Mesopotamia, and the Aegean. He carried out extensive archaeological research but was very much a historian and used the information that he gained from excavation work to explore the relationships among these geographic areas.

From an early age Hall had been offended by the assumption of ancient historians that Greek civilization had emerged and developed in a vacuum, quite separate from its eastern neighbors. In his 1901 publication (above) he was able to integrate his extensive knowledge of Egypt and Mesopotamia with the new information coming to light on Crete (through the work of Sir ARTHUR EVANS) together with the discoveries made previously on the Greek mainland (by HEINRICH SCHLIEMANN); he was thus able to show that many parallels and influences were apparent and that the early Aegean civilizations owed much to the older civilizations of the Near East.

He continued to pursue the idea of the dependence of early Greece on the Near East throughout his career and contributed greatly to further thought in this area.

SOURCES

Hugh Last, "Dr. H. R. Hall," *JEA* 17 (1931): 111–16; Hugh Last, "Harry Reginald Holland Hall 1873–1930," *PBA* (1930): T. E. Peet, 475–485; *DNB*, 1922–30; Dawson and Uphill, *Who Was Who in Egyptology*, 1972; *AJA* (1930): 64; *TL* (October 14, 1930); *NYT* (October 14, 1930).

(Sir) William Hamilton

b: December 13, 1730. Scotland.
d: April 6, 1803. London, England.

APPOINTMENTS AND AWARDS

3rd Regiment of Footguards: Officer (1747–58); Member of Parliament (1761–64); British Envoy Extraordinary, Naples, Italy (1764–1800). Fellow: Royal Society (1766); Society of Antiquaries. Member: Society of Dilettanti (1777). Hon. Degrees: D.C.L., Oxford Univ. (1802). Award: K.C.B (Knight Commander of the Bath, 1772).

PUBLICATIONS

Campi Phlegraei (2 vols.), Naples: W. Tischbein, 1776, supplement, 1779; *Observations on Mount Vesuvius, Mount Etna, and Other Volcanoes* (1772), London: T. Cadell, 1774; *An Account of the Earthquakes in Calabria, Sicily* . . . , 1783 (English and Italian editions).

In spite of the fact that William Hamilton did not author archaeological texts his contributions to Classical scholarship were quite remarkable.

Hamilton was rather unusual with regard to the motivation for his interest in antiquity; he gently mocked the enthusiasm of individuals who found antiquities appealing curiosities and instead saw in them a more relevant value, that is, as models for modern artists to emulate in terms of their high standard of workmanship and artistry. He was also exceptional in that he found ancient vases (specifically Greek) of greater interest than Classical architecture or sculpture.

Subsequent to his appointment as British Envoy Extraordinary to Naples in 1764, Hamilton became interested in the ancient Greek vases that he saw in the homes of wealthy Neapolitans, and having purchased a vase collection, he then began to acquire new pieces which were being exhumed from tombs and excavations around Naples and Sicily. He eventually amassed 730 Greek vases and a large number of ancient coins (six thousand), terracottas, and bronzes. Previously the chief interest in ancient pottery had been the interpretation of its subjects, and publications on this topic generally included very badly drawn renditions of pots and their art work. Hamilton's interest in Greek pottery was more practical than antiquarian and he decided to finance and organize the publication of a scholarly catalog of his vase collection in order that modern artists and craftsmen might more readily perceive their aesthetic value and copy them more correctly. He hired the Frenchman, D'Hancarville (Pierre Francois Hugues) for this project and *Antiquités étrusques, grecques et romaines étirés du cabinet de Mr. Hamilton à Naples* was published in four volumes, with text in French and English, from 1766 to 1767 (a four-volume second edition was issued 1801–08). The book included faithfully drawn diagrams of pottery shapes and large colored drawings of their decoration with written descriptions and commentary by D'Hancarville. This catalogue was the first major publication on Greek pottery.

As the book was only published in Italy it did not result in a wave of European enthusiasm for Greek vases, but after the proofs for the plates became available during printing Hamilton freely distributed them among friends and acquaintances, including his friend Josiah Wedgwood. Through Wedgwood's exposure to these proofs and his subsequent manufacture of Classical style pottery, Hamilton's original intention in publishing the catalogue was realized. Moreover, knowledge of Greek pottery and its aesthetic value had finally reached the general public.

Finding himself in financial straits, Hamilton sold his collection of antiquities to the British Museum in 1772 for £8,400, a purchase which provided the museum with the foundation for its Department of Greek and Roman Antiquities. The British Museum thus became the first public museum to exhibit Greek pottery.

Hamilton again began collecting Greek vases, and before selling this new collection commissioned Wilhelm Tischbein to publish a catalog of it entitled *Collections of Engravings from Ancient Vases mostly of pure Greek workmanship, in the possession of Sir William Hamilton* (text in English and French) in four volumes with a supplementary volume, 1791–95. A second edition, *Pitture di Vasi antiche*, was published 1800–03. Hamilton wrote the introduction to this work in which he firmly states that the vases are of Greek origin and not Italian (at this time they were often regarded as being of Etruscan manufacture).

Stimulated by his desire to procure more artifacts, Hamilton took an active interest in the excavation work that was being carried out at Pompeii and Herculaneum and attempted, without success, to convince the government of Naples that it should support the explorations at these two sites. He made a number of other presentations of ancient artifacts to the British Museum (including some sculpture), and it was Hamilton who purchased the "Portland Vase" in Italy from the Barberini Palace collection and sold it to Margaret Cavendish, Duchess of Portland in 1785 for 1,800 guineas. The vase was purchased by the British Museum in 1810.

Hamilton proved to be instrumental in the success of LORD ELGIN's activities in Athens, for he recommended that the Italian Giovanni Battista Lusieri should accompany Elgin as his architect and artist. Hamilton's wife was the famous Lady Emma Hamilton; their relationship with Admiral Horatio Nelson is well known.

SOURCES

Edwards, *Lives of the Founders of the British Museum* (1870), reprint, 1968; Cust, *History of the Society of Dilettanti*, 1914; Clarke, *Greek Studies in England, 1700–1830*, 1945; *DNB*, Vol. 8; Cook, *Greek Painted Pottery*, 1972, 2d. ed.; Michaelis, *Ancient Marbles in Great Britain*, 1882; Miller, *Greece Through the Ages*, 1972.

GEORGE M(AXIM) A(NOSSOV) HANFMANN

b: November 20, 1911. St. Petersburg, Russia.
d: March 13, 1986. Cambridge, Massachusetts.

EDUCATION

University of Jena.
University of Munich.
Friedrich-Wilhelm-Universität, Berlin, 1934 (Ph.D.).
John Hopkins University, 1935 (Ph.D.).

APPOINTMENTS AND AWARDS

Harvard Univ.: Junior Fellow (1935–38), Instructor (1938–41), Asst. Professor of Fine Arts (1941–43), Assoc. Professor of Fine Arts (1949–56), Professor (1956–71), John E. Hudson Professor of Archaeology (1971–82), Professor Emeritus (1982); Fogg Art Museum, Harvard Univ.: Curator of Ancient Art (1949–74). Fellow: American Academy of Arts and Sciences; Royal Society of Antiquaries (1960); Bollingen Foundation (1956–57); American Council of Learned Societies (1963–64). Member: American Research Center (Egypt); American Academy in Rome; Instituto di Studi Etruschi (Florence); Institute for Advanced Study (Princeton University). Hon. Degree: D. Phil., Freie Universität, Berlin (1982). Award: Gold Medal, Archaeological Institute of America (1978).

EXCAVATIONS

Tarsus, southwest Asia Minor, 1947–48; Field Director, Sardis, Asia Minor, 1958–76.

PUBLICATIONS

Altertruskische plastik: Die minschliche Gestalt in der Rund-plastik bis zum Ausgang der orientalisierenden Kunst, 1936; *The Season Sarcophagus in Dumbarton Oaks* (1951), New York: Johnson Reprint Corp., 1971 (2 vols.); Review of C.F.A. Scha-effer's *Stratigraphie comparée et chronologie de l'Asie Occidentale*, *AJA* 55 (1951): 418; *Observations on Roman Portaiture*, Bruxelles: revue d'études latines, 1953; "The Iron-Age Pottery of Tarsus," in HETTY GOLDMAN, editor, *Tarsus III: The Iron Age*, 1963; *Roman Art: A Modern Survey of the Art of Imperial Rome* (1964), New York: W. W. Norton, 1975 (2d. ed.); *Classical Sculpture*, Connecticut: New York Graphic Society, 1967; *Letters from Sardis*, Cambridge, Mass.: Harvard University Press, 1972; *Sardis: Temple of Artemis, Roman Bath-Gymnasium* (with F. Yegul), 1973; *From Croesus to Constantine: The Cities of Western Asia Minor and Their Arts in Greek and Roman Times*, Ann Arbor, Mich.: University of Michigan Press, 1975; *A Survey of Sardis and the Major Monuments outside the City Walls* (with J. C. Wald-baum), Cambridge, Mass.: Harvard University Press, 1976; *Sculpture from Sardis: The Finds through 1975* (with Nancy Ramage), Cambridge, Mass.: Harvard University Press, 1987; *Sardis from Prehistoric to Roman Times: Results of the Archaeolog-ical Exploration of Sardis, 1958–1975* (contributor), Cambridge, Mass.: Harvard Univeristy Press, 1983.

Hanfmann's early interest was in the Etruscan civilization and its origins, but his focus changed after he was asked to pub-lish the Lydian pottery that had been uncovered by excavations at Sardis in Asia Minor (the excavations at Sardis had been underway since 1910). In order to publish these finds properly Hanfmann realized that more stratigraphic excavation needed to be carried out. With this in mind, he initiated (with A. Henry Detweiler) the resumption of the Sardis excavations in 1958.

Hanfmann's original plans constituted a fairly short-term project but Sardis proved an exceptionally fruitful site and he was to spend almost the next twenty years there. From George Hanfmann's work we know that the occupation of Sardis spanned nearly four thousand years beginning c. 2500 B.C.E. and ending in A.D. 1402 when it was destroyed by the Mongol leader, Tamerlane. During this long period the city was home to a number of successive peoples (Persian, Greek, Roman,

Byzantine, and Islamic) and was an important cultural and commercial center to the peoples of the Mediterranean and Near East throughout its history; it was also a particularly strong center of early Christianity. Sardis's most celebrated ruler was King Croesus who reigned in the sixth century B.C.E. and who was noted for his incredible wealth. The remains of the Lydian period of the city were unearthed under the Roman city in 1958. Upon further examination Hanfmann discovered that Croesus's Sardis was in fact larger than the area later occupied by the Greeks and the Romans.

In addition to the information gained regarding the urban development of this city and the region of Lydia which surrounds it, there have been a number of notable finds made at Sardis which include a Roman mausoleum, a marble-paved commercial street, one of the largest synagogues of the ancient world, an elaborate Roman bath/gymnasium complex, and the tomb of King Gyges, a seventh century B.C.E. Lydian king.

Hanfmann successfully employed an interdisciplinary approach to the Sardis excavations and utilized the most modern tools for archaeological research including laser transits and stereometric balloon photography.

While curator of ancient art at the Fogg Art Museum, George Hanfmann presented several important exhibitions including "Ancient Art in American Private Collections" in 1956 which proved to be instrumental in bringing ancient art and its acquisition to the attention of the general public.

SOURCES

David Gordon Mitten, "George Maxim Anossov Hanfmann, 1911–1986," *AJA* 91 (1987): 259–65; Mitten et al., editors, *Studies Presented to George M. A. Hanfmann*, 1971; Butler, *Sardis*, Vol. 1: *The Excavations. Part 1: 1910–1914*, 1969; *DAS*, 1978; *CB*, 1967; *NYT* (March 15, 1986).

(SIR) CECIL HARCOURT-SMITH

b: September 11, 1859. Staines, Middlesex, England.
d: March 27, 1944. Stoatley Bramley, Surrey, England.

EDUCATION

Winchester College.

APPOINTMENTS AND AWARDS

Department of Greek and Roman Antiquities, British Museum: Assistant (1879–96), Asst. Keeper (1896–1904), Keeper (1904–08); British School at Athens: Director (1895–97); Victoria and Albert Museum: Director (1909–24); Adviser for Royal Art Collections (1925); Surveyor of the Royal Works of Art (1928–36); Hellenic Society: Vice President. Hon. Degrees: LL.D., Univ. of Aberdeen (1895); D. Litt., Oxford Univ. (1928). Awards: K.C.B. (Knight Commander of the Bath, 1909); Commander of the Victorian Order (1917); Knight Commander of the Victorian Order (1934); Grand Cross of the Order of the Phoenix (Greece, 1932).

PUBLICATIONS

The Archaic Artemisia by D. G. HOGARTH (with chapter by Harcourt-Smith), London: The Trustees of the British Museum, 1908; *The J. P. Morgan Antiquities: The Art Treasures of the Nation*, 1929; *The Society of Dilettanti: Its Regalia and Pictures*, 1932.

Best known for his work in reorganizing the collections of the Victoria and Albert Museum, Harcourt-Smith made several contributions to Mediterranean archaeology when he was granted two years leave of absence from his post with the

British Museum to become director of the British School at Athens. This came at a crucial time for the school as it had just begun to receive funding from the British Treasury. Harcourt-Smith had been appointed to the directorship based mainly upon his organizational strengths and his reputation for showing promise as an archaeologist. He had already founded the journal *Classical Review*, and one of his first tasks in Athens was to organize a publication for the school. The *Annual of the British School at Athens* was published for the first time in 1895, and it was under his directorship that the Phylakopi excavations were begun on the island of Melos.[1]

Harcourt-Smith determined that it was important that all students be under one roof and within the boundaries of the school itself. It was under his supervision that the British School was physically enlarged to include the student residence quarters. The building erected during his tenure still forms the core of the present hostel.

SOURCES

Waterhouse, *British School at Athens*, 1986; Stephen B. Luce, "Sir Cecil Harcourt-Smith," *AJA* (1944): 274; James Laver, *DNB*, 1941–50; *WWW*, 1941–50; *TL* (March 29, 1944); *NYT* (March 31, 1944).

NOTE

1. Phylakopi has proved to be one of the most important Bronze Age sites in the Cyclades.

JANE ELLEN HARRISON

b: September 9, 1850. Cottingham, England.
d: April 16, 1928. London, England.

EDUCATION

Cheltenham Ladies' College, 1870.
Newnham College, Cambridge University, 1879.

APPOINTMENTS AND AWARDS

British Museum, South Kensington Museum: Lecturer; Newnham College, Cambridge Univ.: Lecturer in Classical Archaeology (1898–1900), Research Fellow (1900–03), Lecturer in Russian (1917–22). Corresponding Member: Berlin Classical Archaeological Institute (1896). Hon. Degrees: D.Litt, Durham Univ.; LL.D., Univ. of Aberdeen.

PUBLICATIONS

Myths of the Odyssey in Art and Literature, 1882; *Introductory Studies in Greek Art*, London: T. F. Unwin, 1885; *The Mythology and the Monuments of Ancient Athens*, by Margaret de G. Verrall (introduction and archaeological commentary by J. Harrison), London: Macmillan, 1890; *Greek Vase Paintings* (with D. S. MacColl), London: T. F. Unwin, 1894; *Prolegomena to the Study of Greek Religion* (1903), Princeton, N.J.: Princeton University Press, 1991; *Primitive Athens as Described by Thucydides*, Cambridge: Cambridge University Press, 1906; *Themis: A Study of the Social Origins of Greek Religion* (1912), Cleveland, Ohio: World Publishing, 1927; *Mythology* (1924), New York: Cooper Square Publishers, 1963; *Ancient Art and Ritual* (1913), New York: Greenwood Press, 1969; *Epilegomena to the Study of Greek*

Religion (1921), New York: University Books, 1962; *Reminiscences of a Student's Life*, London: Hogarth Press, 1925.

Jane Ellen Harrison was born at a time when scholarly interest in the world of ancient Greece and Rome focused upon the study of the Greek and Latin languages; archaeology was not yet a science and the artifacts gleaned from the few archaeological excavations that had been carried out by that time were viewed as objects to be admired, not analyzed, and were used to support the idealized picture of ancient Greece which scholars had derived from studying only literary sources. Harrison saw archaeological excavation as a means of providing new opportunities to allow us to gain access into the day-to-day lives of the Greeks; her open-mindedness and bold thinking helped change and expand the field of Classical studies to include archaeology and anthropology.

After graduating from Newnham College, Cambridge, she studied Greek vases at the British Museum under the supervision of its then director, Sir CHARLES NEWTON. She noticed that the religious themes that appeared on the vases were often quite different from those depicted in sculpture and in traditional Greek myth; there were examples of lesser deities who were often not part of the known Homeric tradition. Since these lesser gods were often local (gods of the house and local demon types such as those appearing on the Kabeiric vases at Thebes), they were much closer to the people than were the more grandiose and isolated gods of Olympus. This work led Harrison to devote the major part of her career to the study of the origin of ancient Greek religion. Through her work on Greek vases, Harrison illuminated a little known and hithertofore little appreciated aspect of ancient Greek life.

Harrison would eventually incorporate the thinking of contemporary sociologists, anthropologists, and philosophers (including Emil Durkheim and Henri Bergson) into her work. The most complete accounts of her theory were set out in her publications of 1903, 1912, and 1921 (above). Among her close circle while at Cambridge were Gilbert Murray (actually an Oxonian) and Francis McDonald Cornford, both of whom made major contributions to the study of religious thought in Greece.

Harrison visited Greece on three occasions, studying the topography of Athens under WILHELM DÖRPFELD. Her 1906 publication (above) was the result of this period of work.

SOURCES

Harrison, *Reminiscences of a Student's Life*, 1925, 2d. ed.; *AJA* 33 (1929): 109; S. Reinach, "Jane Ellen Harrison," *RA* (1927–28): 131; Turner, *The Greek Heritage in Victorian Britain*, 1981; Stewart, *Jane Ellen Harrison: A Portrait from Letters*, 1959; Peacock, *Jane Ellen Harrison: The Mask and the Self, 1988*; *DNB* 22, Supplement (F. M. Cornford).

HARRIET BOYD HAWES

b: October 11, 1871. Boston, Massachusetts.
d: March 31, 1945. Washington, D.C.

EDUCATION

Smith College, 1892 (B.A.), 1901 (M.A.).
American School of Classical Studies at Athens,
1896–1900.

APPOINTMENTS AND AWARDS

Smith College: Instructor (1900–06); Wellesley College:
Instructor (1920–36). Hon. Degree: Ph.D., Smith College (1910).

EXCAVATIONS

Kavousi, Crete, 1900; Gournia, Crete, 1901, 1903, 1904.

PUBLICATIONS

"Excavations at Kavousi, Crete, in 1901" *AJA* 5 (1901):
125–157; *Gournia, Vasiliki and Other Prehistoric Sites on the
Isthmus of Ierapetra, Crete* (American Exploration Society),
1908; *Crete: Forerunner of Greece* (coauthored with husband
Charles Henry Hawes with preface by ARTHUR J. EVANS)
(1909), London: Harper and Brothers, 1922; "Memoirs of a
Pioneer Excavator in Crete: Part, I" *Archaeology* 18(2), (1965):
94–101; "Memoirs of a Pioneer Excavator in Crete: Part II,"
Archaeology 18(4), (1965): 268–276.

Harriet Boyd Hawes, with encouragement from DAVID
HOGARTH (director, British School at Athens) and

ARTHUR EVANS gained the permission of a reluctant American School of Classical Studies at Athens to lead an excavation at Kavousi in Crete (1900). Hawes was the first woman to direct excavations in the Mediterranean area, and she is most noted for her discovery of the Bronze Age site of Gournia in Crete.

While stationed at Kavousi, a local peasant named George Perakis sent her a sealstone which he had found at a cove called Gournia on the Mirabello Bay. Interested by the well-cut sealstone, Hawes traveled to the nearby site and found what appeared to be the tops of ancient walls and many sherds dating to the Bronze Age. She immediately gathered one hundred workmen and began excavations; during three seasons she uncovered a town which dated mainly to the Late Minoan period. The site covers a few acres and consists of a small palace-like structure at the top of an acropolis, surrounded by winding, cobbled streets. About seventy houses were unearthed, some surviving to a height of four to five feet. Like the major palace sites on Crete, the settlement had been abandoned and then destroyed by fire during the latter fifteenth century B.C.E. The discovery of a town from this period, concurrent with the discoveries of Arthur Evans at the palace of Knossos, served to balance as well as supplement the archaeological picture of the Bronze Age on Crete.

SOURCES

Allsebrook, *Born to Rebel*, 1992; Hawes, *Archaeology*, 18 (2) (1965): 94–101; Hawes, *Archaeology* 18 (4) (1965): 268–76; E. L. Kohler and P. S. Boyer, *NAW*, Vol. 2, 1971; Lord, *History of the American School . . .* , 1947; Fitton, *Discovery of the Greek Bronze Age*, 1995.

JOSEPH HAZZIDAKIS

b: 1848. Melos, Greece.
d: February 16, 1936. Herakleion, Crete.

EDUCATION

University of Athens, 1871 (M.D.).
University of Monaco.
University of Brussels, 1876.

APPOINTMENTS AND AWARDS

Greek Archaeological Service on Crete: Joint-Director
(with Stephanos Xanthoudides); Herakleion Museum:
Director (1883–1923). Award: Medal of the Holy Cross.

EXCAVATIONS

Idaean Cave, 1884; Eileithya Cave, 1886; Gortyn; Tylissos,
1909–13; Gazi; Gournes Pediados, 1915; Mallia, 1915, 1919.

PUBLICATIONS

'Η 'Ιστορία τῆς νησου Μήλ ου; *Catalogue of the Herakleion
Museum* (in Greek), 1888; Hazzidakis's excavation reports on
Mallia appeared in *Prak* (1915): 108ff; *Prak* (1919): 50ff.; exca-
vation reports on Gournes Pediados in *ArchDelt* 4 (1918): 45ff.,
63ff.; *Études de préhistoire crétoise* (with L. Franchet), Paris: P.
Geuthner, 1921; *Les villas minoennes de Tylissos*, 1934.

A man of tremendous energy and vision, Joseph Hazzidakis was a practicing medical doctor, a political activist, and
one of Greece's foremost archaeologists.

In 1878 he organized the Society for the Promotion of Education which in turn founded the Herakleion Museum (then called the Museum of Crete). The museum began in a two room building and under Hazzidakis's direction expanded rapidly. He ensured, through his actions, that all artifacts found by an excavator (including all foreign institutions) were to remain on Crete and were to be housed in the new museum; today it has evolved into a world-class museum (one of Greece's largest) and houses almost all of the antiquities which have been recovered from a hundred years of excavation on the island (most of it dating to the Minoan period).

Hazzidakis made several important archaeological discoveries including the Bronze Age palace at Mallia, three Minoan villas at Tylissos (dating to the Late Minoan I [LM I] Period), and the Eileithya Cave which he identified as being that which Homer refers to in the *Odyssey*.[1]

As codirector of the Greek Archaeological Service on Crete he played a vital role as liaison between the foreign archaeological schools and the government. During this difficult political and social period he assisted and enabled foreign archaeologists to excavate on the island, including ARTHUR EVANS at Knossos (with the British School) and FEDERICO HALBHERR (of the Italian School), who was a close friend and collaborator at a number of important sites including the Idaean Cave, Gortyn, and the Eileithya Cave.

SOURCES

Menolaos E. Detorakeis, "ΙΩΣΗΦ ΧΑΤΖΙΔΑΚΗΣ (1848–1936)," ΠΑΛΙΜΨΗΣΤΟΝ 3 (1986): 127–148; Fitton, *The Discovery of The Greek Bronze Age*, 1995; Sakellarakis, *Herakleion Museum*, 1979; de Grummond, *EHCA*, 1996; Graham, *The Palaces of Crete*, 1972; Leekley and Noyes, *AEGI*, 1975.

NOTE

1. *Odyssey*, Book XIX: 188.

BARCLAY (VINCENT) HEAD

b: January 2, 1844. Ipswich, England.
d: June 12, 1914. London, England.

EDUCATION

The Grammar School, Ipswich.

APPOINTMENTS AND AWARDS

Department of Coins and Medals, British Museum: Assistant (1864–93), Keeper (1893–1906); Royal Numismatic Society: Vice President (1908); *Numismatic Chronicle:* Joint Editor (1869–1910). Hon. Degrees: Ph.D., Heidelberg; D.C.L., Durham Univ. (1887); D.Litt., Oxford Univ. (1905). Member: Correspondant de l'Institute de France and the Royal Prussian Academy of Sciences. Hon. Member: Academia Romana of Bukarest (1914).

PUBLICATIONS

Catalogue of Greek Coins in the British Museum: Italy (with P. GARDNER and R. S. Poole) (1873), *Sicily* (with P. Gardner and R. S. Poole) (1876), *Thrace* (with P. Gardner) (1877), *Macedonia* (edited by R. S. Poole) (1879), *Central Greece* (1884), Bologna: A. Forni, 1963, *Attica, Megaris, Aegina* (1888), Bologna: A. Forni, 1963; *Corinth and her Colonies I* (1889), Bologna: A. Forni, 1963, *Ionia* (1892), Bologna: A. Forni, 1964, *Caria* (1897), Bologna: A. Forni, 1964, *Lydia* (1902), Bologna: A. Forni, 1964, *Phrygia* (1906), Bologna: A. Forni, 1964; *The History of the Coinage of Syracuse,* 1874; *Guide to the Principal Gold and Silver Coins of the Ancients, from circa* B.C. *700 to* A.D. *1* (1881), Chicago: Argonaut, 1968; *Historia Numorum*

(1887) (1911, 2d. ed. assited by G. F. HILL, G. MAC-
DONALD, W. Wroth), Chicago: Argonaut, 1967.

Prior to the work of Barclay Head, ancient numismatics
had been widely regarded by scholars of ancient history as little
more than a pastime for dilettantes. Greek coins, in particular,
were recognized as works of great beauty but little academic
value was placed upon them. Head was the first to recognize
that much could be learned about the commercial and political
history of an ancient city by systematically studying the types,
styles, and chronology of the coins which that city issued over
a lengthy period, and in his 1912 publication on the coinage of
Syracuse he provided a framework for the study of Greek
coinage which has been retained to the present day.

Head's *Historia Numorum* is regarded as his greatest
contribution and stands as one of the classic reference
works on Greek numismatics. He was sole author of eight
volumes of the *Catalogue of Greek Coins in the British Museum*
and co-contributor to three.

Recognition of his contribution was slow to materialize in
Britain (possibly due to his humble educational background)
but he was quickly appreciated by foreign institutions. Upon
his retirement from the British Museum he was presented with
a collection of essays (*Corolla Numismatica*, 1906) written by
thirty contributors. Of these, ten wrote in German, five in
French, one in Italian, and one in Greek. He did not receive his
honorary degree from Oxford University until the age of sixty.

SOURCES

"Barclay Vincent Head," *NC*, Vol. 14, Series 4 (1914):
249–55; *The Athenaeum* (London), No. 4521 (June 20, 1914):
861; G. F. Hill, *DNB* (1912–21): 246; *WWW* (1897–1916); *TL*
(June 13, 1914).

REYNOLD (ALLEYNE) HIGGINS

b: November 26, 1916. Weybridge, Surrey, England.
d: April 18, 1993. England.

EDUCATION

Sherborne School.
Pembroke College, Cambridge University, 1938 (B.A.).

APPOINTMENTS AND AWARDS

Dept. of Greek and Roman Antiquities, British Museum: Asst. Keeper (1947–65), Deputy Keeper (1965–76), Acting Keeper (1976–77); British School at Athens: Visiting Fellow (1969), Chairman, Managing Committee (1975–79); Norton Lecturer (Archaeological Institute of America, 1982–83). Fellow: British Academy (1972). Hon. Degrees: D.Litt., Cambridge Univ. (1964). Award: Order of the Madara Horseman (Bulgaria).

EXCAVATIONS

Mycenae, 1955 (under A.J. B. WACE); Knossos, Crete.

PUBLICATIONS

Catalogue of the Terracottas in the British Museum, Vol. 1 (1954), Vol. 2 (1959), London: British Museum, 1969; "The Archaeological Background to the Furniture Tablets from Pylos," *Bulletin of the Institute of Classical Studies* 3 (1956) (Univ. of London); *Greek and Roman Jewellery* (1961), Berkeley, Calif.: University of California Press, 1980 (2d. ed.); *Greek Terracottas*, London: Methuen, 1967; *Minoan and Mycenaean Art*

(1967), London: Thames and Hudson, 1997 (rev. ed.); "The Facade of the Treasury of Atreus at Mycenae," (with R. Hope Simpson and S. E. Ellis) *BSA* 63 (1968): 331–336; *The Greek Bronze Age* (1970), London: British Museum Publications, 1977; *The Aegina Treasure: An Archaeological Mystery*, London: British Museum Publications, 1979; *Tanagra and the Figurines*, Princeton, N.J.: Princeton University Press, 1986; *The Archaeology of Minoan Crete*, London: Bodley Head, 1973.

Reynold Higgins was considered a leading expert in three fields of archaeological study: Greek terracotta figurines, Greek and Roman jewelry, and the Greek Bronze Age.

His publications on the terracottas in the British Museum (which earned him an honorary doctorate from Cambridge University) are widely held to be the best and most comprehensive account of this genre of ancient art, while his publication on Greek and Roman jewelry remains the standard English work on the subject.

Higgins also achieved recognition by his dating of the so-called "Aegina Treasure." In 1891 the British Museum had acquired a magnificent collection of gold jewelry and ornaments; however, the provenance and date of these objects had eluded some of the leading experts of the day (including ARTHUR EVANS). Higgins reexamined the treasure, comparing it with finds from the Cretan palace of Mallia, and was able to assign the pieces to Crete in the seventeenth to sixteenth centuries B.C.E., thus establishing a provenance and date which have generally been agreed upon by contemporary scholarship.

SOURCES

J. N. Coldstream, "Reynold Alleyne Higgins 1916–1993," *PBA* 87 (1995): 309–24; R. V. Nicholls, *AJA* 61 (1957): 303–306; F. H. Stubbings, *CR* 13 (1963): 103–104; *TL* (April 28, 1993).

BERT HODGE HILL

b: March 7, 1874. Bristol, Vermont.
d: December 2, 1958. Athens, Greece.

EDUCATION

University of Vermont, 1895 (A.B.).
Columbia University, 1900 (M.A.).

APPOINTMENTS AND AWARDS

Newport Academy (Vermont): Principal (1895–98); Boston Museum of Fine Arts: Asst. Curator of Classical Antiquities (1903–06); Wellesley College: Lecturer (1903–06); American School of Classical Studies at Athens: Director (1906–27), Director Emeritus (1927); Archaeological Institute of America, Vice President (1949). Fellow: American Academy of Arts and Sciences. Hon. Member: Archaeological Society of Athens; Austrian Archaeological Institute; German Archaeological Institute; Society for the Promotion of Hellenic Studies. Hon. Degrees: L.H.D., Univ. of Vermont; Ph.D., Univ. of Salonica. Award: Gold Cross, Order of the Redeemer (Greece).

EXCAVATIONS

Corinth; Nemea; Lapithos; Curium (Director, Univ. of Pennsylvania Archaeological Expedition to Cyprus, 1932, 1934–54).

PUBLICATIONS

The Springs: Peirene, Sacred Spring, Glauke, Princeton, N.J.: American School of Classical Studies at Athens, 1964.

One of Hill's major contributions was the introduction and teaching of modern scientific technique in archaeological excavation. He did this at a time when such techniques had just begun to be used, notably by the Germans at Olympia (see ERNST CURTIUS). He paid special attention to the precise recording of all details of a dig and to the problems involved in identifying and differentiating successive strata. Hill's perfected method was passed on to two generations of students of archaeology, including CARL. W. BLEGEN, WILLIAM BELL DINSMOOR, OSCAR BRONEER, RICHARD STILLWELL, and BENJAMIN MERITT.

Known as an able administrator, Hill was director of the American School of Classical Studies at Athens for more than twenty years. His skillful diplomacy led to the initial agreement with the Greek government which permitted the school to excavate the site of the ancient Athenian Agora.

SOURCES

Carl W. Blegen, "Bert Hodge Hill," *AJA* 63 (1958): 193–94; Carl W. Blegen, *Hesperia* 23 (1954): 1–2; Dow, *A Century of Humane Archaeology*, 1979; Lord, *History of the American School* . . . , 1947; J. L. Caskey, "Carl William Blegen (1887–1971)," *APSY* (1972): 121; *NYT* (December 3, 1958).

(Sir) George F(rancis) Hill

b: December 22, 1867. Berhampore, Bengal, India.
d: October 18, 1948. London, England.

EDUCATION

School for the Sons of Missionaries (later Eltham College).
University College, London.
Merton College, Oxford University, 1889 (Class.Mods.),
1891 (Lit.Hum.).

APPOINTMENTS AND AWARDS

Department of Coins and Medals, British Museum: Assistant (1893–1912), Keeper (1912–30); British Museum: Director and Principal Librarian (1931–36); *Journal of Hellenic Studies*: Editor (1898–1912); *Numismatic Chronicle*: Editor (1912–30); Rhind Lecturer (1915). Fellow: British Academy (1917); Society of Antiquaries; University College (London). Hon. Fellow: Merton College, Oxford. Hon. Degrees: D.C.L., Oxford Univ.; Litt.D. Cambridge Univ.; LL.D., Edinburgh Univ.; Litt.D., Univ. of Manchester. Awards: Medallist, Royal Numismatic Society (1915), American Numismatic Society (1923), and Société Française de Numismatique (1934); K.C.B. (Knight Commander of the Bath, 1933); Serena Medal, British Academy (for Italian Studies, 1948).

PUBLICATIONS

Sources for Greek History between the Persian and Peloponnesian Wars, 1897; *Catalogue of Greek Coins in the British Museum* (originally published by the Trustees of the British Museum with later reprint editions noted): *Lycia, Pamphylia and Pisidia*

(1897), Bologna: A. Forni, 1964, *Lycaonia, Isauria and Cilicia* (1900), Bologna: A. Forni, 1964, *Cyprus* (1904), Bologna: A. Forni, 1964, *Phoenicia* (1910), Bologna: A. Forni, 1965; *Palestine (Galilee, Samaria, and Judaea)* (1910), Bologna: A. Forni, 1965, *Arabia, Mesopotamia and Persia* (1922), Bologna: A. Forni, 1965; *Handbook of Greek and Roman Coins* (1899), Chicago: Argonaut, 1964; *A Manual of Greek Historical Inscriptions* (with E. L. Hicks), Oxford: The Clarendon Press, 1901; *Coins of Ancient Sicily*, Westminster: A. Constable and Co., 1903; *Pisanello* (1905), New York: Dover Publications, 1965; *Corolla Numismatica*, London: H. Frowde, 1906; *Historical Greek Coins* (1906), Chicago: Argonaut, 1966; *Historical Roman Coins* (1909), Chicago: Argonaut, 1966; *Historia Numorum* by BARCLAY HEAD (assisted in the second, revised edition), Oxford: The Clarendon Press, 1911; *Portrait Medals of Italian Artists in the Renaissance*, London: P. L. Warner, 1912; *The Development of Arabic Numerals in Europe*, Oxford: The Clarendon Press, 1915; *Medals of the Renaissance*, 1920; *Medallic Portraits of Christ*, Oxford: The Clarendon Press, 1920; *Becker the Counterfeiter*, (1924–25) (2 vols.), New York: Sanford Durst, 1995; *Select Greek Coins: A Series of Enlargements Illustrated and Described*, Brussels, Paris: G. Vanoest, 1927; *How to Observe in Archaeology: Suggestions for Travellers in the Near and Middle East* (editor), London: Trustees of the British Museum, 1929; *A Corpus of Italian Medals before Cellini* (2 vols.), London: British Museum, 1930; *Treasure-Trove: The Law and Practice of Antiquity*, London: H. Milford, 1936; *History of Cyprus* (4 vols., Vol. 4 published posthumously), Cambridge: Cambridge University Press, 1940–52.

Sir George Hill's academic career began at Oxford where he earned his first degree in a record two terms, rather than in the usual five. It was at Oxford that he became greatly interested in ancient numismatics when he came into contact with PERCY GARDNER, and it was with Gardner's advice that he applied for his initial post at the British Museum.

Hill entered the world of ancient numismatics when it was just becoming popular; academics had begun to appreciate the fact that the scientific study of ancient coins could elucidate our understanding and knowledge in many other areas of ancient scholarship (see BARCLAY HEAD). One of Hill's first projects was to continue the publication of the Greek coins in the British Museum. The first volume in the series had been produced by R. S. Poole, P. GARDNER, and BARCLAY HEAD in 1873, and further volumes had been produced by Head and Gardner. Hill changed the format of the catalog by publishing more plates and by expanding the introduction so that each became a monograph on its subject. He also assisted Barclay Head (and others) in the revision and expansion of Head's *Historia Numorum*.

Hill had a far-ranging effect on archaeology as secretary to the Archaeological Joint Committee from its inception in 1920. While in office he participated in the drafting of laws relating to the discovery of antiquities in Iraq, Palestine, and Cyprus.

SOURCES

E. S. G. Robinson, "George Francis Hill 1867–1948," *PBA*, 36 (1950); E. S. G. Robinson, *DNB*, 1941–50: 119; Absalom, et al., *A Tribute to Sir George Hill on his Eightieth Birthday, 1867–1947*, 1948 (contains full bibliography); *WW*, 1940; *TL* (October 20, 1948).

DAVID G(EORGE) HOGARTH

b: May 23, 1862. Lincolnshire, England.
d: November 6, 1927. Oxford, England.

EDUCATION

Oxford University, 1885.
British School at Athens, 1886–87.

APPOINTMENTS AND AWARDS

British School at Athens: Director (1897–1900); Ashmolean Museum, Oxford University: Keeper (1908–27). Hon. Degrees: D.Litt., Oxford Univ. (1918).

EXCAVATIONS

Old Paphos, Cyprus, 1888 (with ERNEST GARDNER); Phylakopi, 1898; Naukratis (Egypt), 1899; Dictaean Cave, Crete, 1900; Knossos, 1901 (with ARTHUR J. EVANS); Kato Zakro, 1901; Temple of Artemis, Ephesus, 1904–05.

PUBLICATIONS

Devia Cypria, London: H. Frowde, 1889; *Koptos* (by W. FLINDERS PETRIE with a chapter by D. Hogan), London: B. Quaritch, 1896; *A Wandering Scholar in the Levant*, 1896; *Philip and Alexander of Macedon: Two Essays in Biography* (1897), Freeport, N.Y.: Books for Libraries Press, 1971; *Authority and Archaeology* (editor) (1899), Freeport, N.Y.: Books for Libraries Press, 1971; *Fayûm Towns and Their Papyri* (by Bernard P. Grenfell, Hogarth, et al.), London: Egypt Exploration Fund, 1900; *The Nearer East*, New York: D. Appleton and Co., 1902; *The Penetration of Arabia: A Record of the Development of Western Knowledge Concerning the Arabian Peninsula* (1904), Connecticut: Hyperion Press, 1981; *The Archaic Artemisia of Ephesus* (with chapters by CECIL HARCOURT-SMITH, et al.), London: Trustees of the British Museum, 1908; *Accidents in an Antiquary's Life*, London: Macmillan, 1910; *Ionia and the East: Six Lectures delivered Before the University of London* (1914), New York: Haskell House, 1969; *Carchemish*, Part 1, 1914; *The Balkans: A History of Bulgaria, Serbia, Greece, Rumania, Turkey* (Hogarth, et al.), Oxford: The Clarendon Press, 1915; *The Ancient East* (1915), New York: Greenwood Press, 1968; *Hittite Seals*, 1920; *Arabia*, Oxford: The Clarendon Press, 1922; *The Wandering Scholar*, Oxford: Oxford University Press, 1925; *Kings of the Hittites*, Oxford: Oxford University Press, 1926 (Schweich Lectures); *The Life of C. M. Doughty: A Memoir* (1928, published posthumously), Michigan: Scholarly Press, 1972.

A capable archaeologist, Hogarth was definitely limited by the outlook of his day. That is to say that he excavated monumental sites and sought artifacts which were aesthetically pleasing but discarded routine, everyday objects as "domestic rubbish." On the other hand his work was extensive (he excavated major sites in Anatolia, Egypt, Melos, Crete, and Syria) and he kept detailed daybooks on his digs, many of which are extant.

He published his excavations quickly and was a very able and prolific writer who influenced Mediterranean archaeology by his seriousness of purpose, his disciplined approach, and by the publication of works which brought the flavor of travel in Mediterranean lands to people in the West.

SOURCES

A. H. Sayce, "David George Hogarth," *PBA* 13 (1927): 379–83; Peter Lock, "D. G. Hogarth (1862–1927): A Specialist in the Science of Archaeology," *BSA* 85 (1990): 175–95; Waterhouse, *British School at Athens*, 1986; *TL* (November 7, 1927).

THOMAS HOWARD
(SECOND EARL OF ARUNDEL)

b: 1585. Finchingfield, Essex, England.
d: October 4, 1646.[1] Padua, Italy.

EDUCATION

Westminister School, London.
Trinity College, Cambridge University.

APPOINTMENTS AND AWARDS

Privy Councilor of Scotland and Ireland (1617); Earl-Marshall of England (1621); various other government posts.

The Earl of Arundel was the first English collector of Classical antiquities and as such initiated a real interest in the acquisition and study of ancient artifacts among the upper classes of seventeenth-century England. From the early part of that century small objects such as carved gems and coins had begun to find their way into Europe but it was Arundel who first obtained and imported larger pieces such as full-sized sculptures and portrait busts.

He had first visited Italy as a young man and had become enamored of the ancient works of art which he found there. When he returned to that country in 1613 he obtained permission to carry out some excavation work in Rome, discovered a large number of portrait busts, and with these finds began collecting antiquities in earnest.

Very few pieces of Greek art had found their way into Italy and the few that Arundel saw caused him to focus on their acquisition, though he continued to acquire Roman objects as well. A number of agents in Greece and western Asia Minor were engaged to obtain any Classical works of art regardless of size or expense and through these agents Arundel was able to obtain sculptures from sites such as Ephesus, Pergamon, Samos, and sites in the Peloponnese.

He housed his collection in the rooms and gardens of Arundel House in London and received much criticism for the way in which he chose to display some of the works; for instance, he had a number of ancient inscriptions incorporated into the garden walls of his estate. Arundel was also an enthusiastic proponent of the restoration of sculptures and this seems to have been carried out without much fidelity to style or original artistic intent. Indeed, it was said of the earl by one of his contemporaries, "[H]e was only able to buy the antiquities, never to understand them."[2]

Despite the criticism he encountered for the treatment of his collection, Arundel was a major catalyst in generating the West's interest in Classical archaeology, for when the upper classes came to view the ancient artifacts in his home they began to plan their own excursions to Italy and later to Greece. The presence of his collection also initiated a scholarly interest in the study of antiquities (as with the Marmora Parium fragment) which culminated in the formation of institutions such as the Society of Dilettanti, founded in London in 1734.

A major portion of Arundel's sculptures and inscriptions were eventually given to Oxford University by the earl's descendants and now reside in the Ashmolean Museum. Among these are a large group of inscriptions which have become known as the "Arundel Marbles" (see RICHARD CHANDLER). The Arundelian Library of Manuscripts was acquired by the British Museum at a later date.

SOURCES

Michaelis, *Ancient Marbles in Great Britain*, 1882; Edwards, *Lives of the Founders of the British Museum* (1870), reprint, 1969; Cust, *History of the Society of Dilettanti*, 1914; Clarke, *Greek Studies in England, 1700–1830*, 1945; *DNB*, Vol. 10.

NOTES

1. Arundel's date of death is erroneously given as September 24, 1646 in Edwards's *Lives of the Founders of the British Museum*, 1870.
2. Michaelis, *Ancient Marbles in Great Britain*.

CHRISTIAN HÜLSEN

b: November 29, 1858. Charlottenburg, Germany.
d: January 19, 1935. Florence, Italy.

EDUCATION

University of Erlangen, 1880.

APPOINTMENTS AND AWARDS

German Archaeological Institute of Rome: Second Secretary (1887–1909); Columbia Univ.: Visiting Professor (1910); Univ. of Heidelberg: Professor Emeritus (1917). Hon. Member: Archaeological Institute of America; Socio onorario della Pontifica Accademia Romana de Archeologia. Hon. Degrees: Litt.D., Columbia Univ.; Litt.D., Oxford Univ.

PUBLICATIONS

Formae Urbis Romae (with H. Kiepert), 1896; *Bilder aus der Geschichte des Kapitols*, 1899; *Das Forum Romanum*, 1904 (English edition, 1906); *Topographie der Stadt Rom in Altertum* (with Henri Jordan) (2 vols.), Berlin: Weidmannsche Buchhandlung, 1871–1907; *La Pianta di Roma dell'Anonimo Einsidlense*, 1907; *Die Thermen des Agrippa*, Rome: Loescher, 1910; *Saggio di bibliografia ragionata delle piante iconografiche e prospettiche di Roma dall 1551 al 1748* (1915), Rome: Bardi, 1969; *Römische Antikengärten des XVI Jahrhunderts*, 1917; *The Forum and the Palatine* (translated by H. H. Tanzer), New York: A. Bruderhausen, 1928.

Christian Hülsen was considered the leading authority on Roman topography specializing in the Ancient, Medieval, and Renaissance periods.

Hülsen studied under some notable teachers including Theodore Mommsen; his first interest was in philology and as a student of Mommsen's, assisted him in his work on the *Corpus Inscriptionum Latinarum*. Hülsen became involved in Roman topography when he was asked to direct the work on *The Topography of the City of Rome in Antiquity* upon the death of H. Jordan (1907, above). Using the same systematic approach with which he tackled philological problems he was able to gain an intimate knowledge of Rome's topographical history.

Roman archaeology was experiencing a period of rapid growth at the time of Hülsen's activity there; since the end of the nineteenth century the city had undergone great expansion during which many ancient ruins and artifacts had been brought to light. The extensive and systematic excavations of the city which ensued attracted many talented scholars to Rome including ESTHER BOISE VAN DEMAN (from the United States) and EUGÉNIE STRONG (from Britain). The Italian archaeologist RODOLFO LANCIANI was also active at this time, and the British archaeologist THOMAS ASHBY proved to be one of Hülsen's most memorable students during this period.

SOURCES

I. Sieveking, "Christian Hülsen," *Jmünch* (1934–35): 39–40; L. Curtius, "Christian Hülsen" (Memorial speech delivered before the Roman Institute, February 20, 1935, supplied by the German Archaeological Institute, Berlin); *NDB*, Vol. 9; Michaelis, *A Century of Archaeological Discoveries*, 1908; *AJA* 1935: 254; *NYT* (January 2, 1935).

L(ILIAN) H(AMILTON) JEFFERY

b: January 5, 1915. Westcliff-on-Sea, England.
d: September 29, 1986. England.

EDUCATION

Cheltenham Ladies' College.
Newnham College, Cambridge University.
British School at Athens, 1937–39.
Lady Margaret Hall, Oxford University, 1951 (Ph.D.).

APPOINTMENTS AND AWARDS

Lady Margaret Hall, Oxford Univ.: Tutor in Ancient History (1952–80); *Annual of the British School at Athens*: Joint Editor (1955–61); Bryn Mawr College: Catharine McBride Guest Lecturer (1971–72). Fellow: Institute for Advanced Study, Princeton Univ. (1951–52); British Society of Antiquaries (1956); British Academy (1965). Hon. Fellow: Lady Margaret Hall, Oxford Univ. (1980).

EXCAVATIONS

Chios; Smyrna, 1949.

PUBLICATIONS

Dedications from the Athenian Akropolis: A Catalogue of the Inscriptions of the Sixth and Fifth Centuries B.C. (edited by A. E. Rabuitschek with the collaboration of L. H. Jeffery), Massachusetts: Archaeological Institute of America, 1949; *The Local Scripts of Archaic Greece: A Study of the Origins of the Greek Alphabet and Its Development from the Eighth to the Fifth*

Centuries B.C., Oxford: The Clarendon Press (1961), 1990; *Archaic Greece: The City-States c. 700–500 B.C.*, New York: St. Martin's Press, 1976.

L. H. Jeffery was an expert in the Archaic period of Greek history, specifically in the development of regional scripts. The Archaic period is of crucial importance in the history of Greece as it marks the time when Greek culture was emerging from a long period of decline often referred to as the "Dark Age." It was a period when those aspects of culture that are signifiers of civilization (such as monumental architecture and sculpture) made a gradual comeback. Writing also reappeared at this time (through the Greeks borrowing of the Phoenician alphabet) and so Jeffery's work focused on the earliest forms of what was to become the Greek alphabet.

In 1939, just before the beginning of World War Two, Jeffery was able to assist A. E. Raubitschek in his major work on archaic inscriptions found on the acropolis at Athens (*Dedications from the Athenian Acropolis*, 1949). After the war she gravitated toward Oxford rather than returning to Cambridge. At this time Oxford led the field in studying archaeological data as a way to learn about ancient Greek civilization; here she was able to study with, among others, J. D. BEAZLEY and Russell Meiggs.

Her interest in the Archaic period culminated in an unusually large-scale dissertation which was later expanded and published as *The Local Scripts of Archaic Greece*. In this singularly important work Jeffery systematically surveyed the extant Greek alphabetic inscriptions dating down to the end of the fifth century B.C.E. in order to produce a chronology of its development. She approached the work first from an archaeological standpoint, considering the dates of pottery, sculpture and archaeological context, and then considered philological and historical arguments. One of her major conclusions was one which supported the view made earlier by RHYS CARPENTER, that the Archaic Greek script had its origins in the eighth century B.C.E. and not earlier as many still insisted. Indeed, her readers at Oxford were surprised by her later dating for the transmission of the alphabet into Greece but, given her painstakingly careful research and supporting data, accepted her thesis.

In addition to providing a vast catalog of early Greek inscriptions, L. H. Jeffery's work enormously increased our understanding of where and how the adaptation of the Phoenician alphabet took place, and of the uses of writing in Archaic Greece.

SOURCES

D. M. Lewis, "Lilian Hamilton Jeffery 1915–1986," *PBA* 63 (1987): 505–16; Susan Treggiari, "Lilian Hamilton Jeffery, 1915–1986," *AJA* 92 (1988): 227–28; A. M. Woodward, *CR* 12 (1962): 257–61; Benjamin D. Meritt, *AJA* 67 (1963): 91–92; *TL* (October 1, 1986).

GEORG KARO

b: January 11, 1872. Venice, Italy.
d: November 12, 1963. Freiburg, Germany.

EDUCATION

Munich, 1892.
Bonn University, 1896 (Ph.D.).

APPOINTMENTS AND AWARDS

Bonn Univ.: University Lecturer (1902–05); German Archaeological Institute, Athens: Asst. Director (1905–10), Director (1910–20, 1930–36); Univ. of Halle: Professor of Archaeology (1920–30); Univ. of Cincinnati: Visiting Professor of Classics and Art History (1939–40); Oberlin College: Professorial Lecturer (1940–42); Pomona College: Visiting Professor of Greek and Roman Art and Archaeology (beg. 1948); Claremont College; *Archaeolgischer Anzeiger*: Editor. Hon. Degree: Ph.D., Univ. of Athens (1937).

EXCAVATIONS

Tiryns, 1910, 1926; Mycenae.

PUBLICATIONS

"Orient und Hellas in archaischer Zeit. I. Die chronologische Grundlagen," *Athenische Mitteilungen* 45 (1920); *Die Kretisch-Mykenische Kultur* (by Diedrich Fimmen, edited by Karo), 1921; *Die Schachtgräber von Mykenai*, 1930; *Greifen am Thron*, 1959.

Georg Karo dug under the direction of WILHELM DÖRPFELD at Tiryns and later worked at Mycenae. He is best remembered for his detailed reexamination of the shaft graves at Mycenae, the findings of which were published in 1930 (above).

HEINRICH SCHLIEMANN'S excavations of the graves had been slipshod; he had not made sketches of the objects as they had been unearthed and, although he did take some measurements, these were in some instances dependent upon objects that had later been moved and so were of little use. Karo examined all of the available data (from Schliemann's work down to the publications of the British School at Athens) and was able to make a number of assertions regarding the shaft graves, such as the graves having contained successive, rather than one-time burials; that the shaft graves were earlier than the beehive tombs (thus lending scientific support to what CHRISTOS TSOUNTAS had postulated much earlier), and that the encircling wall was built during the fourteenth century B.C.E., at the same time as the Lion Gate (the great entranceway to the palace). He also recognized that much of the decorative art found at Mycenae betrayed a Minoan influence. In the second part of *Die Schachtgräber von Mykenai* he listed all of the objects recovered from the graves so that the work is invaluable to anyone who studies the site today.

An early interest of Karo's had been the relationship between the ancient civilizations of the Near East and Greece; his efforts in this area provided a basis for further work by individuals such as HUMFRY PAYNE.

SOURCES

Friedrich Matz, "Georg Karo," *Gnomon* (1964): 637–40; Sp. Marinatos, "Necrology," *AJA* 70 (1966); Carl W. Blegen, *AJA* 35 (1931): 356–57; *DAS*, 1951, 2d. ed.; Vermeule, *Greece in the Bronze Age*, 1972; McDonald, *The Discovery of Homeric Greece*, 1967.

(SIR) FREDERIC G(EORGE) KENYON

b: January 15, 1863. London, England.
d: August 23, 1952. London, England.

EDUCATION

Winchester School, 1882.
New College, Oxford University, 1883 (B.A.),
1886 (Lit. Hum.).

APPOINTMENTS AND AWARDS

Dept. of Manuscripts, British Museum: Assistant
(1889–98), Asst. Keeper (1898–1909); British Museum:
Director (1909–30); Royal Academy: Professor of Ancient History (1918). Fellow: British Academy (1903). Hon. Fellow:
Magdalen and New College, Oxford Univ. Member: Hellenic
Society, President (1919–24); British Academy, President
(1917–21). Awards: K.C.B. (Knight Commander of the Bath,
1912); Grand Cross of the Order of the British Empire (1925).

PUBLICATIONS

Classical Texts from Papyri in the British Museum, London:
Trustees of the British Museum, 1891; *Aristotle on the Constitu-
tion of Athens*, London: G. Bell, 1901; *Palaeography of Greek
Papyri* (1899), Chicago: Ares Publishers, 1998; *Catalogue of
Greek Papyri in the British Museum*, Vol. 1 (1891), Vol. 2 (1898),
Vol. 3 (1907); *Our Bible and the Ancient Manuscripts* (1895), New
York: Harper, 1958; *Facsimiles of Biblical Manuscripts in the
British Museum*, 1900; *Handbook of the Textual Criticism of the
New Testament*, 1901; *Recent Developments in the Textual Criticism
of the Greek Bible*, Oxford: Oxford University Press, 1933; *The*

170

Bible and Modern Scholarship, London: J. Murray, 1948; *Books and Readers in Ancient Greece and Rome* (1931), Oxford: The Clarendon Press, 1951. Works on the poetry of the Brownings include: *The Brownings for the Young*, 1886; *The Letters of Elizabeth Barrett Browning* (2 vols., edited and with biographical additions by Kenyon), New York: Macmillan Co., 1899; *Robert Browning and Alfred Domett* (editor), 1906.

Kenyon published the first discussion regarding the palaeography of Greek papyri and was one of the first to support papyrological studies as a distinct discipline. Among his major contributions was the initial publication of the British Museum's holdings of papyri, and one of his most spectacular identifications was that of the lost treatise of Aristotle, *The Constitution of Athens*. Other important papyri which Kenyon edited include works by Bacchylides, Hyperides, Herodas, and Isocrates.

In addition to his interest in ancient manuscripts he admired the poetry of Elizabeth and Robert Browning (see publications, above).

SOURCES

H. I. Bell, "Sir Frederic George Kenyon 1863–1952," *PBA* 38 (1952): 269–94; *TL* (August 25, 1952).

R(ICHARD) PAYNE KNIGHT

b: 1750. England.
d: April 23, 1824. London, England.

APPOINTMENTS AND AWARDS

Member of Parliament (1780–1806); Society of Antiquaries: Vice President. Member: Society of Dilettanti (1781).

PUBLICATIONS

An Account of the Remains of the Worship of Priapus lately existing in Isernia to which is added a Discourse on the Worship of Priapus, and its Connexion with the Mystic Theology of the Ancients, London: T. Spilsbury, 1786; *An Analytical Essay on the Greek Alphabet*, London: J. Nichols, 1791; *Carmina Homerica, Ilias et Odyssea* (1808), London: Valpianis, 1820 (reprinted with text); *An Analytical Inquiry into the Principles of Taste*, 1808; *Specimens of Antient Sculpture, selected from several Collections in Great Britain*, 1809; *An Inquiry into the Symbolical Language of Ancient Art and Mythology* (1818), New York: J. W. Bouton, 1876 (with new and complete index by Alexander Wilder); *Sexual Symbolism: A History of Phallic Worship by Richard Payne Knight and Thomas Wright* (with introduction by Ashley Montagu), New York: Julian Press, 1957.

R. Payne Knight was one of the most influential connoisseurs of ancient art in eighteenth century England and as such was a pioneer of Classical archaeology.

He was born into a wealthy family but, due to an extremely weak constitution as a child, did not attend any public schools or go on to university. As a result, he did not begin his study of Greek until the age of seventeen. At this young age he also made

172

his first journey to Italy where he stayed for approximately six to seven years. He returned to Italy many times over the next twenty years and became a close friend of SIR WILLIAM HAMILTON and his wife who were then living in Naples.

While in Italy Knight began collecting small ancient bronzes and coins, especially Greek coins from southern Italy and Sicily. He became an avid collector and subsequently amassed the finest collection of ancient coins and bronzes in Britain. At the time of his death his collections were valued at between £30,000 and £60,000. Knight bequeathed all of his antiquities to the British Museum which, with his collections, became the rival of the Royal Museum of Paris for Greek coins and of the Museum of Naples for bronzes. Up to that time the Naples Museum had held the finest collection of Greek bronzes in the world.

Knight had a penchant for small objects of art and in fact was quite hostile toward large pieces of sculpture, even if they were of ancient Greek manufacture. He was known to have held the opinion that the best Greek artists had seldom lowered themselves to work in large pieces of stone. When he viewed the Elgin Marbles in London he observed that they were overrated, and at a dinner party told LORD ELGIN that he had "lost his labour"[1] in bringing the sculptures from Athens to London. Later he appeared before the House of Commons and tried to dissuade the British government from purchasing the marbles from Lord Elgin and, although he did not succeed, was able to persuade the government to pay a much lower price for the sculptures.

Despite his inability to perceive what the rest of the world saw in the sculptures of the Parthenon, Knight, as a leading member of the Society of Dilettanti for more than forty years, had a profound effect upon European taste and upon the West's readiness to embrace ancient art. He ensured that the society's interests focused squarely upon the art of antiquity rather than in other areas. Knight produced several interesting and unique publications (his 1786 publication caused great indignation among its readers, in no small part due to its subject matter) and his bequest to the British Museum resulted in its becoming a world-class institution, as it added greatly to the foundation previously provided by the collections of WILLIAM HAMILTON, LORD ELGIN, and CHARLES TOWNELEY. Knight was also one of the earliest scholars to appreciate the usefulness of coins in studying the history of the ancient world.

SOURCES

Michaelis, *Ancient Marbles in Great Britain*, 1882; Cust, *History of the Society of Dillettanti*, 1914; Edwards, *Lives of the Founders of the British Museum* (1870), reprint, 1969; Clarke, *Greek Studies in England 1700–1830*, 1945; *DNB*, Vol. 11.

NOTE

1. *DNB*, p. 260.

COLIN (MacKennal) Kraay

b: March 23, 1918. Hampstead, England.
d: January 27, 1982. England.

EDUCATION

Ascham St. Vincent's School, England.
Lancing College.
Magdalen College, Oxford University, 1947 (B.A.), 1953 (Ph.D.).

APPOINTMENTS AND AWARDS

Heberden Coin Room, Ashmolean Museum, Oxford Univ.: Temporary, part-time Asst. Keeper (1948), Asst. Keeper (1952–62), Senior Asst. Keeper (1962–75), Keeper (beg. 1975); Oxford Univ.: University Lecturer in Greek Numismatics (1959–70); Royal Numismatic Society, President (1970–74); Centro Internazionale di Studi Numismatici, Naples, President (1974–79); Univ. of British Columbia: Visiting Professor (1981). Fellow: Royal Numismatic Society (1948); Wolfson College (Oxford Univ., 1966); British Academy (1978); Society of Antiquaries. Awards: Medallist, Royal Numismatic Society (1978); Huntington Medal (American Numismatic Society, 1980).

EXCAVATIONS

Mycenae, 1939 (under A.J.B. WACE).

PUBLICATIONS

Collection of Greek Coins in the Heberden Coin Room, Ashmolean Museum, Oxford (4 vols.), Oxford: Oxford University Press,

1951–81; "The aes coinage of Galba," *ANSNM* 133 (1956): 1–56; *The Composition of Greek Silver Coins: Analysis by Neutron Activation*, 1962 (with a chapter by V. M. Emeleus); *Greek Coins*, New York: H. N. Abrams, 1966; *Essays in Greek Coinage, Presented to Stanley Robinson* (edited by C. M. Kraay and G. K. Jenkins), Oxford: The Clarendon Press, 1968; *Greek Coins and History: Some Current Problems* (1966), New York: Barnes and Noble, 1969; *The Heberden Coin Room: Origin and Development* (with C. H. V. Sutherland), Oxford: Ashmolean Museum, 1972; *The Hellenistic Kingdoms: Portrait Coins and History* (with Norman Davis), London: Thames and Hudson, 1973; *An Inventory of Greek Coin Hoards* (with M. Thompson and O. Mørkholm), New York: American Numismatic Society, 1973; *Archaic and Classical Greek Coins*, London: Methuen, 1976.

Colin Kraay was regarded as one of the world's experts in a difficult area of ancient numismatics, Greek coinage. He specialized in the coinage of the sixth and fifth centuries B.C.E. and had the unique ability to connect the many strands of information regarding the coinage of this period and was able to produce a detailed and integrated picture. His publication of 1976 (above) is widely considered the most comprehensive treatment of Archaic and Classical Greek coinage ever produced.

Kraay had become interested in archaeology (specifically Egyptology) as a young schoolboy and his initial interest in ancient numismatics had been in Roman Imperial bronzes. This interest changed to Greek when he became assistant keeper in the Coin Room of the Ashmolean Museum at Oxford University. He was receptive to new techniques for dating coinage and soon adopted the idea that the chronology of coins could be derived from a comparative study of different coin hoards; he also used the comparatively new method of neutron activation in his analyses.

SOURCES

C. H. V. Sutherland, "Colin MacKennal Kraay 1918–1982," *PBA* 68 (1982): 591–605; *WW*, 1982; Correspondence with the American Numismatic Society; *TL* (January 28, 1982).

RODOLFO (AMEDEO) LANCIANI

b: January 1, 1847. Montecelio, near Rome, Italy.
d: May 21, 1929. Rome, Italy.

EDUCATION

Jesuit Collegio Romano.
University of Rome.

APPOINTMENTS AND AWARDS

Municipal Archaeological Commission: Secretary (1872–76); Museo Karcheriano: Asst. Director (1876); Univ. of Rome: Professor of Roman Topography (1878–1927); Univ. of St. Andrews: Gifford Lecturer. Member: Italian Senate; Academia dei Lincei; Academia di S. Luca; Academie Royale de Belgique. Hon. Degrees: D.C.L., Oxford Univ.; LL.D., Univ. of Aberdeen; LL.D., Harvard Univ.; LL.D., Univ. of Glasgow; Ph.D., Univ. of Rome; Ph.D., Univ. of Wurzburg.

EXCAVATIONS

Rome (Director), 1877–90; Tivoli; Ostia.

PUBLICATIONS

Frontino intorno le acque e gli aquedotti, 1880; *Ancient Rome in the Light of Recent Excavations* (1888), New York: B. Blom, 1967; *Pagan and Christian Rome* (1892), New York: B. Blom, 1967; *Forma Urbis Romae*, Rome: 1893–1901; *Ruins and Excavations of Ancient Rome* (1898), New York: Bell Publishing Co., 1979; *New Tales of Old Rome*, 1901; *Storia degli Scavi di Roma* (4 vols.) (1902–12), Rome: Quasar, 1994; *The Golden Days of the Renaissance in Rome, from the pontificate of Julius II to that of Paul III*, 1906; *Wanderings in the Roman Campagna* (1909), New York: Houghton Mifflin Co., 1924; *The Roman Forum*, Rome: Frank and Co., 1910; *Wanderings Through Ancient Roman Churches*, 1924; *Ancient and Modern Rome* (1925), New York: Cooper Square Publishers, 1963.

Lanciani was a pioneer in the field of Roman archaeology and was particularly interested in topographical studies. He carried out the first excavations at the House of the Vestals and excavated extensively at Ostia and in Rome itself.

He published a large number of scholarly works, his most monumental undertaking being accomplished between 1893 and 1901 (see above). This entailed the publication of a forty-six page plan of the city of Rome on a 1:1,000 scale which showed the city with its modern streets and buildings in relation to the buildings of the Classical and medieval periods.

For his *Storia degli Scavi di Roma*, Lanciani had intended to present a survey of excavations carried out in Rome from the eleventh century to the late nineteenth century, but he was only able to complete it to 1605.[1] This work required valuable research into obscure, little known, and often unpublished documents.

Appointed to the Royal Commission for the Reorganization of the City of Rome, Lanciani worked hard to protect the integrity of the ancient sites against modern incursion, particularly in the area of the Baths of Caracalla. He was a respected and popular speaker and carried out several lecture tours in Britain and in the United States.

SOURCES

S. Reinach, "Ridolfo Amedeo Lanciani," *RA* 30 (1929): 128–29; de Grummond, (David L. Thompson), *EHCA*, 1996; *AJA* 34 (1930): 62; *TL* (May 23, 1929), (May 30, 1929); *NYT* (May 23, 1929).

NOTE

1. The completion of this work, together with a reprinting of the previously published sections, is currently being carried out under the editorship of L. M. Campeggi.

WILLIAM MARTIN LEAKE

b: January 14, 1777. London, England.
d: January 6, 1860. Brighton, England.

EDUCATION

Royal Military Academy, Woolwich, England.

APPOINTMENTS AND AWARDS

Royal Regiment of Artillery: Second Lieutenant, Captain, Lieutenant Colonel (1813); Royal Society of Literature, Vice President. Fellow: Royal Society; Royal Geographic Society. Member: Society of Dilettanti (1814). Hon. Member: Royal Academy of Sciences, Berlin. Correspondent: Institute of France. Hon. Degree: D.C.L., Oxford University (1816).

PUBLICATIONS

Researches in Greece, 1814; *The Topography of Athens* (1821), London (privately printed for the author 1841, 2d. ed.); *Journal of a Tour in Asia Minor with comparative remarks on the ancient and modern geography of that country,* London: J. Murray, 1824; *An Historical Outline of the Greek Revolution,* 1825, 1826; *An Edict of Diocletian fixing a Maximum of Prices,* 1826; *Travels in the Morea* (3 vols.) (1830), Amsterdam: A. M. Hakkert, 1968; *Travels in Northern Greece* (4 vols.), 1835; *Peloponnesiaca: a supplement to the Travels in the Morea* (1846), Amsterdam: A. M. Hakkert, 1967; *Numismatica Hellenica: A Catalogue of Greek Coins Collected by William Martin Leake,* London: J. Murray, 1856 (supplement, 1859); *On some disputed Questions of Ancient Geography,* 1857.

William Leake traveled extensively throughout the Near East, Asia Minor, and Greece as a colonel in the British military. He took copious notes regarding the topography of the countries he visited, and those that have proved especially useful include his descriptions of the less traveled areas of Greece, particularly northern Greece and the Peloponnese (he was one of the earliest visitors to the Treasury of Atreus at Mycenae and provided a finely detailed description of it).

He had a great interest in ancient coins of which he collected many, especially bronze. His personal collection was carefully cataloged and described in *Numismatica Hellenica* in 1854. While engaged in his military assignments in Greece, he also sought out ancient vases, gems, inscriptions, sculpture, and bronzes. He presented his collection of ancient sculpture and inscriptions to the British Museum in 1839, and the rest of his collection was purchased by Cambridge University after his death.

SOURCES

Cust, *History of the Society of Dilettanti*, 1914; *DNB*, Vol. 11; Miller, *Greece Through the Ages*, 1972; Michaelis, *Ancient Marbles in Great Britain*, 1882; Weber, *Voyages and Travels . . .* , 1952; Clarke, *Greek Studies in England, 1700–1830*, 1945.

KARL LEHMANN

b: September 27, 1894. Rostock, Germany.
d: December 17, 1960. Basel, Switzerland.

EDUCATION

University of Tübingen, 1913.
University of Munich, 1913–14.
University of Göttingen, 1914.
University of Berlin, 1922 (Ph.D.).

APPOINTMENTS AND AWARDS

German Archaeological Institute, Athens: Fellow (1922–23); Univ. of Berlin: Instructor (1924); German Archaeological Institute in Rome: Asst. Director (1924–25); Univ. of Heidelberg: Instructor, Acting Director (1925–29); Archaeological Museum, Münster: Professor, Director (1929–33); Institute of Fine Arts, New York Univ.: Professor of Classical Archaeology (1935–60). Awards: Knight Commander of the Royal Greek Order of the Phoenix (1951); Honorary Citizen, Samothrace, Greece.

EXCAVATIONS

Samothrace (Director), 1938–60.

PUBLICATIONS

Die antiken Hafenanlagen des Mittelmeeres Beiträge zur Geschichte des Städtebaues im Altertum, (*Klio*, Beiheft 14) 1923; *Die Trajanssaüle Ein römisches Kunstwork Zu Beginn der Spätantike* (2 vols.), Berlin, Leipzig: W. de Gruyter and Co.,

1926; *Die antiken Großbronzen* (with K. Kluge) (3 vols.), Berlin, Leipzig: W. de Gruyter and Co. 1927; *Corpus Vasorum Antiquorum, Italia, Regio Museo Archeologico di Firenze*, Milan: Bestetti and Tumminelli, 1931 (Vols. 1–5); *Bauge-schichtliche Untersuchungen am Stadtrand von Pompeii* (with F. Noack) 1936; *Plinio Il Giovane, Lettere scelte, con commento archeologico*, 1936; *Dionysiac Sarcophagi in Baltimore* (with E. Olsen), New York: Institute of Fine Arts, 1942; "The Impact of Ancient City Planning on European Architecture," *JSAH* 3 (1943): 22–29; "The Dome of Heaven," *The Art Bulletin* 27 (1945): 1–27; *Thomas Jefferson, American Humanist* (1947), University Press of Virginia, 1985; "The Mystery Cult of Samothrace, Excavations in 1953," *Archaeology* 7 (1954): 91–95; *Samothrace. A Guide to the Excavations and the Museum* (1955), New York: J. J. Augustin, 1975 (4th ed, revised and enlarged); *Samothrace* series edited by Karl Lehmann and his wife Phylis Williams Lehmann, published by Pantheon Books, New York: Vol. 1: *The Ancient Literary Sources* (edited and translated by Naphtali Lewis), 1959; Vol. 2, Part 1: *The Inscriptions on Stone*, by P. M. Fraser, Part 2: *The Inscriptions on Ceramics and Minor Objects*, 1960; Vol. 3: *The Hieron* (3 vols., by Phyllis Williams Lehmann and Martin R. Jones), 1969; Vol. 4, Part 1: *The Hall of Votive Gifts*, Part 2: *The Altar Court* (with D. Spittle), 1963; Vol. 5: *The Temenos* (with Phyllis Williams Lehmann and D. Spittle); Posthumous publications: "Piranesi as Interpreter of Roman Architecture," *Piranesi*, Northampton, Mass., (1961): 88–98; *Samothracian Reflections: Aspects of the Revival of the Antique* (with Phyllis Williams Lehmann), Princeton, N.J.: Princeton University Press, 1973.

Karl Lehmann established his expertise in the fields of Roman art and archaeology with his 1926 two volume publication on Trajan's column; it has become a standard reference on the subject of Roman historic relief.

Lehmann's career was interrupted by the events of prewar Germany when he was dismissed from his post in Münster by the Hitler regime. He moved first to Italy and then in 1935 to the United States, becoming an American citizen in 1944. His interests expanded to Greek art and religion, and in 1938 he began his life's major work, the excavation of the sanctuary of the "Great Gods" on the island of Samothrace.

One volume on these excavations was published before his death, and he had prepared a large amount of work for future volumes which were completed and later published by others.

Another lifelong interest was the survival and revival of ancient art in the Medieval and Renaissance periods.

SOURCES

Von Blanckenhagen, "Necrology," *AJA* 65 (1961): 307–308; Phyllis Pray Bober, "Karl Lehmann," *Gnomon* 33 (1961): 526–28; Sandler, editor, *Essays in Memory of Karl Lehmann*, 1964; *EJ*, Vol. 11, 1982; *AAB*, 1962; *WWA*, 1958–59; Leekely and Noyes, *AEGI*, 1975; correspondence with New York University.

DORO (TEODORO) LEVI

b: June 1, 1898. Trieste, Italy.
d: July 3, 1991. Rome, Italy.

EDUCATION

University of Florence, 1920 (Ph.D.).
Italian School of Archaeology at Athens, 1921–24.

APPOINTMENTS AND AWARDS

Archaeological Superintendency of Etruria: Inspector,
Director (1926–35); Univ. of Florence: Lecturer (1931); Univ.
of Cagliari: Professor of Archaeology (1935–38); Superinten-
dent of Antiquities of Sardinia (1935–38); Italian Archaeolog-
ical School at Athens: Director (1947–77); *Bollettino d'Arte*:
Editor (1948–74). Fellow: Guggenheim Fellow (1941–43).
Member: Institute for Advanced Study, Princeton Univ.
(1938–45). Foreign Hon. Member: Archaeological Institute of
America (1974); German Archaeological Institute; Greek
Archaeological Society, Honorary Vice President. Hon.
Degree: Ph.D., Univ. of Athens (1988).

EXCAVATIONS

Various sites in Italy (1926–31) including Chiusi and
Volterra; Kardiani, Tenos, 1923; Kos; Phaistos, Crete,
1949–67; Gortyn, Crete, 1954–61; Iasos, Turkey, 1960–72.

PUBLICATIONS

"La necropoli etrusca del Lago dell' Accesa," *Mont. Ant. Linc*
35 (1933); *Early Hellenic Pottery of Crete* (1945), Amsterdam: A.

M. Hakkert, 1969; *Antioch Mosaic Pavements* (1947), Rome: L'Erma di Bretschneider, 1971 (2 vols.); *The Italian Excavations in Crete and the Earliest European Civilization*, 1963; "The Recent Excavations at Phaistos," *SIMA* 11, 1964; *Festos: e la civilta minoica*, Rome: Edizioni dell'Ateneo, 1976–88 (6 vols.).

Doro Levi's career focused upon the prehistory of Crete where he began his excavation of Phaistos (the second largest Minoan palace on Crete) in 1949. The site had originally been dug by the Italian Archaeological Mission to Crete under the supervision of FEDERICO HALBHERR, beginning in 1900, and had yielded extensive remains of the palace and surrounding town; L. Pernier (who later supervised the Phaistos excavations) had concluded his work during the 1930s by carrying out a partial restoration of the site. Levi dug to the west and south and uncovered a large part of the First Palace and some of the ancient Minoan town which had surrounded it.

He made a major archaeological discovery at Iasos in Caria (Turkey) when he uncovered the remains of Minoan houses and pottery. This provided evidence of an early link, previously unknown, between Anatolia and Crete. He also discovered Mycenaean pottery at this site, thereby establishing positive proof of early relations between Anatolia and prehistoric mainland Greece.

In 1947 Levi was presented with a difficult task when he was appointed director of the Italian School of Archaeology at Athens; the buildings of the school had been destroyed during the Second World War and its holdings scattered. Due to Levi's determined and concentrated efforts, however, the school was able to offer courses again by 1950, and he continued as its director for a total of thirty years.

SOURCES

Clelia Laviosa, "Doro Levi, 1898–1991," *AJA* 97 (1993): 165–66; Leekley and Noyes, *AEGI*, 1975; Vincenzo La Rosa, "Teodoro Levi," *ASAtene* 68–69 (1995): 1–3; *IWW*, 1981–82; *WWWorld, 1981–82*; *EJ*, 1982.

GEORG LOESCHCKE

b: June 28, 1852. Penig, Saxony.
d: November 26, 1915. Baden Baden, Germany.

EDUCATION

University of Leipzig, 1873.
Bonn University, 1876.

APPOINTMENTS AND AWARDS

Univ. of Dorpat: Professor of Philology and Archaeology
(1879–87); German Archaeological Institute at Athens:
Director (1887–89); Bonn Univ. (1889–1912); Univ. of Berlin
(beg. 1912).

EXCAVATIONS

Mycenae; Pergamon; German *limes*.

PUBLICATIONS

Mykenische Thongefäße (with A. FURTWÄNGLER),
Berlin: A. Asher and Co., 1879; *Mykenische Vasen* (with A.
Furtwängler), Berlin: A. Asher and Co., 1886.

Georg Loeschcke, together with his colleague ADOLF
FURTWÄNGLER, is recognized as having changed the course
of archaeological investigation during the last quarter of the
nineteenth century with his work on Mycenaean pottery.

At this time archaeology still focused upon the study of the
most aesthetically appealing antiquities and paid no attention
to the ubiquitous small sherds of pottery which were found

alongside these lovelier objects. Loeschcke, influenced partly by the highly astute Furtwängler, emphasized a different approach; he saw that the value of archaeological artifacts lay not only in their aesthetic appeal, but more importantly, in their ability to tell us something about the history of an excavation site. He and Furtwängler believed that by examining the developments in the fabric, shape, and most especially the decorative patterns on pottery sherds (together with a consideration of their archaeological context) one could begin to work out a chronology. Loeschcke's emphasis on the study of the most meager artifacts led one of his colleagues to remark that "(to Loeschcke) even a post-hole in the ground becomes a monument."[1]

In their first collaboration (1879, above) they made great headway by identifying Mycenaean pottery as being separate from Geometric (at the time the two were deemed to be the same). In their second joint work (1886) they provided a classification and an analysis of all Mycenaean pottery known to date; through this landmark publication the two provided a foundation for all future scholarship in prehistoric pottery and established the fact that pottery was to provide the basis of archaeological excavation. The work of ARTHUR EVANS, CARL W. BLEGEN, and A.J. B. WACE later rested on this premise.

Following his endeavors in prehistoric pottery, Loeschcke turned his attention to Roman culture on the Rhine, especially the Roman *limes* (frontiers). Archaeological excavation had already been carried out at many sites in the Rhineland but with his enlightened approach (i.e., the examination of the most simple remains) Loeschcke was able to procure new information, information that had largely been ignored by previous excavators because it had been deemed too meager to bear any scholarly fruit.

While Furtwängler continued an active career in excavation, Loeschcke chose to disseminate his knowledge through teaching. He was considered a brilliant and inspiring teacher and drew students from around the world including DAVID M. ROBINSON, T. LESLIE SHEAR, and GEORGE KARO, as well as Germany's own MARGARETE BIEBER.

Loeschcke is also remembered (along with U. Köhler) for having identified a number of fragments of an Athenian building inscription as having come from the Parthenon; these fragments gave us our evidence for the starting date of construction on this temple (447 B.C.E.) and its final completion date (432 B.C.E.). The inscription stated that the temple proper took nine years to build while an additional five years were needed to fully complete it (presumably to situate the pedimental sculptures and to sculpt the Ionic frieze).

SOURCES

Ernst Langlotz, "Georg Loeschcke, 1852–1915" in *150 Jahre Rheinische Friedrich-Wilhelms-Universtät zu Bonn, 1818–1968*, (1968): 233–38; Oelmann, "Zum hundertsten Geburtstage Georg Loeschcke," in *Bonn Jahrbücher* (1952): 5–12; Lullies and Schiering, *Archäologenbildnisse*, 1988; Michaelis, *A Century of Archaeological Discoveries*, 1908; Cook, *Greek Painted Pottery*, 1972, 2d. ed.; Stillwell, editor, *PECS*, 1976.

NOTE

1. Langlotz, p. 233.

(SIR) GEORGE MACDONALD

b: 1862. Elgin, Scotland.
d: August 9, 1940. Edinburgh, Scotland.

EDUCATION

Edinburgh University, 1882 (M.A.).
Balliol College, Oxford University, 1887 (Lit. Hum.).

APPOINTMENTS AND AWARDS

Kelvinside Academy: Classical Master (1887–92); Univ. of Glasgow: Senior Asst. (to Gilbert Murray), Lecturer in Classical Archaeology (1892–1904), Hon. Curator, Hunterian Museum (1905–40); Dept. of Education for Scotland: Asst. Secretary (1904–22), Secretary (beg. 1922); Society for the Promotion of Roman Studies, President (1921–26); Royal Numismatic Society, President (1935–36). Hon. Degree: LL.D., Oxford Univ. (1935).

EXCAVATIONS

Bar Hill, Croy, 1901 (with Alexander Park); Castle Cary, 1902; Rough Castle, 1903; Glenmailen, Aberdeenshire, 1913; Haverfield; Raedykes, Angus, 1914; Mumrills, near Falkirk, 1923–27.

PUBLICATIONS

Catalogue of Greek Coins in the Hunterian Collection (3 vols.), Glasgow: J. Maclehose and Sons, 1899–1905; "Early Seleucid Portraits," *JHS* 23 (1903): 92–116; *Coin Types, their Origin and Development* (1905), Chicago: Argonaut, 1969 (The Rhind Lectures, 1904); "Early Seleucid Portraits, II," *JHS* 27 (1907): 145–159; *The Roman Forts on the Bar Hill, Dumbartonshire* (with Alexander Park), Glasgow: J. Maclehose, 1906; *Historia Numorum* (contributor), Oxford: The Clarendon Press, 1911 (2d. ed.); *The Roman Wall in Scotland* (1911), Oxford: The Clarendon Press, 1934 (revised and enlarged edition); *The Evolution of Coinage* (1916), Chicago: Obol International, 1980; *The Silver Coinage of Crete: A Metrological Note* (1919), Chicago: Obol International, 1974; "The Agricolan Occupation of North Britain," *JRS* 9 (dated 1919, issued 1921): 111–138; "The Building of the Antonine Wall: a fresh study of the inscriptions," *JRS* 11 (dated 1921, issued 1923): 1–24; *The Romanization of Roman Britain* (1923), Westport, Conn.: Greenwood Press, 1979; *Roman Occupation of Britain* (co-contributor), 1924; *Agricola in Britain*, London: J. Murray, 1932.

Sir George MacDonald's major contribution was in the field of ancient Greek numismatics and his three large volumes (above, 1899–1905) made this important collection accessible to scholars for the first time. He was particularly interested in the coinage of the Seleucid kingdom. He also added greatly to our knowledge of Roman settlements in Scotland, with special regard to the Antonine Wall. MacDonald had been engaged in writing a comprehensive two part work on the prehistory of Scotland, but only two chapters were finished at the time of his death. In addition to his work in the fields of archaeology and numismatics, MacDonald made major contributions to education in Scotland.

SOURCES

A. O. Curle, "Sir George MacDonald 1862–1940," *PBA* 27 (1941): 432–51; J. G. C. Anderson, "Sir George MacDonald: A Bibliographical Supplement," *JRS 32* (1941): 129–32; *JRS* 20 (1932) 1–8; *TL* (August 12, 1940).

DUNCAN MACKENZIE

b: May 17, 1861. Aultgowrie, Scotland.
d: August 25, 1934. Rome, Italy.

EDUCATION

Edinburgh University, 1889 (MA).
University of Vienna, 1895 (Ph.D.).
British School at Athens, 1895–98.

APPOINTMENTS AND AWARDS

Edinburgh Univ.: Carnegie Fellow in History (1903–06); Palestine Exploration Fund: Director (1910–13); Archaeological Curator, Knossos (1926–28).

EXCAVATIONS

Phylakopi, Melos, 1896–99; Knossos, 1900–10, 1922–25; Ains Shems, Palestine, 1910, 1912.

PUBLICATIONS

"Ancient Sites in Melos," *BSA* 3 (1896–7): 71–88; "The Pottery of Knossos," *JHS* 23 (1903): 157–205; "The Successive Settlements at Phylakopi in their Aegeo-Cretan Relations," *Excavations at Phylakopi in Melos*, *JHS*, Supplementary Paper 4, 238–272 (T.D. Atkinson, et al.); "Cretan Palaces and the Aegean Civilization," Part 1: *BSA* 11 (1904–05): 181–223, Part 2: *BSA* 12 (1905–06): 216–258, Part 3: *BSA* 13 (1906–07): 423–445, Part 4: *BSA* 14 (1907–08): 343–422; "The East Pediment Sculptures of the Temple of Aphaia at Aegina," *BSA* 15

(1908–09): 274–307; "The Dolmens, Tombs of the Giants, and Nuraghi of Sardinia," *PBSR* 5 (1910): 87–137.

The key role that Duncan Mackenzie played in the excavation of the palace of Knossos has often been overshadowed by that of ARTHUR EVANS; nonetheless, Mackenzie did contribute enormously to the outcome of these excavations. Evans had had very little experience in actual excavation work when he began at Knossos, while Mackenzie had largely supervised the British excavation at Phylakopi for four years and had thus been trained in the new methods of archaeological field work for which Phylakopi is known (see RICHARD C. BOSANQUET).

In his 1903 publication on the pottery of Knossos (above), Mackenzie set out the three-part division of Minoan pottery (Early, Middle, and Late) with the further three subdivisions (I, II, and III) for each major division. These terms were allotted certain spans of time and dates which have stood to the present day with little change.

It seems that Mackenzie's views on the last stage of settlement at Knossos eventually differed from those of Evans. Evans firmly held to the belief that Knossos was never overthrown by a foreign people and that its eventual demise occurred as the result of internal strife. Mackenzie, in his 1904 publication on Phylakopi (above), however, states that Crete, like Phylakopi, might finally have been destroyed by invaders from the Greek mainland. Despite the fact that this position evidently caused some friction between the two men, they remained in fairly close contact after the excavations were finished; Mackenzie lived at Evans's home in Oxford, England during part of World War One, and was later appointed to the position of archaeological curator at Knossos by Evans.

Mackenzie's meticulously kept daybooks and pottery notebooks made during his tenure at Knossos provide the only continuous record for the excavations there and as such have recently become important in the debate (raised by L. R. Palmer) over the date of the Linear B tablets found at this site.

SOURCES

Nicoletta Momigliano, "Duncan Mackenzie: A Cautious Canny Highlander," in Christine Morris, editor, *Klados: Essays*

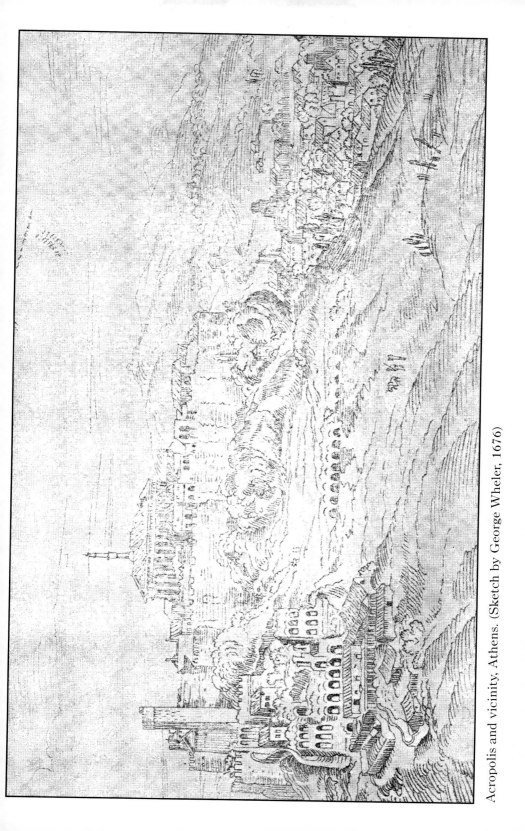

Acropolis and vicinity, Athens. (Sketch by George Wheler, 1676)

Born in Prussia the son of a cobbler, Johann Joachim Winckelmann (1717-1768) went on to become one of the most influential figures in the history of art, especially Classical archaeology. (Staatsbibliothek, Bildarchive, Berlin. Artist: Anton Raphael Mengs)

Retired businessman Heinrich Schliemann (1822-1890), untrained as an archaeologist and often ridiculed by his countrymen, was responsible for uncovering some of the most fabulous treasures of the Homeric "Heroic Age," including the site of Troy and the so-called Treasure of Priam. (Photo courtesy of the Deutsches Archäologisches Institut, Berlin)

Sophie Schliemann wearing jewelry from the "Treasure of Priam" discovered by Heinrich Schliemann at the site of Troy.

The remains of Troy: trench dug by Heinrich Schliemann. (Photo courtesy of Marvin W. Kushnet)

Heinrich Schliemann discovered Grave Circle A at Mycenae in 1876. The photograph shows the actual shafts of the graves that lie within the circle. (Photo courtesy of Marvin W. Kushnet)

With his discovery of the Minoan culture of Bronze Age Crete, Sir Arthur Evans (1851-1941) joined Heinrich Schliemann as one of the true "founding fathers" of Mediterranean archaeology. (Photo courtesy of the British Academy)

Sir Arthur Evans (left) with Theodore Fyfe and Duncan Mackenzie (1861-1934) who, with Evans, played a key role in the excavation of the Palace of Minos at Knossos. (Photo permission of the Ashmolean Museum, Oxford)

Sir Arthur Evans (with Duncan Mackenzie to his left) on the steps of the Grand Staircase at the Palace of Minos, Knossos. (Photo permission of the Ashmolean Museum, Oxford)

Einar Gjerstad was one of Sweden's foremost archaeologists. He directed the excavations of the Swedish Cyprus Expedition (1927-1931) which are generally considered to be the most important archaeological excavations to have been carried out on the island. (Photo permission of University of Uppsala Library, Uppsala, Sweden)

Archaeologist Hetty Goldman (1881-1972), shown here (center, back row) in 1922, was the first female professor to teach at Princeton's Institute for Advanced Study. Carl Blegen (left, back row) was one of her students. (Photo permission of the American School of Classical Studies at Athens)

Swedish archaeologist Arne Furumark (1903-1982) produced one of the most important reference works on the classification, analysis, and chronology of Mycenaean pottery. (Photo courtesy of Mrs. Dagmar Furumark)

Frigidarium, Villa Imperiale, Piazza Armerina, Sicily, excavated by Paolo Orsi in 1929. (Photo by Marvin W. Kushnet)

Carl Blegen (1887-1971) is regarded as one of the foremost American archaeologists, whose discovery of hundreds of Linear B tablets on the Greek mainland helped rewrite the history of prehistoric Greece. (Photo permission of the American School of Classical Studies at Athens)

"The Boxers Fresco" from Akrotiri, Thera, Greece. The site of Akrotiri was excavated by the Greek archaeologist Spyridon Marinatos from 1967-1974. (Photo by Linda Medwid)

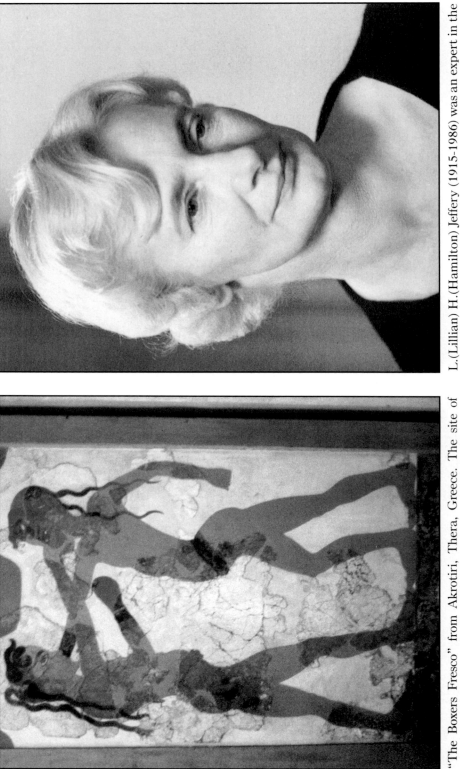

L.(Lillian) H.(Hamilton) Jeffery (1915-1986) was an expert in the Archaic period of Greek history, specifically in the development of regional scripts. (Photo courtesy of the British Academy)

Adolf Furtwängler (1853-1907), a monumental figure in the history of ancient art and Classical archaeology, was the first to recognize that pottery could be used as a basis for the chronological dating of ancient sites. (Photo courtesy of the Deutsches Archäologisches Institut, Berlin)

Wilhelm Dörpfeld (1853-1940) considered one of the greats of Classical archaeology, is best known for his immense contribution to our knowledge of the Greek Bronze Age. (Photo courtesy of the Deutsches Archäologisches Institut, Berlin)

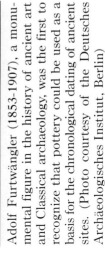

T. B. Mitford's (1905-1978) work in the Cypriot Classical syllabic script greatly assisted Michael Ventris in his decipherment of the Bronze Age script known as Linear B. (Photo permission of the British Academy)

The Third Style of Pompeiian wall painting, House of Loreias Tiburtinus, Pompeii. The classification of Roman wall painting was worked out by August Mau, based on his work at Pompeii. (Photo by Marvin W. Kushnet)

The Mausoleum at Halicarnassus (Bodrum), Turkey. The site was discovered by Charles Newton in 1856.(Photo by Marvin W. Kushnet)

A portion of the Parthenon frieze, British Museum. (Photo by Linda Medwid)

Temple of Aphrodite, Palaeopaphos, Cyprus, 1888. (Photo from Hogarth, *A Wandering Scholar in the Levant*, 1896)

Erik Sjöqvist (1903-1975), who did valuable work excavating ancient Cyprus, later joined the faculty at Princeton University where he turned his attention to the history of ancient Sicily and the city of Morgantina. (Photo courtesy of the Medelhavs-museet, Stockholm, Sweden)

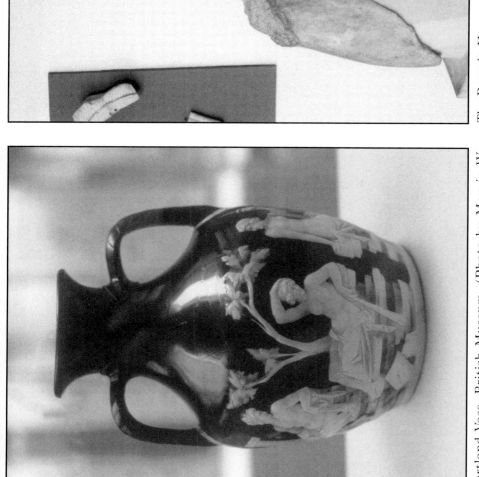

The Portland Vase, British Museum. (Photo by Marvin W. Kushnet)

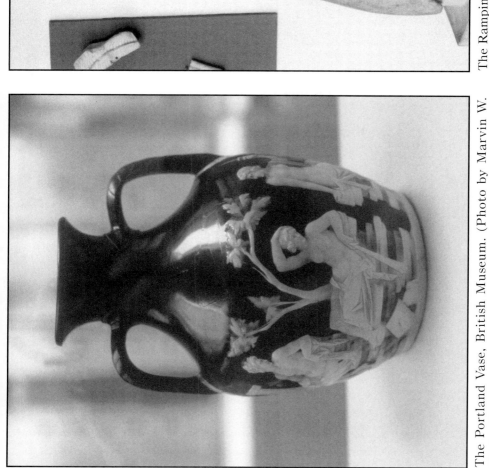

The Rampin Horseman, Acropolis Museum, Athens. (Photo by Marvin W. Kushnet)

Housteads Fort Granary, Hadrian's Wall, England (Roman Borcovicium). Richard Bosanquet began excavations at the site in 1898. (Photo by Marvin W. Kushnet)

The Neolithic settlement at Sesklo, Greece, excavated by Christos Tsountas during the 1901-1902 seasons. (Photo by Marvin W. Kushnet)

Caerwent, Wales (Roman Venta Silurum), excavated by Thomas Ashby beginning in 1899. (Photo by Marvin W. Kushnet)

The Forum Romanum, Rome. (Photo by Marvin W. Kushnet)

Michael Ventris (1922-1956) successfully deciphered Bronze Age Linear B script and demonstrated that it was an early form of Greek.

Luigi Palma di Cesnola (1832-1904) provided New York's Metropolitan Museum of Art with the nucleus of its now world-caliber collection of ancient art; however, he is one of the most controversial figures in the history of Classical archaeology.

in Honour of J. N. Coldstream (1995): 163–70; "Necrology" *AJA* 39 (1935): 378–79; *BSA* 4 (1897–98): 121; Palmer, *On the Knossos Tablets*, 1963; McDonald, *The Discovery of Homeric Greece*, 1967; Fitton, *The Discovery of the Greek Bronze Age*, 1995; Pendlebury, *A Guide to the Stratigraphical Museum in the Palace at Knossos*, 1933; Cleator, *Archaeology in the Making*, 1976.

Amedeo Maiuri

b: January 7, 1886. Veroli, Italy.
d: April 7, 1963. Naples, Italy.

EDUCATION

University of Naples.
University of Rome, 1908.
University of Athens.

APPOINTMENTS AND AWARDS

Member, Italian Archaeological Mission to Crete
(1911–14); Director of Antiquities in the Dodecanese
(1914–24); Inspector of Antiquities, Campagna (1924–61);
Univ. of Naples: Professor of Greek and Roman Archaeology
(1942–61). Hon. Degrees: Ph.D., The Sorbonne.

EXCAVATIONS

Gortyn, Crete; Halicarnassus, Caria; Pompeii, 1924–61
(Director); Herculaneum, 1927–61 (Director); Paestum; Velia;
Cuma; Stabia; Capri; Pozzuoli; various sites on Rhodes
including Ialysos.

PUBLICATIONS

Guida di Rodi, 1921; *Nuova silloge epigrafica di Rodi e Cos*,
1925; "Ialysos. Scavi della Missione arch. ital. a Rodi,"
ASAtene (1926) Vols. 6–7; *Il Diomede di Cuma*, 1930; *La Villa dei
Misteri* (1931), Rome: Instituto Poligrafico dello Stato, 1960
(3d. ed.); *La Casa del Menandro e il suo tesoro di argenteria*, Rome:
La Libreria dello Stato, 1933; *Pompei: I nuovi scavi e la villa dei*

misteri, Rome: La Libreria dello stato, 1937; *L'ultima fase edilizia di Pompeii*, 1942; *Pompei ed Ercolano. Tra easa e abitanti*, Padova: Le Tre Venezie, 1950; *Pompeii*, Paris: F. Nathan, 1952; *Roman Painting*, Geneva: Skira, 1953, (*La peinture romaine*, 1954); *Ercolano* (4th ed.), 1954; *Ercolano: I nuovi scavi (1927–58)*, 1958; *The Phlegraean Fields: From Virgil's Tomb to the Grotto of the Cumaea Sibyl* (translation by V. Priestley), Rome: Instituto Poligrafico dello Stato, 1958; *Herculaneum*, Rome: Instituto Poligrafico dello Stato, 1959; *Painting in Italy: From the Origins to the Thirteenth Century* (with Lionello Venturi et al.), New York: Skira, 1959; *Capri: Its History and Its Monuments*, Rome: Instituto Poligrafico dello Stato, 1958; *Pompeian Wall Paintings*, Berne: Hallwag, 1960.

Amedeo Maiuri is best remembered for his longtime work at the Roman sites of Herculaneum and Pompeii.

Originally a student of Byzantine philology, he became interested in archaeology as a student of FEDERICO HALB-HERR whom he accompanied on the Italian Archaeological Mission to Crete from 1911 to 1914, excavating the nymphaeum and theater at Gortyn. His experience in Crete served him well when he was appointed director of antiquities in the Dode-canese where the focus of his work was on the island of Rhodes, including the important Classical acropolis at Ialysos and its nearby *necropoleis* which date from Mycenaean through Roman times. Before leaving the Dodecanese to return to Italy in 1924, Maiuri founded the archaeological museum on Rhodes.

As director of antiquities for Campagna, he became director of excavations at Pompeii, a site which provides us with the best and fullest information we have about life in an affluent Roman town of the first century. Large parts of the site had already been cleared but many areas still remained covered under a thick layer of volcanic ash; during the next thirty-seven years Maiuri succeeded in laying bare much of the site, in the process of which he uncovered the House of Menander (with its treasury of silver), the large palaestra (adjacent to the amphitheater), and finished excavating the Villa of the Mysteries which had been abandoned after its ini-tial excavation in 1909. Maiuri's careful and detailed analysis of this villa showed that it had passed through six phases of development, the original dating to c. 200–150 B.C.E.; by the time of its destruction by the eruption of Mt. Vesuvius in C.E.

79 the villa was one of the grandest in Pompeii and still serves as a major source for our knowledge of Roman wall painting.

In addition to his work at Pompeii, Maiuri directed the excavation of the nearby site of Herculaneum. Here he was presented with a much more difficult problem: while Pompeii had been covered by a fairly shallow layer of soft volcanic ash, Herculaneum had been enveloped by a layer of volcanic mud (in some places to a depth of 12 meters). Despite the difficulties, however, he was largely able to uncover the orthogonal plan of the city during thirty-one years of excavation.

Maiuri carried out important excavations at other sites including Stabia, Paestum (where he uncovered the city walls), and Capri where he discovered the imperial villa of the emperor Tiberius. He was the author of more than three hundred publications.

SOURCES

Alfonso de Franciscis, "Amedeo Maiuri," *Bollettion d'Arte* 48 (1963): 287–88; Charles Picard, "Amedeo Maiuri (1886–1963)," *RA* 1 (1965): 104–106; Kraus, *Pompeii and Herculaneum: The Living Cities of the Dead*, 1973; Leekley and Noyes, *AEGI* 1975; MacKendrick, *The Mute Stones Speak*, 1960; Stillwell, editor, *PECS*, 1976; *NYT* (April 8, 1963); *TL* (April 8, 1963).

SPYRIDON N. MARINATOS

b: November 4, 1901. Lexourion, Kephallenia, Greece.
d: October 1, 1974. Santorini, Greece.

EDUCATION

University of Athens (Ph.D.), 1921.
University of Berlin.
University of Halle.

APPOINTMENTS AND AWARDS

Archaeological Museum, Herakleion, Crete: Assistant, Antiquities Department (1919–25), Conservator (1925–29), Director (1929–37); Director of Antiquities on Crete (1929–37); Director of Antiquities and Historic Monuments (Athens) (1937–40, 1955–58); Univ. of Athens: Professor of Archaeology (1939), Rector (1958–59), Pro-Rector (1960–62), Emeritus Professor (1962); Greek Archaeological Services and Restoration of Monuments: Inspector General (1967–73); Norton Lecturer (1958–59); Academy of Athens (beg. 1955), President. Member: British Academy. Hon. Member: Academy of Vienna; Archaeological Institute of America; Gottfried V. Herder Preis (1967). Foreign Member: American Philosophical Society (1966). Award: Gold Medal, French Academy of Science (1967).

EXCAVATIONS

Crete; Kephallenia; Thermopylae; Marathon; Pylos; Thera (Santorini), 1967–74.

PUBLICATIONS

Pictorial Representations of the Sea in the Cretan-Mycenaean Age, 1925 (Dissertation); *Cretan Civilization*, 1927; "The Volcanic Destruction of Minoan Crete," *Antiquity* 13 (1939): 425–439; *Greece and Greek Civilization as the Results of Economic Expansion*, 1946; *Thermopylae: A Guide*, 1951; *Kreta und das Mykenische Hellas*, 1959 (English edition: *Crete and Mycenae*, New York: H. N. Abrams, 1960); *Two Interplanetary Phaenomena of 468 B.C.*, 1963; "The Volcanic Origin of Linear B," *Europa* (1967): 204–210 (*Grumach Festschrift*); *Archaeologia Homerica*, 1967; *Thera* 1–7, Athens: Athenais Archaeologike Hetaireia, 1967–73; *Some Words About the Legend of Atlantis*, Athens: Rhodi Bros., 1969; *Kreta, Thera und das mykenische Hellas*, Munich: Hirmer, 1973; *Die Ausgrabungen auf Thera und ihre Probleme*, Wien: Verl D. Österr, 1973.

Spyridon Marinatos excavated near Akrotiri on the island of Thera from 1967 until his death in 1974. This site has yielded one of the most perfectly preserved Bronze Age settlements in the area and thus has provided us with some of the most complete wall paintings and architectural remains from this period to be found anywhere.

Marinatos was led to the site through his investigation into the cause of the collapse of the Minoan civilization on Crete and he hypothesized (1939, above) that Crete's destruction had been brought about by the volcanic eruption that took place on Thera c.1500 B.C.E. He went to the island to investigate his theory and, after a careful survey, discovered the settlement which at some points was covered by as much as sixty meters of volcanic ash. Many of the buildings were preserved from the basement to the first floor and sometimes even to the second.

The exact role of the Theran volcanic eruption in the destruction of Minoan Crete has never been settled. At present the consensus is that the chronology of the two events does not coincide.

Marinatos died in a fall while working in a trench at Akrotiri.

SOURCES

Homer A. Thompson, "Spyridon Marinatos—November 4, 1901–October 1, 1974," *Archaeology* 28, No. 1 (1979): 59; Benjamin D. Meritt, "Spyridon N. Marinatos (1901–1974)," *APSY* (1975): 144–48; Doumas, *Thera: Pompeii of the Aegean*, 1983; *IWW*, 1973–74 (37th edition); *SIMA* 23 (1971): 52–53; *NYT* (October 2, 1974), (October 3, 1974).

HAROLD MATTINGLY

b: December 24, 1884. Sudbury, England.
d: January 26, 1964. Chesham, England.

EDUCATION

Leys School, Cambridge.
Gonville and Caius College, Cambridge University, 1907.
University of Berlin.
University of Freiburg.

APPOINTMENTS AND AWARDS

Dept. of Coins and Medals, British Museum: Dept. of
Printed Books (1910–12), Asst. Keeper (1912–48); *Numismatic
Chronicle*: Editor (1936–52); Royal Numismatic Society, Presi-
dent (1942–48; Hon. Vice President [1953]); Society for the
Promotion of Roman Studies, Vice President (beg. 1938).
Fellow: Royal Numismatic Society (1912); British Academy
(1946). Hon. Fellow: Gonville and Caius College, Cambridge
Univ. Visiting Fellow of Classics: Univ. of Dunedin, New
Zealand (1954–55). Hon. Degree: D.Litt., Univ. of Dunedin
(1955). Awards: Chancellor's Medal for Classics, Cambridge
Univ. (1907); Archer M. Huntington Medal, American Numis-
matic Society (1938); C.B.E. (Commander of the British
Empire, 1960).

PUBLICATIONS

The Imperial Civil Service of Rome (1909), Connecticut:
Hyperion Press, 1979; *Outlines of Ancient History: From the
Earliest Times to the Fall of the Roman Empire in the West*, A.D.
476, Cambridge: Cambridge University Press, 1914; *Roman*

Imperial Coinage (co-editor and contributor), London: Spink, 1923–51; *Coins of the Roman Empire in the British Museum (1923–1950)* (5 vols.), London: Trustees of the British Museum, 1975 (reprinted with revisions); *Roman Coins from the Earliest Times to the Fall of the Western Empire* (1928), London: Methuen, 1967; *The Defences of the Roman Fort at Malton* (by Philip Corder, with Mattingly as contributor), Leeds: The Yorkshire Archaeological Society, 1930; *The Date of the Roman Denarius and Other Landmarks in Early Roman Coinage* (with E. S. G. Robinson), London: H. Milford, 1933; *The Man in the Roman Street* (1947), New York: W. W. Norton, 1966; *Christianity in the Roman Empire: Six Lectures*, Dunedin, New Zealand: University of Otago, 1955; *Roman Imperial Civilization*, New York: St. Martin's Press, 1957.

Harold Mattingly is credited with having revolutionized the study of Roman coinage. When he entered the field in the early part of the twentieth century he was faced with a mass of badly organized and uncritical published works along with much material awaiting publication. Through a steady stream of books and articles he created a new, scholarly approach to the discipline and almost single-handedly succeeded in making Roman numismatics a legitimate and integral part of the study of ancient Roman history and civilization.

He laid the foundation for this new approach in his *Roman Imperial Coinage* series (above) which he initially undertook in collaboration with E. A. Sydenham. It had been traditional to publish coinage of the emperors in alphabetical order, but in this 1923 work Mattingly listed the emperors chronologically and focused upon the mints that produced the coinage, listing the issues also in chronological order. The result was a clear and concise picture of the development of the Roman monetary system. This new structure became the blueprint for Mattingly's British Museum catalogues on the same subject; these catalogues were made even more useful by the provision of lengthy discussions regarding historical context, mints, and Roman denominational systems in addition to the inclusion of relevant coins not held by the British Museum. Although there have been many works on the subject published since, these volumes remain the standard two reference works on Roman Imperial coinage.

SOURCES

R. A. G. Carson, "Harold Mattingly 1884–1964," *PBA* 50 (1964): 331–40; R. A. G. Carson, "Harold Mattingly 1884–1964," *NC*, 7th series, 5 (1965): 239–54; *WWW*, 1961–1970; *TL* (February 1, 1964), (February 4, 1964), (February 12, 1964).

AUGUST MAU

b: October 15, 1840. Kiel, Germany.
d: March 6, 1909. Rome, Italy.

EDUCATION

University of Kiel, 1863 (Ph.D.).
University of Bonn.

APPOINTMENTS AND AWARDS

School of Learning, Glückstadt: Teacher; German Archaeological Institute in Rome: Assistant (1873–87), Librarian
(beg. 1887).

PUBLICATIONS

Pompejanische Beiträge, 1879; *Geschichte der dekorativen
Wandmalerei in Pompeii*, Berlin: G. Reimer, 1882; *Das Pri-
vatleben der Römer* (1886 with Joachim Marquardt), reprint,
1964; "Scavi di Pompei, 1894–95, reg. VI, isola ad E della 11
Casa dei Vettii," RM 11 (1896): 3–97; *Pompeii in Leben und
Kunst*, 1900 (English ed., Pompeii: Its Life and Art, trans. by
Francis W. Kelsey, New York: Macmillan, 1902 [revised. ed.]);
Führer durch Pompeii, 1928 (6th edition).

Mau was not an archaeologist by profession but his publication on Pompeian wall painting (1882, above) neverthe-
less proved to be one of the most influential works ever
written on Roman art.

Mau had been trained in Classical theology but was
forced to move from his native Germany to Italy for health
reasons at the age of thirty-two. There he came into contact

with Theodore Mommsen and gained employment at the German Archaeological Institute at Rome studying ancient inscriptions from Pompeii.

At this time the Pompeian excavations were under the supervision of Giuseppe Fiorelli, who had been working at Pompeii since 1860. Fiorelli was the first excavator at Pomepeii to approach the task in a methodical way; he had worked to clear a large part of the site and had superimposed a grid over it which broke up the area into nine districts (*regiones*) so that it could be studied in a systematic way for the first time.

Fiorelli was studying the various phases of Roman construction at Pompeii and, when Mau became interested in the stylistic development of the wall paintings, Fiorelli's studies provided a good foundation for his work. Mau applied the same concentrated effort to the paintings that he had formerly given to the inscriptions and in the process was able to discern four distinct styles of Roman painting beginning with what he termed the "First Style" which was purely decorative (imitation marble, and so on) and ending with the florid "Fourth Style" which combined three-dimensionality and decorative art (based in Roman theater). The "Four Styles" described by Mau more than one hundred years ago still provide the basis for all studies of Roman wall painting.

SOURCES

Lullies and Schiering, *Archäologenbildnisse*, 1988; Studniczka, "August Mau: 15. X. 1840–6. III. 1909," *RM 23* (1908): 269–74; Michaelis, *A Century of Archaeological Discovery*, 1908; Kraus, *Pompeii and Herculaneum*, 1973; Maiuri, *Roman Painting*, 1953; *TL* (June 10, 1909).

BENJAMIN D(EAN) MERITT

b: March 31, 1899. Durham, North Carolina.
d: July 7, 1989. Austin, Texas.

EDUCATION

Hamilton College, New York, 1920 (A.B.), 1923 (A.M.).
American School of Classical Studies at Athens, 1920–22.
Princeton University, 1923 (M.A.), 1924 (Ph.D.).

APPOINTMENTS AND AWARDS

Univ. of Vermont: Instructor in Greek (1923–24); Brown
Univ. (1924–25); Princeton Univ.: Asst. Professor of Greek
(1925–26); American School of Classical Studies at Athens:
Asst. Director (1926–28); Univ. of Michigan: Assoc. Professor
of Greek and Latin (1928–29), Professor (1929–33); American
School of Classical Studies at Athens: Visiting Professor
(1932–33, 1969–70); Johns Hopkins Univ.: Francis White Pro-
fessor of Greek (1933–35); Institute for Advanced Study,
Princeton Univ.: Professor of Greek Epigraphy (1935–69), Pro-
fessor Emeritus (1969). Fellow: American Academy of Arts and
Sciences. Visiting Professor: Univ. of Texas at Austin (beg.
1973). Visiting Lectureships: Martin Lecturer, Oberlin College
(1939), Eastman Professor, Oxford Univ. (1945–46), Sather
Professor, Univ. of California (1959), Semple Lecturer, Univ. of
Cincinnati (1967). Member: American Philosophical Society;
German Archaeological Institute. Hon. Degrees: Oxford Univ.
(1936); Hamilton College (1937); Princeton Univ. (1947);
Glasgow Univ. (1948); Univ. of Pennsylvania (1967); Univ. of
Athens (1970); Brown Univ. (1974). Awards: Commander of the
Order of the Phoenix (Greece); Order of George I (Greece).

EXCAVATIONS

Colophon, 1922; Corinth, 1927 (Director).

PUBLICATIONS

The Athenian Calendar in the Fifth Century (1928), Freeport, N.Y.: Books for Libraries Press, 1969; *Supplementum Epigraphicum Graecum*, Vol. 5 (with A. B. West), 1931; *Corinth*, Vol. 8, Part 1: "Greek Inscriptions," Cambridge, Mass.: Harvard University Press, 1931; *Athenian Financial Documents of the Fifth Century*, Ann Arbor, Mich.: University of Michigan Press, 1932; *The Athenian Assessment of 425 B.C.*, Ann Arbor, Mich.: Univeristy of Michigan Press, 1934; *The Athenian Tribute Lists* (with M. F. McGregor and H. T. Wade-Gery) (4 vols.), Cambridge, Mass.: Harvard University Press, 1939–53; *The Chronology of Hellenistic Athens* (with William Kendrick Pritchett), Cambridge, Mass: Harvard University Press, 1940; *The Athenian Year*, Berkeley, Calif.: University of Califronia, 1961 (Sather Lecturers of 1958/9); *Inscriptions: The Athenian Councillors* (with J. S. Traill), Princeton, N.J.: American School of Classical Studies at Athens, 1974.

Meritt was considered one of the world's foremost epigraphers. His work centered around fifth century B.C.E. Greece and his many publications have become required sources in any study of the history of the Athenian Empire and of the Athenian calendar year. His most notable publication was an analysis and discussion of the Athenian tribute lists. These lists, which were written on more than one hundred fragments, were discovered during excavations on the Athenian acropolis after the Greek War of Independence. The lists cover the forty years which comprise the "Golden Age" of Greece and name the tributees and their various allotted payments to Athens as members of the Delian League (which effectively became the Athenian Empire after the removal of the League's treasury from Delos to Athens in 454 B.C.E.); as such the lists provide invaluable information regarding the Athenian Empire and its relation to its subject-states. The fragments had been reconstructed during the nineteenth century, but when Meritt reexamined the tablets (with Allen B. West[1]), it was concluded that they had been incorrectly pieced together. The two were able to convince the director of the Epigraphical Museum in Athens of the poor reconstructions and were subsequently granted permission to rearrange them. This proved to be the beginning of a monumental undertaking which was to culminate in Meritt's landmark publications of 1939–53 (together with coauthors Wade-Gery and McGregor).

Meritt was a prolific writer and produced more than two hundred articles and reviews for scholarly journals.

SOURCES

John S. Traill, "Benjamin Dean Meritt, 1899–1989," *AJA* 94 (1990): 483–84; Lord, *History of the American School . . .*, 1947; *WW*, 1977; W. S. Ferguson, *AJA* 33 (1929): 340–41; *CR* 77 (1963): 334–35; Russell Meiggs, *CR* 69 (1955): 113; MacKendrick, *The Greek Stones Speak*, 1981; Dow, *Fifty Years of Sathers Lectures*, 1965; *NYT* (July 9, 1989).

NOTE

1. Allen B. West's promising career was cut short when he was killed in an automobile accident in 1936.

T(ERENCE) B(RUCE) MITFORD

b: May 5, 1905. Yokohama, Japan.
d: November 8, 1978. Scotland.

EDUCATION

Dulwich College.
Jesus College, Oxford University.

APPOINTMENTS AND AWARDS

St. Andrews University, Scotland: (Temporary) Asst. Professor, Warden, St. Salvator's Hall (1932–36), Lecturer in Humanity, Reader in Humanity and Classical Archaeology (1952–73), Hon. Emeritus Professor and Research Fellow (1973). Fellow: British Academy (1974); Society of Antiquaries. Corresponding Fellow: Austrian Academy (1978). Member: Institute of Advanced Study, Princeton University (1961, 1967). Corresponding Member: German Archaeological Institute; Austrian Archaeological Institute. Hon. Degree: D.Litt, Oxford University (1973).

EXCAVATIONS

Kafizin, Cyprus, 1949 (with P. DIKAIOS); Kouklia, Cyprus, 1950–55 (with J. F. Iliffe).

PUBLICATIONS

"Contributions to the Epigraphy of Cyprus," *JHS 57* (1937): 28–37; *Studies in the Signaries of South-Western Cyprus*, London: Institute of Classical Studies, 1961; *Journeys in Rough Cilicia* (with G. E. Bean) in *Denkschriften der Wiener Akademie*,

1965, 1970; *The Inscriptions of Kourion*, Philadelphia: American Philosophical Society, 1971; "The Cypro-Minoan Inscriptions of Old Paphos," *Kadmos* 10 (1971): 87–96; *The Greek and Latin Inscriptions from Salamis* (with I. Nicalaou), 1974; *The Nymphaeum of Kafizin. The Inscriptions of a Hellenistic Cult Site in Central Cyprus*, 1980 (published posthumously).

Mitford was the foremost scholar in Cypriot epigraphy. He first visited Cyprus in the 1930s and eventually became fascinated with the development of the syllabic scripts found there. Since the Greek alphabet was not used by the ancient Cypriots until the end of the fourth century B.C.E., a thorough knowledge of their syllabic scripts is vital to learning the early history of the island. Mitford was a pioneer in this field.

At Kouklia he unearthed more than two hundred fifty Archaic Paphian syllabic texts which had been incorporated into a siege ramp erected by a Persian army in 498 B.C.E. This was a particularly important find since this phase of development represents a transition between the Cypriot script of the Late Bronze Age and that of the Classical period; a line could now be traced backward from the Classical syllabic script to the Cypro-Minoan script of the Late Bronze Age.[1]

When the political situation on Cyprus in the late 1950s required the termination of his work there, Mitford turned his attention to an area of epigraphical study which had long interested him, that of western Cilicia and Pamphylia, in Asia Minor. During his journeys into this wild, mountainous country, he was able to find many previously unknown inscriptions and some Classical sites that had eluded earlier searchers.

Mitford served in the defense of Crete in World War Two under J. D. S. PENDLEBURY, and was one of the last to escape the island when it fell. As a note of interest, Mitford bore a rather striking resemblance to busts of the emperor Vespasian.

SOURCES

Franz Georg Maier, "Terence Bruce Mitford 1905–1978," *PBA* 67 (1981): 433–442; *SIMA* 23 (1971): 86; *TL* (November 24, 1978).

NOTE

1. MICHAEL VENTRIS had used Cypriot Classical syllabic script to aid his decipherment of the Bronze Age Linear B script found on Crete and in Greece.

GEORGE E(MMANUEL) MYLONAS

b: December 9, 1898. Smyrna (modern Izmir), Turkey.
d: April 15, 1988. Athens, Greece.

EDUCATION

University of Athens, 1927 (Ph.D.).
Johns Hopkins University, 1929 (Ph.D.).

APPOINTMENTS AND AWARDS

Department of Art and Archaeology, Washington University: Asst. Professor, Professor, Chairman, Distinguished Univ. Professor (1933–68); Archaeological Society, Athens: Secretary General (beg. 1968); Archaeological Institute of America: resident (1956–60). Member: American Academy of Arts and Sciences. Hon. Member: Society of Antiquaries (London). Hon. Degrees: Ohio State Univ.; Washington Univ.; Univ. of Illinois. Awards: Gold Medal, Archaeological Institute of America (1970); Grand Commander, Royal Order of the Phoenix (Greece).

EXCAVATIONS

Corinth (under B. H. HILL); Nemea and Aghiorghitika, 1923–28 (under C. W. BLEGEN); Aghios Kosmas, 1930–31, 1952; Olynthus, 1932–33 (with D. M. ROBINSON); Eleusis, 1931–34, 1950–57; Mycenae, 1951–54 (with J. PAPADIMITRIOU), beg. 1958.

PUBLICATIONS

Excavations at Olynthus, Baltimore, Md.: Johns Hopkins Press, 1929–52; *Proistoriki Eleusis*, 1932; *The Hymn to Demeter and Her Sanctuary at Eleusis*, St. Louis, Mo.: Washington University Press, 1942; *The Balkan States: An Introduction to Their History*, Missouri: Eden Publishing House, 1947; *Studies Presented to David Moore Robinson on His Seventieth Birthday* (co-editor) (2 vols.), St. Louis, Mo.: Washington University Press, 1951–53; *Ancient Mycenae: The Capital City of Agamemnon*, Princeton, N.J.: Princeton University Press, 1956; *Aghios Kosmas: An Early Bronze Age Settlement and Cemetery in Attica*, Princeton, N.J.: Princeton University Press, 1959; *Eleusis and the Eleusinian Mysteries*, Princeton, N.J.: Princeton University Press, 1961; *Grave Circle B of Mycenae*, Lund: C. Bloms, 1964; *Mycenae and the Mycenaean Age*, Princeton, N.J.: Princeton University Press, 1966; *The Cult Center of Mycenae*, 1972; *The West Cemetery of Eleusis*, 1975; *Mycenaean Religion*, 1977.

George Mylonas excavated at sites throughout Greece over a sixty year period. For the last thirty years of his life he worked at the Bronze Age site of Mycenae and this important work bridged the earlier, partly unpublished excavations of CHRISTOS TSOUNTAS and the work of A. J. B. WACE.

Mylonas's excavations earned him a worldwide reputation and he lectured extensively in countries as far afield as Australia, New Zealand, and Japan.

In addition to being noted for his quick and precise publication of excavation material, he produced comprehensive books on more general topics such as the temple site of Demeter at Eleusis and on life during the Mycenaean Bronze Age. Professor Mylonas was buried, at his own request, at Mycenae.

SOURCES

Spyros Iakovidis, "George Emmanuel Mylonas, 1898–1988," *AJA* 93 (1989): 235–237; *CA*: 125; *WWA*, 1982–83; *DAS* 1, 1974; Leekley and Efstratiou, *AECNG*, 1980; Mylonas, *Eleusis and the Eleusinian Mysteries*, 1961; Stillwell, editor, *PECS*, 1976; de Grummond, *EHCA*, 1996; *NYT* (May 3, 1988).

(SIR) J(OHN) L(INTON) MYRES

b: July 3, 1869. Preston, Lancashire, England.
d: March 6, 1954. Oxford, England.

EDUCATION

New College, Oxford University, 1890 (Class. Mod.), 1892 (Lit.Hum.).
British School at Athens beg. 1892.

APPOINTMENTS AND AWARDS

Christ Church, Oxford Univ.: Lecturer in Ancient History (1895–1907); Univ. of Liverpool: Gladstone Professor of Greek and Lecturer in Ancient Geography (1907–10); New College, Oxford Univ.: Wykeman Professor (1910–39), Emeritus Professor of Ancient History (1939); Univ. of California: Sather Professor (1914, 1927); British School at Athens: Chairman of the Managing Committee (1933–47); Royal Anthropological Institute: President (1928–31). Fellow: Society of Antiquaries; British Academy (1923). Hon. Degrees: D.Sc., Univ. of Wales (1920); D.Sc., Univ. of Manchester (1933); Ph.D., Univ. of Athens (1937). Awards: Victoria Medal, Royal Geographical Society (1953); Commander of the Order of George I (Greece) (1918); K.C.B. (Knight Commander of the Bath, 1943).

EXCAVATIONS

Alchester, Oxfordshire, 1892; Ayia Oaraskevi (Nicosia), Kalopsida, Turabi Tekke (Larnaca), Amathus, Kition, Cyprus, 1894; Crete, 1895 (with Arthur Evans), 1898 (with Arthur Evans and DAVID HOGARTH); Palaikstro, Crete, 1903; Bamboula, Lapithos, Enkomi, Cyprus, 1913.

213

PUBLICATIONS

A Catalogue of the Cyprus Museum with a chronicle of excavation undertaken since the British Occupation (with M. OHNEFALSCH-RICHTER), 1899; *A History of Rome*, 1902; *The Dawn of History*, London: Williams and Norgate, 1911; *A Handbook of the Cesnola Collection of Antiquities from Cyprus* (1914), New York: Arno Press, 1974; *The Political Ideas of the Greeks* (1926), New York: AMS Press, 1971; *Who Were the Greeks?* (1930), New York: Biblo and Tannen, 1967 (Sather Lectures); *Mediterranean Culture*, Cambridge: Cambridge University Press, 1943; *Herodotus, Father of History* (1953), Chicago: H. Regnery Co., 1971; *Geographical History in Greek Lands* (1953), Westport, Conn.: Greenwood Press, 1974; *Homer and His Critics*, London: Routledge and Paul, 1959 (edited by Dorothea Gray, posthumously published); *Inscriptions in the Minoan Linear Script of Class A*, Oxford: Oxford University Press, 1961 (edited by W. C. Brice from the notes of SIR ARTHUR EVANS and Sir John Myres).

John Myres's archaeological interests centered upon two Aegean Mediterranean islands which were both home to early Hellenic civilization: Cyprus and Crete.

Myres has often been referred to as the "Father of Cypriot Archaeology" because it was he who first put this field on a firm, scientific basis. During the mid-nineteenth century, Cyprus had achieved international attention through the excavations of individuals such as CESNOLA; but Cesnola, and others like him, had simply been interested in procuring antiquities for the purpose of selling them to museums around the world. Excavations had not been conducted in a systematic way, and no interest at all was shown in recording the archaeological context of finds. As a result, by the time John Myres first visited Cyprus in 1894, Cypriot archaeology was in a state of complete chaos. This all changed, however, with his presence; from the beginning, Myres displayed the professional approach and scientific method that had hitherto been wholly lacking. He carried out careful excavations of key sites and in 1899 coauthored (with MAX OHNEFALSCH-RICHTER) the first catalog of Cypriot antiquities in which a chronology of Cypriot archaeology was presented for the first time; it was this catalog that later provided the basis for the important work of EINAR GJERSTAD. Myres's publication (in 1914) of the Cesnola collection in the Metropolitan Museum of Art in New York firmly established him as the world's leading authority in Cypriot archaeology.

Myres first became interested in the archaeology of Crete when he met ARTHUR EVANS at Oxford in 1892, and it was this meeting that began the collaboration and friendship which would last throughout their long careers. On Crete, it was Myres who recognized that sherds of Kamares ware were of the same type as those discovered by FLINDERS PETRIE at Kahum in Egypt and this provided another link in the relatively firm dating for the prehistory of the Aegean.

Evans died before completion of the *Scripta Minoa* series (Evans had published Volume 1 in 1909) and Myres subsequently provided the complete text to Volume 2 (published in 1952).

It was this publication which later enabled MICHAEL VENTRIS and John Chadwick to carry out their pioneering work on the "Minoan" script. Myres died while Volume 3 of the series was in proof; it was eventually edited by W. C. Brice and published in 1961.

Myres was instrumental in aiding Evans in his major reorganization of the Ashmolean Museum at Oxford and was knighted in 1943.

SOURCES

T. J. Dunbabin, "Sir John Myres 1869–1954," *PBA* 41 (1955): 349–66; Porphyrios Dikaios, "Sir John L. Myres," ΚΥΠΙΑΚΑΙ ΣΠΟΥΔΑΙ ΙΖ, 1953 (1954): 107–10; Casson, *Ancient Cyprus*, 1937; Myres and Ohnefalsch-Richter, *Catalogue of the Cyprus Museum*, 1899; *WWW*, 1951–60; Waterhouse, *British School at Athens*, 1986; *TL* (March 8, 1954).

EDWARD T(HEODORE) NEWELL

b: January 15, 1886. Kenosha, Wisconsin.
d: February 18, 1941. New York, New York.

EDUCATION

Harvard School, Chicago.
Yale University, 1907 (B.A.), 1909 (M.A.).

APPOINTMENTS AND AWARDS

American Numismatic Society: President (beg. 1916); *American Journal of Archaeology*: Associate Editor. Fellow: Royal Numismatic Society; British Numismatic Society. Hon. Member: Société Royale de Numismatique de Belgique. Awards: Gold Medal, Royal Numismatic Society; Archer M. Huntington Medal, American Numismatic Society (1918); Prix Allier de Hauteroche, Académie Française (1929).

PUBLICATIONS

The Reattribution of Certain Tetradrachms of Alexander the Great, 1912; *The Dated Alexander Coinage of Sidon and Ake* (1916), New York: AMS Press, 1980; *Tarsus Under Alexander*, 1919; *The First Seleucid Coinage of Tyre*, New York: American Numismatic Society, 1921; *The Coinages of Demetrius Poliorcetes*, Oxford: Oxford University Press, 1927; *The Pergamene Mint under Philetairos*, 1936; *Royal Greek Portrait Coins*, New York: W. Raymond, Inc., 1937; *The Coinage of the Eastern Seleucid Mints* (1938), New York: American Numismatic Society, 1978; *Late Seleucid Mints in Ake-Ptolemais and Damascus*, New York: The American Numismatic Society, 1939; *The Coinage of the Western Seleucid Mints* (1941), New York: American Numismatic Society, 1977.

Newell is widely regarded as the greatest numismatist that America has ever produced. He became interested in ancient coins, especially Greek, while an undergraduate at Yale and because of his personal wealth was able to accumulate a vast collection of his own.

In addition to being an avid collector he was a serious scholar and published a number of works which laid the foundation for further study of the coins of Alexander the Great and his successors. Newell was also considered an authority on Islamic and Indian coinages.

At the time of his death Edward T. Newell possessed a total of sixty thousand Greek, two thousand, three hundred Roman, and two thousand Byzantine coins; these coins now comprise the major part of the American Numismatic Society's collection. His interests extended beyond coinage and he also amassed ancient gems, scarabs, seal cylinders, and Greek and Roman glass. In 1938 he presented Yale University with his collection of fifteen hundred Babylonian and Assyrian cuneiform tablets.

SOURCES

D. M. Robinson, "Necrology," *AJA* (1941): 284; Alfred L. Bellinger, *DAB*, Supplement 3 (1941–45): 551–52; *Numismatist*, April 1941.

(SIR) CHARLES T(HOMAS) NEWTON

b: September 16, 1816. Bredwardine, Herefordshire, England.
d: November 28, 1894. Westgate-on-Sea, England.

EDUCATION

Shrewsbury School.
Christ Church, Oxford Univ., 1837 (B.A.), 1840 (M.A.).

APPOINTMENTS AND AWARDS

Dept. of Antiquities, British Museum: Junior Assistant (1840–52); Vice Consul, Mytilene (1852); Acting Consul, Rhodes (1853–54); Consul, Rome (1860–61); Dept. of Greek and Roman Antiquities, British Museum: Keeper (1861–85); University College, London: Yates Chair of Classical Archaeology (1880–85). Honorary Fellow: Worcester College, Oxford (1874). Member: Society of Dilettanti (1863). Corresponding Member: Institute of France. Honorary Member: Accademia dei Lincei (Rome). Hon. Degrees: D.C.L., Oxford Univ. (1875); LL.D., Cambridge Univ. (1879); Ph.D., Univ. of Strasbourg (1879). Awards: C.B. (Companion of the Bath, 1875); K.C.B. (Knight Commander of the Bath, 1887).

EXCAVATIONS

Calymnos, 1852, 1854–55; Halicarnassus (Bodrum) beg. 1856; Cnidus, 1858–59; Branchidae (near Miletus).

PUBLICATIONS

Map of British and Roman Yorkshire, London: Royal Archaeological Institute of Great Britain and Ireland, 1847; *Method of the Study of Ancient Art,* 1850; *History of Discoveries at Halicarnassus, Cnidus and Branchidae* (with R. P. Pullan), London: Day and Son, 1862–63; *Travels and Discoveries in the Levant* (2 vols.), London: Day and Son, 1865; *Collection of Ancient Greek Inscriptions in the British Museum* (1874), Milano: Instituto editoriale Cisalpino-La goliardica, 1977; "Dr. Schliemann's discoveries at Mycenae," *Edinburgh Review,* 1878; *Synopsis of the Contents of the British Museum: Department of Greek and Roman Antiquities: Second Vase Room* (2 vols.), London: Trustees of the British Museum, 1878; *Essays on Art and Archaeology,* London: Macmillan and Co., 1880.

Charles T. Newton made major contributions to Classical archaeology both as an excavator and as a pivotal figure in the development of the British Museum's collections of Classical antiquities. He was widely regarded as Britain's leading scholar on ancient Greece and, as its most able practical archaeologist, was often likened to WINCKELMANN in his scientific approach to the study of ancient art.

At the time of his stay at Oxford, Classical pursuits centered around the study of Greek and Latin but Newton declared that literary sources only served to give a very partial and one-sided view of ancient culture. He believed that much could be learned about Greek life through careful and systematic study of vase paintings, coins, and inscriptions; one of his most famous students at the British Museum was JANE ELLEN HARRISON who, after studying Greek vases under Newton, went on to develop her important theories regarding the origin of ancient Greek religion.

Newton was appointed vice consul at Mytilene and later acting consul at Rhodes, with the intention that he would explore the area's ancient sites and perhaps return to Britain with more artifacts with which to increase the British Museum's collections; he did not disappoint his superiors. He began excavating at present-day Bodrum in southwestern Asia Minor and discovered the famous Hellenistic Mausoleum of Halicarnassus, one of the seven wonders of the ancient world. In 1857 he unearthed the colossal statues of Mausolus and his wife Artemisia as well as several high relief sculpted slabs from the building's principal frieze. It was not difficult to obtain *firmans* from the Turkish government for the removal of antiquities at this time, and so Newton was able to bring all of these finds back to Britain for their installation in the British Museum.

Shortly after leaving Asia Minor he was appointed keeper of the British Museum's new Department of Greek and Roman Antiquities. Due to his influence and leadership he greatly increased the British government's funding to the museum and, through the contacts that he had made during his travels, was able to procure many more ancient artifacts for the department's collection. Newton's presence in the British Museum at this time was extremely important because Britain lagged far behind other nations (e.g., France and Germany) in its collection of Classical antiquities. It was due to Newton's influence that the museum was made to recognize the importance of acquiring more Classical artifacts; as a result, its Greek and Roman collection achieved world-class stature under his direction.

Newton took an active interest in HEINRICH SCHLIE-MANN'S excavations at Troy and Mycenae and kept up a regular correspondence with him. He was able to assist Schliemann regarding the provenance of some of the pottery which was being exhumed from the site, and he helped organize Schliemann's lectures in London.

In addition, Newton conducted a careful excavation to recover the city plan of ancient Cnidus, the first investigation of its kind. He was also one of the earliest archaeologists to use photography extensively in his excavations, though he published in lithographic form. He was a founding member of the Society for the Promotion of Hellenic Studies in London and contributed to the founding of the British School at Athens.

SOURCES

Cust, *History of the Society of Dilettanti*, 1914; Edwards, *Lives of the Founders of the British Museum* (1870), reprint, 1969; Turner, *The Greek Heritage in Victorian Britain*, 1981; Fitton, "Charles Newton and the Discovery of the Greek Bronze Age," in Christine Morris, editor, *Klados: Essays in Honour of J. N. Coldstream* (1995): 73–78; Eugénie Sellers, "Sir Charles Newton," *CR* (1895): 81–85; Michaelis, *A Century of Archaeological Discoveries*, 1908; Waterhouse, *British School at Athens*, 1986; Daniel, *A Hundred and Fifty Years of Archaeology*, 1975; *DNB*, Vol. 4; *TL* (November 30, 1894).

Max (Hermann) Ohnefalsch-Richter

b: April 7, 1850. Sohland, Germany.
d: February 6, 1917. Berlin, Germany.

EDUCATION

Görlitz Gymnasium, 1866.
Halle University, 1872.

APPOINTMENTS AND AWARDS

Journalist; various British governmental positions on Cyprus.

EXCAVATIONS

Larnaca; Kition, 1879; Salamis, 1882; Akhna, 1882; Ormidhia; Xylotymbou; Idalian, 1883; Alambra; Tamassos, 1884; Ayios Heraklidios; Nicosia, 1884; Marion, 1885, 1886.

PUBLICATIONS

"Neue Funde auf Cypern. Die Akropolis von Kition und ein Sanctuarium der syrischen Astarte," *Das Ausland* LII/49 (1879): 970–74; "Ein altes Bauwerk bei Larnaka," *AZ* 39 (1881): 311–14; "A prehistoric building at Salamis," *JHS* 4 (1883): 112–16; *Kypros, the Bible and Homer*, London: Asher and Co., 1893; *A Catalogue of the Cyprus Museum with a chronicle of excavation undertaken since the British Occupation* (with JOHN L. MYRES), 1899; "Nues über die auf Cypern mit Unterstützung Seiner Majestät des Kaisers, der Berliner Museen und der Rudolf Virchow Stiftung angestellten Ausgrabungen," *Verhandlungen der Berliner Gesellschaft für Anthropologie, Ethnologie und Urgeschichte* (1899): 29ff.

Max Ohnefalsch-Richter was one of the earliest excavators of Cyprus and, although he has been denounced as a "gold-seeker" in recent times,[1] can also be viewed as having helped provide a foundation for the development of modern Cypriot archaeology.

Ohnefalsch-Richter went to Cyprus in 1878 as a newspaper correspondent and, after becoming aware of the antiquities which abounded everywhere, became obsessed with acquiring artifacts himself. In 1879 he began excavations in the Larnaca-Kition area, and was hired by several museums from around the world (including those in Paris, Berlin, and London) to procure more antiquities. He subsequently excavated hundreds of ancient tombs, with the consequence that thousands of ancient Cypriot artifacts were shipped overseas with little recorded information regarding their archaeological context.

In spite of this wholesale export of Cypriot antiquities, Ohnefalsch-Richter's actions reflect an overall intention to make a serious contribution to Cypriot studies. In 1883, through correspondence with the well-known philhellenist W. E. Gladstone (who had just become Prime Minister of Great Britain), he helped found the Cyprus Museum and later consulted with experts of the day, including JOHN L. MYRES, WILHELM DÖRPFELD and ADOLF FURTWÄNGLER (with whom he worked at Idalion) in an effort to further scholarship in Cypriot archaeology.

Ohnefalsch-Richter coauthored (with John L. Myres) the initial catalog of the Cyprus Museum (see 1895, above) which was the first scholarly attempt to present a comprehensive account of Cypriot archaeology including the shapes, decoration, and chronology of Cypriot pottery. The nomenclature devised for this publication was later considered by EINAR GJERSTAD to be appropriate enough to be retained with only minimal modification.

Max Ohnefalsch-Richter was an avid admirer of HEINRICH SCHLIEMANN and at one time had planned to dig with him at Troy. In keeping with the times his view of archaeology tended toward the romantic; but in spite of the fact that he himself excavated tombs at break-neck speed, often selling the booty to foreign museums, he publicly denounced individuals such as LOUIS di CESNOLA as "gold-diggers." What seems to have separated Ohnefalsch-Richter from the likes of Cesnola is the fact that he took practical measures in order to help foster a scholarly attitude toward Cypriot antiquities and personally oversaw the progress of his excavations, something which Cesnola neglected completely.

SOURCES

Malecos, *Studies in Cyprus*, 1994; Gjerstad, *Studies in Prehistoric Cyprus*, 1926; Merrillees, "Einar Gjerstad: Reflections on the Past and the Present," *Meldelhavsmuseet* 9 (1994): 45–53; Åstrom, et al., *The Fantastic Years on Cyprus, the Swedish Cyprus Expedition and Its Members*, 1994; Michaelis, *A Century of Archaeological Discoveries*, 1908; McFadden, *The Glitter and the Gold*, 1971; Goring, *A Mischievous Pastime*, 1988; Casson, *Ancient Cyprus: Its Art and Archaeology*, 1937; Fitton, *The Discovery of the Greek Bronze Age*, 1995; Correspondence with the German Archaeological Institute, Berlin.

NOTE

1. Åstrom in Åstrom, et al., *The Fantastic Years on Cyprus . . .* , 1994, p. 26.

PAOLO ORSI

b: 1859. Rovereto, Italy.
d: November 8, 1935. Rovereto, Italy.

APPOINTMENTS AND AWARDS

National Museum, Syracuse: Assistant (1888–91), Director (beg. 1891).

EXCAVATIONS

Stentinello; Finocchito; Thapsos; Cozz del Pantano; Castelluccio, 1892, 1893; Gela; Calabria; Piazza Amerina, 1929; Croton; Leontini; Megara Hyblaea.

PUBLICATIONS

"La necropoli sicula di Castelluccio (Siracusa). Il sepolcreto di Tremenzano," *BPI* 17, 1892; "Scarichi del villaggio siculo di Castelluccio," *BPI* 19, 1893; "Necropoli Sicula presso Siracusa con vasi e bronzi micenei (Cozzo Pantano)," *Mon.Ant.Linc.*, 2, 1893; "Siculi e Greci in Leontini," *RM* 15 (1900): 62ff.; "Gela," *MA* 17, 1906; "Sepolcri di transizione dalla civiltà Sicula alla Greca," *RM* 24 (1909): 59ff.; "Croton," *NSc* (1911) Suppl: 77–124; "Scavi di Calabria nel 1911," *NSc* (1912) Suppl.; "Scavi di Calabria nel 1913," *NSc* (1913) Suppl.; "Megara Hyblaea; Villaggio neoliltico e tempio greco e di taluni singolarissimi vasi di Paternò," *Mont.Ant.Linc.* 27, 1921; "Le necropoli preeleniche calabrese di Torre Galli e di Canale, Ianchina, Patariti," *MA* 21 (1926) 5ff.; *Templum Apollinis Alaei*, Rome, 1933; *La necropoli di Passo Marinaro a Camarina: campagne di scavo, 1904–1909*, Rome: Academia nazionale dei Lincei, 1990.

Paolo Orsi has been described as "the great discoverer of prehistoric, . . . Christian and Byzantine Sicily,"[1] and he is one of the most respected of the earlier generation of Classical archaeologists.

He was drawn to Sicily not by an interest in the Greek remains but rather by the urge to discover what he could about the two pre-Greek populations of Sicily, the Sikels, and the Sikans (Sicans). Using a modern and scientific approach to excavation that was uncommon at the time and through his careful regard for stratigraphy and distributions of specific pottery types within strata, Orsi developed a five-stage chronological framework for prehistoric Sicily which began with the Neolithic period followed by four "Siculan" periods dating from c. 2400 B.C.E. (Early Bronze Age) through the fourth Siculan period, c. 500 B.C.E. (Iron Age). Thus his research revealed much evidence regarding the indigenous pre-historic cultures of Sicily, as well as the Greek colonists who began settling on the island in the eight century B.C.E.

Orsi followed closely the publications of FLINDERS PETRIE (regarding Mycenae), CHRISTOS TSOUNTAS, ADOLF FURTWÄNGLER, and GEORG LOESCHCKE, and was the first to demonstrate Sicilian trade with the Bronze Age Mycenaean culture of mainland Greece.

SOURCES

Robert Leighton, "Paolo Orsi (1859–1935) and the prehistory of Sicily," *Antiquity* 60 (1896): 15–20; Brea, *Sicily Before the Greeks*, 1966, 2d. ed.; Dunbabin, *The Western Greeks: The History of Sicily and South Italy from the Founding of the Greek Colonies to 480 B.C.*, 1948; Arias, *Quattro Archeologi del Nosro Secolo*, 1976; Michaelis, *A Century of Archaeological Discoveries*, 1908; Holloway, *The Archaeology of Ancient Sicily*, 1991; Stillwell, editor, *PECS*, 1976.

NOTE

1. Brea, *Sicily Before the Greeks*, p. 16.

MASSIMO PALLOTTINO

b: November 9, 1909. Rome, Italy.
d: February 7, 1995. Rome, Italy.

EDUCATION

University of Rome, 1931.

APPOINTMENTS AND AWARDS

Dept. of Antiquities of Rome: Inspector (1933); Museo
Nazionale di Villa Giulia: Director (1937); Univ. of Rome:
Lecturer, Acting Professor (1938–40); Univ. of Cagliari: Professor of Classical Archaeology (1940–45); Univ. of Rome: Professor of Etruscology and Italic Antiquities (beg. 1946); *Archeologia Classica*: Chief Editor. Hon. Fellow: Society of Antiquaries (London) (1965); Istituto di Studi Etruschi ed Italici:
President (1972–95). Member: British Academy. Award: International Prize, Balzan for Sciences of Antiquity (1982).

EXCAVATIONS

Cerveteri, 1937; Veii; Porto Torres (Sardinia); Pyrgi.

PUBLICATIONS

Elementi di Lingua Etrusca, 1936; *Tarquinia*, 1937; *Etrus-
cologia* (1942), Milan: U. Hoepli, 1975 (English edition: *The
Etruscans*, translated by J. Cremona, Indiana University Press,
1975, revised and enlarged); *La scuola di Vulca*, 1945; *L'Origine
degli Etruschi*, Rome: Tumminelli, 1947; *La peinture etrusque*,
1952 (English ed.: *Etruscan Painting*, trans. by M. E. Stanley
and Stuart Gilbert, Geneva: Skira, 1952); *Testimonia linguae*

Etruscae, 1954; *Art of the Etruscans*, London: Thames and Hudson, 1955; *The Meaning of Archaeology* (trans. by Peggy Martin), London: Thames and Hudson, 1968; *La necropoli di Cerveteri* (1939), Rome: Ist Poligrafico dello Stato, 1968 (7th ed.); *Arte in Sardegna*, Milan: Electa, 1969; *La langue étrusque: problémes et perspectives*, Paris: Belles Lettres, 1978; *Storia della prima Italia*, Milan: Rusconi, 1985 (Jerome Lectures, English edition: *A History of Earliest Italy*, trans. by M. Ryle and K. Soper, Ann Arbor, Mich.: University of Michigan Press, 1990); *Les Etrusques et l'Europe*, Paris: Réunion des musées nationaux, 1992; *Origine e storia primitiva di Roma*, 1993.

Massimo Pallottino is regarded as the founder of modern Etruscan studies. "Etruscology" had come into existence as a discipline during the eighteenth century and since that time one of the main foci of scholarship had been the question of Etruscan origins. The fifth century B.C.E. historian, Herodotus, had influenced this train of inquiry by his statement that the Etruscan people had originated from Lydia in Asia Minor. The Etruscan language and some of the apparently unique aspects of its culture seemed to support such a contention and indeed, this was the prevailing theory up to the first half of the twentieth century (see DAVID RANDALL-MACIVER). As a result of the assumption that Herodotus had been correct, the Villanovan culture of early Iron Age Italy had been perceived as having died out at the time that Etruscan culture began to flourish.

In 1926 the Italian archaeologist, Luigi Pareti, argued that the Etruscan culture was a later development of the Villanovan; his argument fell on deaf ears and it was not until the publication of Pallottino's *L'Origine degli Etruschi*, in 1947, that the archaeological world was finally convinced that the Etruscans represented the final flowering of an indigenous culture that had passed through several stages, including the Villanovan. With this publication, Pallottino had succeeded in totally changing the way this ancient culture was viewed.

Pallottino's excavations at Pyrgi in 1964 unearthed a sixth century B.C.E. gold tablet which was inscribed with both Phoenician and Etruscan scripts; this discovery served to greatly enhance our understanding of Etruscan history, religion, and trade, as well as our knowledge of the Etruscan language itself.

SOURCES

Larissa Bonfante, "Massimo Pallottino, 1909–1995," *AJA* 100 (1996): 157–59; David Ridgway, *PBA* 69 (1983): 559ff. (Obituary of David Randall-MacIver); Pallottino, *The Etruscans*, 1974; *IWW*, 1991–92; *NYT* (February 20, 1995).

JOHN PAPADIMITRIOU

b: August 22, 1904. Skyros, Greece.
d: April 11, 1963. Athens, Greece.

EDUCATION

University of Athens, 1946 (Ph.D.).
University of Berlin.
University of Munich.

APPOINTMENTS AND AWARDS

Greek Archaeological Service: Epimelete (1929), Ephor (1934), Director General (beg. 1958). Member: Institute for Advanced Study, Princeton University (1955–56).

EXCAVATIONS

Epidauros; Boeotia; Euboea; Mycenae, 1952–54; Brauron, Attica, beg. 1948.

PUBLICATIONS

Excavation reports on Brauron appeared in *Prakt* in the following years: 1945 through 1950, 1955 through 1957, 1959; Excavation reports on Mycenae appeared in *Prakt* in the following years: 1950 through 1954.

Dr. Papadimitriou was fortunate enough to make a number of major archaeological discoveries. During the 1952 campaign at Mycenae, with his colleagues GEORGE MYLONAS and D. Theocharis, he discovered a second grave circle (Grave Circle B) just outside the wall of the palace; the grave circle dates from the Middle Helladic III period and contained artifacts which rivaled the finds of SCHLIE-MANN almost a century earlier.

In 1958 Papadimitriou discovered the Sanctuary of Artemis at Brauron in Attica, excavating a temple and stoa as well as many fine pieces of sculpture and votive reliefs. These ruins date mainly from the fifth century B.C.E. but some go back as far as the Geometric period. Also in 1958, he discovered a cave near Marathon which he designated the Cave of Pan. There are many references made to this cave in ancient literature.

In addition to carrying out these important excavations, Papadimitriou played a major role in the reorganization and development of the Greek Archaeological Service.

SOURCES

John L. Caskey, "Necrology," *AJA* 67 (1963): 301; Charles Picard, "J. Papadimitriou (1904–1963)," *RA* 2 (1963): 206–207; Leekley and Noyes, *AESG*, 1976; Stillwell, editor, *PECS*, 1976; *Americana Annual* (1964): 743; Vermeule, *Greece in the Bronze Age*, 1972.

HUMFRY (GILBERT GARTH) PAYNE

b: February 19, 1902. Wendover, England.
d: May 9, 1936. Athens, Greece.

EDUCATION

Westminster School, London, England.
Christ Church, Oxford University, 1922 (Hon.Mods.), 1924 (Lit.Hum.).

APPOINTMENTS AND AWARDS

Ashmolean Museum: Assistant (1926–28); British School at Athens: Director (1929–36); Oxford Univ.: University Scholar in Mediterranean Archaeology (1924–26); Research Student of Christ Church (1926–31). Award: Conington Prize (1927).

EXCAVATIONS

Eleutherna, Crete, 1929 (Director, with DAVID G. HOGARTH); Perachora, 1930–33 (Director); Knossos, Crete, 1933; Fortetsa, Crete, 1935.

PUBLICATIONS

Necrocorinthia: A Study of Corinthian Art in the Archaic Period (1931), Maryland: McGrath Publishing Co., 1971; *Corpus Vasorum Antiquorum, Oxford, II,* (with J. D. BEAZLEY), 1931; *Protokorinthische Vasenmalerei* (1933), Mainz: P. von Zabern, 1974; *Archaic Marble Sculpture from the Acropolis,* London: Cresset Press, 1936 (text by Payne); *Perachora: The Sanctuaries of Hera Akraia and Limenia,* Vol. 1, 1940 (contributor, ed. by T. J. Dunbabin), Vol. 2, 1962 (both published posthumously, Oxford: The Clarendon Press).

Payne's specialty was the art of the Greek Archaic period and, being very much aware that more specimens needed to become available for study, he began an excavation at Perachora where he discovered a major Corinthian Archaic site. This was all the more exciting for Payne because it had not been overlaid with many Roman remains. While engaged in describing the excavation work at Perachora he contracted a staphlococcal infection and died at the age of thirty-four. He was buried at Mycenae.

J. D. BEAZLEY considered Payne to be one of his most promising students and believed that he had provided a new foundation for the study of Archaic art with his 1931 publication (above). Moreover, BERNARD ASHMOLE noted that in his 1936 opus (above) Payne had produced one of the most sensitive English works on Archaic Greek sculpture ever published.

Payne's vision was acute and his memory encyclopedic. He had never been to the Museum at Lyons, but while researching his 1936 publication on the Athenian acropolis marbles, he came across a photograph of the head and upper torso of a *kore* known as the "Aphrodite of Marseilles." He immediately saw that it could belong to the lower torso and a shoulder of a *kore* which were housed in the Acropolis Museum in Athens, and requested that a plaster cast be made of the fragment in Lyons. When the cast was received in Athens, the three pieces fit together perfectly. With the same acute perception, he saw that the head of the Rampin horseman (in the Louvre) fit an equestrian base that had been discovered on the Athenian acropolis fifty years earlier.

SOURCES

J. D. Beazley, *DNB*, 1931–40; Powell, *The Traveller's Journey is Done*, 1943; *WWW*, 1929–1940; *PBA* 56 1970 (Obituary on J. D. Beazley); Waterhouse, *British School at Athens*, 1986; Leekley and Noyes *AEGI*, 1975; Leekley and Noyes, AESG, 1976; TL (May 11, 1936).

J(OHN) D(EVITT)
S(TRINGFELLOW) PENDLEBURY

b: October 12, 1904. London, England.
d: c. May 22, 1941.[1] Candia, Crete.

EDUCATION

Winchester School, 1918–23.
Pembroke College, Cambridge University, 1927.
British School at Athens, 1927–28.
Macmillan Student, 1928–29.

APPOINTMENTS AND AWARDS

Curator, Knossos (1930–34); British Vice Consul, Candia, Crete (beg. 1940).

EXCAVATIONS

Macedonia, 1928; Armant, Tell el-Amarna, 1928–29; Tell el-Amarna, 1930–36 (Director); Mt. Dikte, Crete, 1936 (Director); Karphi Lasithi, Crete, 1936–39.

PUBLICATIONS

"Egypt and the Aegean in the Late Bronze Age," *JEA* 16 (1930): 75–92; *Aegyptiaca, a Catalogue of Egyptian Objects in the Aegean Area*, Cambridge: Cambridge University Press (1930), Chicago: Ares Publishers, 1992 (2 vols.); "Two Protopalatial Houses at Knossos," *BSA* 25 (1932): 53–73 (with H. Pendlebury); *A Handbook to the Palace of Minos*, London: Macmillan and Co., 1933; *A Guide to the Stratigraphical Museum in the Palace of Knossos*, 1933; *I. City of Akhenaton, II. The North Suburb and the Desert Altars* (with H. Frankfort), 1933; *III. The*

Central City and Official Quarters (2 vols.), posthumously published by H. W. Fairman, et al., 1951; *Dating the Pottery in the Stratigraphical Museum* (with E. Eccles and M. Money-Coutts), 1934; *Dating the Pottery in the Stratigraphical Museum: The Plans* (with M. Money-Coutts), 1935; *Tell el-Amarna*, London: L. Dickson and Thompson, 1935; *The Archaeology of Crete* (1939), New York: Biblo and Tannen, 1963.

J. D. S. Pendlebury produced a number of major works, and in his first publication, *Aegyptiaca*, he blended his two main interests, ancient Egyptian and early Greek archaeology. Here Pendlebury cataloged the many Egyptian objects found throughout the Aegean area (except Rhodes) describing and dating each; this work gives an important ready reference for the basis of dating early Greek strata.

The Archaeology of Crete (1939) is the product of first-hand information gathered from years of excavation on the island. In this work Pendlebury compiled all of the available data into a clearly and concisely written tome that covers the prehistoric through the historic periods. His work on the *Stratigraphical Museum* has become even more valuable in light of the disturbances which occurred during the Second World War. In it he presents the evidence for dating the various parts of the palace of Knossos.

It is not surprising that ARTHUR EVANS regarded Pendlebury as his successor and the leading authority on Bronze Age Crete. Pendlebury was killed in action during the German invasion of the island in 1941.

SOURCES

S. R. K. Glanville, "J. D. S. Pendlebury," *JEA*, 28 (1942): 61–63; *BSA* 41 (1946): 5–8 (Obituaries by A. J. B. WACE and Pierson Dixon); Waterhouse, *British School at Athens*, 1986; Dawson and Uphill, *Who Was Who in Egyptology*, 2d. ed., 1972; *WWW*, 1941–50; Leekley and Noyes, *AEGS*, 1975; Pendlebury, *Handbook to Palace of Minos*, 1979.

NOTE

1. J. D. S. Pendlebury was killed in action; the specific date of his death is unknown.

Francis C(ranmer) Penrose

b: October 29, 1817. Bracebridge, Lincolnshire, England.
d: February 15, 1903. Wimbledon, England.

EDUCATION

Bedford Grammer School, 1829.
Winchester College, 1835.
Apprentice in Architecture to Edward Blore, 1835–39.
Magdalene College, Cambridge University, 1842.

APPOINTMENTS AND AWARDS

Magdalene College: Traveling Bachelor (1842–45); St. Paul's Cathedral: Surveyor (beg. 1852); British School at Athens: Director (1886–87, 1890–91); Royal Institute of British Architects, President (1894–96). Fellow: Royal Institute of British Architects (1848); Royal Society (1894). Hon. Fellow: Magdalene College (1884). Member: Society of Dilettanti (1852). Hon. Degrees: Litt. D., Cambridge Univ.; D.C.L., Oxford Univ. Awards: Royal Gold Medal, Royal Institute of British Architects (1883); Knight of the Order of the Saviour of Greece.

PUBLICATIONS

Anomalies in the Construction of the Parthenon, 1847; *An Investigation of the Principles of Athenian Architecture: or, The Results of a Survey Conducted Chiefly with Reference to the Optical Refinements Exhibited in the Construction of the Ancient Buildings at Athens* (1851, 1888, 2d. ed.) Washington: McGrath Publishing Co., 1973; *The Prediction and Reductions of Occultations and Eclipses*, 1868 (1902, 2d. ed.); *On a Method of Predicting by Graphical Construction Occultations of Stars by the*

Moon, and Solar Eclipses, for Any Given Place, London: Macmillan and Co., 1869.

Penrose's work broke new ground with regard to our understanding of the subtleties involved in Classical architecture. Early on in his career he showed an observant and critical eye when he noted that the pitch of the Pantheon in Rome did not seem "right"; fifty years later it was established by another scholar that the pediment of the Pantheon had indeed been altered from its original design in antiquity.

Initially interested in the Gothic period, Penrose turned his attention to Classical architecture when he visited Greece in 1845. After an exhaustive study of Greece's ancient buildings, he concluded that the architects of some of the Greek temples of the Classical period had incorporated a number of subtle refinements into their designs which are not readily discernible but which produce a greater sense of harmony and energy in the buildings as a whole. In his publication on the Parthenon (1851) he recognized that although the columns appear to be vertical, they are instead inclined and that seemingly horizontal lines which appear straight (such as the stylobate and architrave) are actually slightly curved.

Penrose was also an able architect in his own right, having designed the entrance to Magdalene College, Cambridge, the first building of the British School at Athens (now the Director's House), and many interior elements of St. Paul's Cathedral in London.

SOURCES

Cust, *History of the Society of Dilettanti*, 1914; *Journal of the Royal Institute of British Architects*, 10 (1903): 213–14, 337–46; *DNB*, Supplement, Vol. 3; Waterhouse, *British School at Athens*, 1986.

AXEL W(ALDEMAR) PERSSON

b: June 1, 1888. Kvidinge, Sweden.
d: May 8, 1951. Uppsala, Sweden.

EDUCATION

University of Lund, 1915.
French School at Athens, 1920–21.

APPOINTMENTS AND AWARDS

Uppsala Univ.: Professor of Greek (1920–24), Professor of Classical Archaeology and Ancient History (beg. 1924); Sather Professor of Classical Literature (1940–41); Secretary to the King of Sweden. Member: Royal Academy of Letters, History and Antiquities (Stockholm); Royal Societies of Lund and Uppsala. Hon. Member: Archaeological Society of Athens.

EXCAVATIONS

Asine, 1922, 1924, 1926, 1930; Dendra (Midea), 1926, 1930, 1937; Berbati (Prosymna), 1935–37; Labraunda, Caria (S.W. Turkey), 1951.

PUBLICATIONS

Zur Textgeschichte Xenophons, Lund: C. W. K. Gleerup, 1915; *Vorstudien zu einer Geschichte der Attischen Sakralgesetzgebung*, 1918; *Asine, Recherches preliminaires en vue des fouilles suedoises*, 1921; *Neuerverbungen der Antikensammlung der Universitat Lund*, 1922; *Aperçu provisoire des résultats obtenus au cours des fouilles d'Asine faites en 1922*, 1923; *Rapport préliminaire sur les fouilles d'Asine; Sceaux et empreintes de sceaux d'Asine*, 1924; *Staat und*

Manufaktur im romischen Reich (1923), New York: Arno Press, 1979; *Schrift und Sprache in Altkreta*, 1930; *The Royal Tombs at Dendra near Midea*, Lund: C. W. K. Gleerup, 1931; *Eisen und Eisenbereitung in altester Zeit, etimologisches und sachliches*, 1934; *Asine, Results of the Swedish Excavations, 1922–1930* (with O. Frodin), 1938; *New Tombs at Dendra near Midea*, Lund: C. W. K. Gleerup, 1942; *The Religion of Greece in Prehistoric Times*, Berkeley, Calif.: University of California Press, 1942 (Sather Classical Lectures); "Swedish excavations at Labraunda, 1948," *Kungl. Vetenskapssamfundet i Lund, Arsberattelse 1948–1949*, 1949: 24–32.

Axel W. Persson was a leading figure in the development of Sweden's important role in the archaeology of the Mediterranean area. He was an industrious excavator who dug at a number of sites including the famous Dendra; the finds at Dendra were the richest in gold and silver objects in Greece since the work of HEINRICH SCHLIEMANN at Mycenae during the previous century. Together with the Crown Prince of Sweden (later King Gustaf VI Adolf) and the Greek Department of Antiquities, Persson led Sweden's first excavation in Greece at the site of Asine (mentioned in Homer's "Catalogue of Ships"). This proved an important dig for other reasons as well; A.J.B. WACE and CARL W. BLEGEN had only recently published their work concerning the chronology of prehistoric mainland Greece, and the work at prehistoric Asine proved vital for comparing and verifying their conclusions. Persson's publications on the site became doubly important after the events of World War Two when the area was plundered by Italian forces for its stone.

At Dendra, Persson excavated an undisturbed Mycenaean *tholos* tomb which had been discovered the previous year by Dorothy Burr (Thompson); here he found gold and silver vessels, weapons, and Late Helladic pottery. In later seasons he went on to uncover a number of Mycenaean chamber tombs (see 1931 and 1942, above). With regard to the objects that he discovered at Dendra, Persson was led to infer more of an Egyptian influence on Mycenaean art than has generally been accepted.

Persson was led to excavate at Labraunda (Caria) in the hope of finding connections between southwest Turkey and Crete; he thought that the name "Labraunda" and the Greek word "labarinthos" could be etymologically connected. He began excavations there in 1948 and while he did not find any remains as early as the Bronze Age, he was able to examine the admixture of Greek and Carian cultures from the sixth century B.C.E., and especially the little known architecture of the time of Mausolus (fourth century B.C.E.). He was preparing to leave for another season's work at Labraunda when he died in Uppsala.

Axel Persson was instrumental in organizing the highly successful Swedish Cyprus Expedition (1927–31) led by EINAR GJERSTAD.

SOURCES

M. P. Nilsson, "Axel Waldemar Persson (1888–1951)" *RA* 43 (1954): 217–21; Gullög C. Nordqvist, "Fragments of A. W. Persson: An Exhibition at the Swedish Institute at Athens, June 1–24, 1988," Svenska Institute, Athens, 1988; Sturer Brunnsåker, "Classical Archaeology and Ancient History," *Uppsala University. 500 Years: History, Art and Philosophy*, 1976: 19–33; David M. Robinson, "Necrology" *AJA* 56 (1952): 67–68; Leekley and Noyes, *AESG*, 1976; C. G. Styrenius, "Some Notes on the New Excavations at Asine," *OpAth* 11:10 (1975): 1; Åström, et al., "The Fantastic Years on Cyprus: The Swedish Cyprus Expedition and Its Members," *SIMA-PB* 79 (1994).

(Sir) W(illiam) (Matthew) Flinders Petrie

b: June 3, 1853. Charlton, Kent, England.
d: July 28, 1942. Jerusalem.

APPOINTMENTS AND AWARDS

University College, London: Edwards Professor of Egyptology (1892–1933), Professor Emeritus (1933). Fellow: Royal Society (1902); British Academy (1904). Member: American Philosophical Society (1905). Hon. Degrees: D.C.L., Oxford Univ. (1892); LL.D, Edinburgh Univ. (1896); Ph.D., Strasbourg Univ. (1897); Litt.D., Cambridge Univ. (1900); LL.D., Univ. of Aberdeen (1906). Award: K.C.B. (Knight Commander of the Bath, 1923).

EXCAVATIONS

Stonehenge, 1872 (survey); Giza, 1880–82; Tanis, 1883; Naukratis, 1884–85; Daphnae, 1886; Nebesha, 1886; Hawara, Biahmu, Arsinoe, 1888; Gurob, Egypt, 1889–90; Maidum, 1891, 1909; Tell el-Amarna, 1891–92; Dendera, 1897–98; Memphis, 1908–13; Sidmant, 1920–21; Silbury, England, 1923; Gaza, 1927–34.

PUBLICATIONS

Flinders Petrie published more than 100 books and approximately 900 articles and reviews for scholarly journals including: "The Egyptian Bases of Greek History," *JHS* 11 (1890): 271ff; *Inductive Metrology*, 1877; *The Pyramids and Temples of Gizeh*, 1883; *Naukratis. Part I. 1884–85* (with E. GARDNER and others), 1886; *Hawara, Biahmu, Arsinoe*, 1889; *A History of Egypt* (3 vols.) (1894–1905), Freeport, N.Y.: Books for Libraries Press, 1972;

Egyptian Decorative Art, 1895; *Diospolis Parva. The Cemeteries of Abadiyeh and Hu, 1898–99* (with A. C. Mace), 1901; *Methods and Aims in Archaeology* (1904), New York: B. Blom, 1972; *Personal Religion in Egypt before Christianity*, London: Harper, 1909; *Arts and Crafts of Ancient Egypt* (1910), New York: Attic Books, 1974; *The Status of the Jews in Egypt*, London: Allen and Unwin, 1922; *Ancient Weights and Measures*, 1926; *Seventy Years in Archaeology* (1931), New York: Greenwood Press, 1969; *Shabtis*, London: British School of Egyptian Archaeology, 1935; *Egyptian Architecture*, London: British School of Archaeology in Egypt, 1938.

Although primarily known as an archaeologist of Egypt and Palestine, Flinders Petrie's discovery of Mycenaean sherds at Tell el-Amarna provided the basis for establishing a chronology for Aegean prehistory. In addition, he is credited with having brought about the transition from antiquarianism to modern archaeology; although generated by Near Eastern excavations, his formulation of a scientific archaeological method provides the backbone of all current research in Classical archaeology.

When Petrie first went to Egypt at the age of thirty, he was confronted by improperly supervised excavations for which no records were kept; he saw tombs which had been dynamited in order to gain quick access to the precious works of art that were imagined to lie within. In his native Britain he had already witnessed the amassing of thousands of pieces of Egyptian works of art by museums where no attention was paid to their dating or provenance. In short, he was outraged by the practices of nineteenth-century archaeology and set out, consciously, to change them. In formulating these new procedures for excavation work, Petrie had no guidelines to follow, relying solely on his own experience and trial and error.

As ADOLF FURTWÄNGLER had recognized the importance of pottery decoration in establishing the chronology of a site, so Flinders Petrie perceived that by observing very carefully the style and shape of pottery (even undecorated), one could come to know the sequences, and thus work out a chronology. At Tell el-Hesi in Palestine, he was confronted with a *tell* with more than sixty feet of occupation depth. In order to work out its chronology, Petrie noted that various strata with their differing styles of pottery, cross-dated a number of sherds from different levels that were of the same type found at sites in Egypt, and developed, by way of establishing absolute dates at different depths, a chronology for all sixty feet of occupation. He was thus the first person to use stratigraphy in such an exacting and extensive manner.

In 1889, in Gurob, Egypt, Petrie found Mycenaean and pre-Mycenaean pottery sherds mixed with 18th Dynasty Egyptian material; the following year he found more pre-Mycenaean wares at the site of Kahun, this time mixed with Twelfth Dynasty Egyptian sherds. In 1891, accompanied by ERNEST GARDNER, he visited Mycenae where he recognized imported Egyptian objects dating to the Eighteenth Dynasty. After discovering a large amount of Mycenaean sherds at Tell el-Amarna (dating to the time of the pharaoh Akhenaten [1380–1360 B.C.E.]) the following year, Petrie was able to state with confidence that the Bronze Age civilization of Greece had evolved by about 2500 B.C.E. and that the late period of Mycenaean civilization dated to between 1500 and 1000 B.C.E. He thus provided absolute dates which could then be used as a framework for establishing a chronology for the prehistoric Aegean. Petrie's dating by way of cross-referencing Egyptian with Mycenaean with pre-Mycenaean artifacts was one of the earliest examples of the use of comparative archaeology.

In addition to the above, Petrie was among the first to emphasize the importance of the immediate publication of excavations and of keeping meticulous field notes. He also stressed the need to draw illustrations of where artifacts were found and the need to take careful measurements. Like HEINRICH SCHLIEMANN, he saw that in order for us to truly learn how a civilization existed, all finds from an excavation must be examined, recorded, and preserved, and that nothing should be discarded.

SOURCES

Sidney Smith, "Sir Flinders Petrie 1853–1942," *PBA* 28 (1942): 307–24; H. E. Winlock, "Sir William Matthew Flinders Petrie (1853–1942)," *APSY* (1942): 358–62; Petrie, *Seventy Years in Archaeology*, 1931 (autobiography); Daniel, *A Hundred and Fifty Years of Archaeology*, 1975; Cleator, *Archaeology in the Making*, 1976; Waterhouse, *British School at Athens*, 1986; Dawson and Uphill, *Who Was Who in Egyptian Archaeology*, 1972, 2d. ed.; Michaelis, *A Century of Archaeological Discoveries*, 1908; Leonard Woolley, *DNB* (1941–1950): 666–67; Percy E. Newberry, "William Matthew Flinders Petrie, Kt., F.R.S., F.B.A.," *JEA* 29 (1943): 67–70; *TL* (July 30, 1942).

(SIR) A(RTHUR) W(ALLACE) PICKARD-CAMBRIDGE

b: January 20, 1873. Bloxworth, England.
d: February 7, 1952. London, England.

EDUCATION

Weymouth College, 1890.
Balliol College, Oxford University, 1893, 1929, (D.Litt.).

APPOINTMENTS AND AWARDS

Oriel College, Oxford Univ.: Fellow and Classical Tutor (1895–97); Balliol College, Oxford Univ.: Classical Tutor (1897–1927); Univ. of Edinburgh: Professor of Greek (1927–30); Jowett Lecturer in Greek (1901); Jowett Fellow (1916). Fellow of the British Academy (1934). Hon. Degrees: D.Litt., Oxford Univ. (1929); D.Litt, Sheffield University; LL.D., Edinburgh Univ. (1933).

PUBLICATIONS

The Attic Theater, by A. E. Haigh (3d. ed., revised and in part re-written by Pickard-Cambridge) (1907), New York: Krause Reprint Co., 1969; *Demosthenes* (1914), New York: Arno Press, 1979; *Education, Science and the Humanities* (1916); *The Use and Abuse of Classical Studies,* 1916; *Dithyramb, Tragedy, and Comedy* (1927), Oxford: The Clarendon Press, 1962 (2d. ed., revised by T. B. L. Webster); *The Theatre of Dionysus,* Oxford: The Clarendon Press, 1946; *The Dramatic Festivals of Athens* (1953, published posthumously), Oxford: The Clarendon Press, 1988.

In conjunction with the discussions of contemporary scholars such as J. D. BEAZLEY and HUMFRY PAYNE, Sir

Arthur Pickard-Cambridge was able to further our knowledge of the origins, history, archaeological development, and performance of ancient Greek drama. His 1946 publication on the Theater of Dionysus in Athens is the most detailed account of this theater ever to have been published. The work discusses the structure from its beginnings through its various modifications to its last phase during the Roman period when its orchestra was made watertight for the staging of mock sea-battles.

In addition to his work in Greek theater, Pickard-Cambridge published a number of works on the role of the Classics in education (above).

SOURCES

Cyril Bailey, "Sir Arthur Wallace Pickard-Cambridge 1873–1952," *PBA* 38 (1952): 303–36; Margarete Bieber, "Necrology," *AJA* 57, No. 2 (1953): 113; *TL* (February 9, 1952), (March 10, 1952).

LEON POMERANCE

b: August 2, 1907. New York.
d: November 11, 1988. New York, New York.

EDUCATION

New York University School of Law.

APPOINTMENTS AND AWARDS

Forest Paper Company, President; Archaeological Institute of America, Vice President (1973–77).

PUBLICATIONS

The Pomerance Collection of Ancient Art (catalogue to an exhibition), Brooklyn, N.Y.: Brooklyn Museum, 1966; *Final Collapse of Santorini (Thera): 1400 B.C. or 1200 B.C.?*, Gothenburg: P. Åström, 1970; *The Phaistos Disc: An Interpretation of Astronomical Symbols*, Gothenburg: P. Åström, 1976; Studies in Aegean Chronology, by Paul Åström, Leon Pomerance and L. R. Palmer, Gothenburg: P. Åström, 1984.

Leon Pomerance was neither a professional archaeologist nor an art historian but he made significant contributions to Mediterranean archaeology in his funding of the study of the Aegean Bronze Age.

Upon graduation from law school he joined his father in the family business where he remained until his retirement in 1979. He and his wife, Harriet, had become collectors of ancient artifacts and in 1966 their collection was displayed in the Brooklyn Museum. By way of his close association with the Archaeological Institute of America, he introduced the

Gold Medal for Distinguished Archaeological Achievement in 1965–66, and in 1980 established the Pomerance Award for Scientific Contributions to Archaeology.

Pomerance played a major role in the discovery and excavation of the Bronze Age Minoan palace site of Kato Zakro. Earlier, DAVID HOGARTH had searched for the remains of the palace but had been unable to locate them. Upon his first visit to Crete, Pomerance became familiar with the notion of the existence of this palace and subsequently corresponded with Nicholas Platon. It was with the joint sponsorship of Leon Pomerance and the Greek Archaeological Society that the site was uncovered and excavations carried out under Platon's direction. Pomerance also supported excavations at Sardis, Kommos, Archanes, Pseira, and a reinvestigation of Troy.

SOURCES

Joseph W. Shaw, "Leon Pomerance, 1907–1988," *AJA* 93 (1989): 459–60; Platon, *Zakros*, 1971; *NYT* (November 14, 1988).

(François Paul) Edmond Pottier

b: August 13, 1855. Sarrebruck, France.
d: July 4, 1934. Paris, France.

EDUCATION

University of Paris.
French School at Athens, 1877–80.

APPOINTMENTS AND AWARDS

Univ. of Rennes: Professor of Classical Antiquity; Univ. of Toulouse: Professor of Classical Antiquity; Louvre Museum: Keeper of Ceramics, and School of the Louvre: Professor (both beg. 1884); *Revue archéologique*: Co-editor (beg. 1914); Louvre Museum: Honorary Curator. Member: Academie des Inscriptions et Belles-Lettres (1899). Award: Commander of the Legion of Honor.

EXCAVATIONS

Myrina (near Smyrna); Athens.

PUBLICATIONS

Les Lekythes blancs attiques à représentations funéraires, Paris: E. Thorin, 1883; *La Nécropole de Myrina* (with S. Reinach) (2 vols.), Paris: E. Thorin, 1887; *Catalgue des Vases antiques de terre cuite* (3 vols.), Paris: Librairies-imprimeries réunies, 1896–1906; *Catalogue des Vases antiques du Louvre* (2 vols.), Paris: Hachette et cie, 1897–1922; *Douris et les Peintres des Vases Grecs*, Paris: H. Laurens, 1905; Diphilos et les modeleurs de terres cuites grecques, Paris: H. Laurens, 1909; Douris and the Painters of Greek Vases (trans. by Bettina Kahnweiler), London: J. Murray, 1909; *L'Art Hittite* (2 vols.), 1926.

Edmond Pottier's early archaeological excavations in Asia Minor sparked two lifelong interests: one in the study of the minor arts (which in his day included vase painting) and the other in the interplay between the cultures of ancient Greece and the East.

He produced the multivolume catalog of the best painted Greek vases in the Louvre and through his writings challenged the then-current notion that somehow Classical Greek culture had evolved in a vacuum. He emphasized the point that the accomplishments of Classical Greece were not lessened if one acknowledged that some of these achievements had their beginnings in the cultures of Greece's Near Eastern neighbors.

His discovery of more than a thousand terracotta figurines at Myrina (a number that rivaled those discovered at Tanagra in Boeotia) instilled in Pottier a sympathy and understanding for the value of other minor arts. He felt strongly that the study of vase painting and objects such as terracotta figurines is actually of greater importance to the study of ancient civilization than that of the major arts (sculpture and architecture), since these lesser objects tell us more about the everyday existence of the people who produced them.

Pottier was somewhat of a pioneer in attempting to establish the development of Classical vase painting styles and in attributing specific pots to specific artists. ADOLF FURTWÄNGLER was a contemporary and did more important work in this regard but nonetheless, Pottier's publication on the painter Douris was a sensitive and edifying monograph written for the benefit of both the expert and the lay person. It remains popular to this day.

SOURCES

R. Lantier and Charles Picard, "Edmond Pottier (1855–1934)," *RA* 4 (1934): v–xvii; David M. Robinson, "Necrology," *AJA* 38 (1934): 584; Cook, *Greek Painted Pottery*, 1972, 2d. ed.; Stillwell, editor, *PECS*, 1976; *CR* 19 (1905): 377–78; *TL* (July 7, 1934).

MARTIN J(ESSOP) PRICE

b: March 27, 1939. London, England.
d: April 28, 1995. London, England.

EDUCATION

The King's School, Canterbury, England.
Queens College, Cambridge University, 1961 (B.A.), 1964 (M.A.), 1967 (Ph.D.).
British School of Archaeology (Macmillan Studentship).
Research Fellow, Downing College, Cambridge University, 1964.

APPOINTMENTS AND AWARDS

Dept. of Coins and Medals, British Museum: Assistant Keeper (1966–78), Merit Deputy Keeper (1978–84), Administrative Deputy Keeper (1984–90), Research Deputy Keeper (1990–94); Royal Numismatic Society: Secretary (1977–83); Hon. Professor: Sydney Univ. (1985); British School at Athens: Director (beg. 1994). Fellow: Royal Numismatic Society (1964); Society of Antiquaries (1979). Hon. Fellow of the Romanian, Swiss and Hellenic Numismatic Societies. Corresponding Fellow: German Archaeological Institute (1985). Visiting Fellow: Institute of Advanced Studies, Princeton Univ. (1986–87). Awards: Bjornstad Medallist, Oslo Univ. (1981); Medalist, Hellenic Numismatic Society (1992); Gold Medal, Royal Numismatic Society (1992).

EXCAVATIONS

Palaikastro, east Crete; Lefkandi; Euboea; Tocra, Libya (site photographer); British School at Athens's campaigns during the 1960s.

PUBLICATIONS

Coins of the Macedonians, London: British Museum, 1974; *Coins and the Bible*, 1975; *Archaic Greek Silver: The 'Asyut' Hoard* (with N. Waggoner), London: V. C. Vecchi, 1975; *Coins and Their Cities: Architecture on the Ancient Coins of Greece, Rome and Palestine* (with Bluma Trell), London: Vecchi, 1977; *Coins: An Illustrated Survey 650 B.C. to the Present Day* (editor), New York: Methuen, 1978; *Coins, Culture, and History in the Ancient World, Numismatic and Other Studies in Honor of Bluma L. Trell* (editor, with L. Casson), Detroit: Wayne State University Press, 1981; *Coinage in the Greek World* (with I. Carradice), London: Seaby, 1988; *The Seven Wonders of the Ancient World* (editor, with P. Clayton), London: Routledge, 1988; *Survey of Numismatic Research, 1978–1984*, editor, 1986 (editor); *The Coinage in the Name of Alexander the Great and Philip Arrhidaeus*, 1991 (2 vols.); *Sylloge Nummorum Graecorum*, 1975–94 (editor of eight vols., author of four including *SNG IX: The British Museum, Part I: The Black Sea*, 1993); *Essays in Honour of Robert Carson and Kenneth Jenkins* (editor with A. Burnett and R. Bland), 1993.

Martin J. Price was a leading scholar in the field of ancient numismatics, especially Greek coinage. His interest focused on three areas of study: the earliest development of coinage (see 1975 publication, above, Price and Waggoner), the transformations which occurred during the Hellenistic Age, and the survival of Greek coinage under the domination of Rome (see 1977 publication, above).

Price produced several monumental works but his two-volume study on the coinage of Alexander the Great (1991, above) is widely felt to be his greatest contribution and achievement. This catalog deals with one of the most complex periods in ancient history and is written in a clear and concise style which makes it comprehensible to both the scholar and lay person. In 1975 he founded the periodical *Coin Hoards*.

SOURCES

CNR 20–2 (1995): 9–10; William Metcalf, *ANSN* 16 (1995): 8; *The Celator* (June, 1995): 28; *TL* (May 10, 1995).

DAVID RANDALL-MACIVER

b: October 31, 1873. London, England.
d: April 30, 1945. New York, New York.

EDUCATION

Radley School, England.
Queen's College, Oxford, 1896 (Litt.Hum.).

APPOINTMENTS AND AWARDS

Worcester College, Oxford Univ.: Laycock Scholar in Egyptology (1900–06); The Museum, Univ. of Pennsylvania: Curator of Egyptology (1907–11); American Geographical Society: Librarian (1911–14). Fellow: Society of Antiquaries (1907); British Academy (1938).

EXCAVATIONS

Dendera (under F. Petrie); Abydos, 1900–01 (Egyptian Exploration Fund); Zimbabwe, Africa, 1905; Nubia, 1907–11 (Director, Univ. of Pennsylvania excavations).

PUBLICATIONS

The Earliest Inhabitants of Abydos: A Craniological Study, Oxford: The Clarendon Press, 1901; *Libyan Notes* (with Anthony Wilkin), London: Macmillan and Co., 1901; *El Amrah and Abydos, 1899–1901* (with A. C. Mace), London: Egypt Exploration Fund, 1902; *The Ancient Races of Thebaid* (with Sir Arthur Thompson), 1905; *Mediaeval Rhodesia* (1906), London: Cass, 1971; *Areika* (with C. Leonard Wooley), Oxford: Oxford University Press, 1909; *Churches in Lower Nubia*, by G. S. Mileham,

(Randall-MacIver, editor), Philadelphia: University Museum, 1910; *Karanòg: the Romano-Nubian cemetery* (2 vols.), Philadelphia: University Museum, 1910; *Buhen* (with C. Leonard Woolley) (2vols.), Philadelphia: University Museum, 1911; *The Villanovans and Early Etruscans*, Oxford: The Clarendon Press, 1924; *The Iron Age in Italy* (1927), Westport, Conn.: Greenwood Press, 1974; *The Etruscans* (1927), New York: Cooper Square Publishers, 1972; *Italy before the Romans* (1928), New York: Cooper Square Publishers, 1972; *Greek Cities in Italy and Sicily* (1931), Westport, Conn.: Greenwood Press, 1970.

David Randall-MacIver was introduced to the latest methods of archaeological investigation through his work in Egypt with FLINDERS PETRIE and in 1905 was called upon to put these skills into practice in Africa. Much speculation had arisen over the sophisticated architectural styles found in and around Zimbabwe in Southern Rhodesia. Among the various theories put forward was the idea that Zimbabwe architecture had its roots in ancient Phoenician culture (see J. THEODORE BENT). At this early stage in the development of archaeology, it would have been tempting for Randall-MacIver to have latched on to a radical diffusionist theory such as this one, but after spending some months in Africa he was able to pronounce that Zimbabwe architecture had its origins in the Medieval period and indeed was the product of a highly sophisticated (and native) Bantu civilization (see 1906, above). He received high praise for his objective approach to this work and for its prompt publication.

After World War One he turned to a little known area of study, that of Iron Age Italy, and it was now that he produced his most famous works. His 1924 publication (above) examines the material finds in Villanovan cemeteries in the areas of Bologna and Etruria and gives an account of the growth of Etruscan culture before 650 B.C.E. In *The Iron Age in Italy* (1927) he focused on the same aspects, but on early Italic cultures other than Villanovan and Etruscan.

Unfortunately, despite his thorough and objective approach, many of the conclusions reached by Randall-MacIver in these publications on Iron Age Italy have since been disproved (including his separation of Villanovan and Etruscan, see MASSIMO PALLOTTINO). This should not, however, detract from an appreciation of the clarity which he brought to the discussion of pre-Roman Italy. No one prior to him had attempted to collate all of the disparate evidence found scattered in various Italic publications, and Italian archaeologists had seemed reluctant to enter into any discussion which would serve to facilitate the assimilation of their diverse observations. Randall-MacIver changed this by opening up the debate and by setting the discussion on a clear and reasonable foundation.

SOURCES

David Ridgway, "David Randall-MacIver 1873–1945," *PBA* 69 (1983): 559–77; *AJA* 49 (1945): 359–60; T. C. Hencken, *DNB*, 1941–50; *WWWE*; *TL* (May 3, 1945).

NICHOLAS REVETT

b: 1720. Suffolk, England.
d: June 3, 1804.

APPOINTMENTS AND AWARDS

Independent architect. Member: Society of Dilettanti (1751).

PUBLICATIONS

The Antiquities of Athens measured and delineated by James Stuart, F.R.S. and F.S.A., and Nicholas Revett, Painters and Architects (1762), New York: B. Blom, 1968; *Ionian Antiquities; or, Ruins of Magnificent and Famous Buildings in Ionia* (with Richard Chandler) (2 vols.), London: T. Spilsbury and W. Haskell, 1769–97; *Ionian Antiquities*, London: W. Bulmer and W. Nicol, 1821.

Like his earlier collaborator JAMES STUART, Nicholas Revett is considered to be one of the founders of Classical archaeology (for a fuller discussion, see James Stuart).

Revett journeyed to Rome in 1742 to study art under the painter Cavaliere Benefiale. It was in Rome that he first met James Stuart and had the idea of organizing a trip to Athens in order to draw and measure its ancient buildings in detail and to learn the mathematical subtleties of the different Classical orders. After gaining financial support for the trip from a number of Englishmen who were living in Italy, the two left Rome in 1750 bound for Greece but were delayed for several months after they missed their connecting ship in Venice. They eventually reached Greece in 1751 and spent most of the next two years in Athens before they were forced to leave the city due to the political tensions of the time. They returned to Britain by a circuitous route which included visits to Chios and Delos and a quick return to Athens to see if it was safe to resume work there (it was not). From there they went on to Smyrna and back to Britain where they arrived in 1755.

In 1762 the two men published volume one of *The Antiquities of Athens*; this work was met with high acclaim but the two became estranged and Revett did not make further contributions to the next volumes, selling his rights to the material to Stuart.

Because of the initial success of the Stuart/Revett undertaking, Revett was selected by the Society of Dilettanti (he was a member by this time) to accompany RICHARD CHANDLER and William Pars on a trip to western Asia Minor. Revett was the architect for the expedition and drew and measured the ancient remains found there. This trip took slightly more than two years, and the party arrived back in London in 1766. Upon the group's return all material written, drawn, and painted by the three men became the property of the Society of Dilletanti which divided it up between Chandler and Revett so that they could prepare it for publication. After completing his portion of the first volume of *Ionian Antiquities* (see 1769, above) Revett seems, as he did on his joint work with Stuart, to have desisted from any further work on the project, and the society was forced to repossess the material. A second volume was eventually issued by the society in 1797. Revett continued to work as an architect but he died in relative poverty in 1804.

Nicholas Revett never achieved the public recognition that his fellow collaborators did partly due to the fact that he reportedly had a somewhat difficult personality. Nonetheless, he is the one who first formulated the idea of going to Greece to carry out a meticulous study of its ancient buildings and it was he, therefore, who was largely responsible for setting the study of Classical archaeology on a serious and scholarly footing and for bringing Greece and its antiquities to the attention of eighteenth-century western Europe.

SOURCES

Chandler, *Richard Chandler: Travels in Asia Minor*, edited by E. Clay, 1971; *DNB*, Vol. 16; Clarke, *Greek Studies in England, 1700–1830*, 1945; Edwards, *Lives of the Founders of the British Museum* (1870), reprint, 1969; Stuart and Revett, *The Antiquities of Athens*, Vol. 1, 1762; Michaelis, *Ancient Marbles in Great Britain*, 1882; Cust, *History of the Society of Dilettanti*, 1914; Miller, *Greece Through the Ages*, 1972; Weber, *Voyages and Travels . . .* , 1953.

GISELA M(ARIE) A(UGUSTA) RICHTER

b: August 15, 1882. London, England.
d: December 24, 1972. Rome, Italy.

EDUCATION

Girton College, Cambridge University, 1904 (B.A.).
British School at Athens, 1904–05.

APPOINTMENTS AND AWARDS

Dept. of Greek and Roman Art, Metropolitan Museum of Art (New York): Assistant (temporary) (1906–10), Assistant Curator of Classical Art (1910–22), Associate Curator (1922–25), Curator (1925–48). Hon. Degrees: Litt.D., Trinity College, Dublin (1913); A.M., Litt.D., Cambridge University (1933); L.H.D., Smith College (1935); L.H.D., Oxford Univ. (1952).

PUBLICATIONS

Greek, Etruscan and Roman Bronzes, New York: The Gilliss Press, 1915; *Catalogue of Engraved Gems of the Classical Style*, New York: Metropolitan Museum of Art, 1920; *The Craft of Athenian Pottery: An Investigation of the Technique of Black-figured and Red-figured Athenian Vases*, New Haven: Yale University Press, 1923; *Ancient Furniture: A History of Greek, Etruscan and Roman Furniture*, Oxford: The Clarendon Press, 1926; *Sculpture and Sculptors of the Greeks* (1929), New Haven: Yale University Press, 1970 (revised. ed.); *Animals in Greek Sculpture: A Survey*, New York: Oxford University Press, 1930; *Red-Figured Athenian Vases in the Metropolitan Museum of Art* (2 vols.), New Haven: Yale University Press, 1936; *Kouroi: Archaic Greek Youths* (1942), London: Phaidon Press, 1960; *The Archaic*

Gravestones of Attica (1944), New York: Phaidon Publishers, 1961; *Archaic Greek Art Against Its Historical Background: A Survey*, New York: Oxford University Press, 1949; *Handbook of the Greek Collection* (1917), New York: Gilliss Press for the Metropolitan Museum of Art, 1953; *Ancient Italy: A Study of the Interrelations of Its Peoples as Shown in Their Arts*, Ann Arbor: University of Michigan Press, 1955; *Catalogue of Engraved Gems, Etruscan and Roman*, 1956; *Catalogue of Greek and Roman Antiquities in the Dumbarton Oaks Collection*, Cambridge, Mass.: Harvard University Press, 1956; A *Handbook of Greek Art* (1959), New York: De Capo Press, 1987; *The Portraits of the Greeks* (3 vols., 1965), Ithaca, N.Y.: Cornell University Press, 1984 (abridged and revised by R. R. R. Smith); *The Furniture of the Greeks, Etruscans and Romans*, London: Phaidon Press, 1966; *Korai: Archaic Greek Maidens*, London: Phaidon, 1968; *Perspective in Greek and Roman Art*, London: Phaidon, 1970; *My Memoirs: Recollections of an Archaeologist's Life*, Rome, s.n. 1972.

Gisela Richter came to America in 1905 at the suggestion and encouragement of HARRIET BOYD HAWES. At the age of twenty-eight she became assistant curator of the Metropolitan Museum of Art in New York. She made major purchases for the Metropolitan Museum including the "New York *Kouros*" in 1932. Specializing in Archaic art, she produced a number of publications on this subject beginning with *Kouroi* in 1942, and became a leading authority on the chronology of the sculpture of the Archaic period of ancient Greece. This chronology has withstood the test of new knowledge with only slight modification.

SOURCES

Evelyn B. Harrison, *NAW*, Vol. 4, 1980; Richter, *My Memoirs, Recollections of an Archaeologist's Life*, 1972; *WWA*, 1972–73; *Archaeology*, June 1952; *NYT* (December 26, 1972).

DAVID M(OORE) ROBINSON

b: September 21, 1880. Auburn, New York.
d: January 2, 1958. Oxford, Mississippi.

EDUCATION

Polytechnic Institute, Brooklyn, New York, 1894.
University of Chicago, 1898 (A.B.), 1904 (Ph.D.).
American School of Classical Studies at Athens, 1901–02,
(Fellow, 1903–04).
University of Halle, 1902.
University of Berlin, 1903–04.
University of Bonn, 1909.

APPOINTMENTS AND AWARDS

Dept. of Classics, Illinois College: Asst. Prof. of Greek,
(and Chair) (1904–05); Johns Hopkins Univ.: Assoc. in Classical Archaeology (1905–08), Assoc. Prof. (1908–12), Prof. in
Greek Archaeology and Epigraphy (1912–13), Professor, Classical Archaeology and Epigraphy (1913–20), W. H. Collins
Vickers Prof. of Archaeology and Epigraphy (1920–47), Prof.
Emeritus, Art and Archaeology (1947), Research Prof. in
Classics (1947–48); Archaeological Institute of America:
Charles Eliot Norton Lecturer (1924, 1925, 1928, 1929);
Univ. of Mississippi: Prof., Classics and Archaeology (beg.
1948). Member: American Academy of Arts and Sciences;
Royal Numismatic Society; German Archaeological Institute
of Sciences; American Geographic Society. Hon. Degrees:
Jamestown College (1915); L.H.D., Trinity College (1925);
Litt.D., Syracuse Univ. (1933); Ph.D., Univ. of Thessalonica,
Greece (1951).

EXCAVATIONS

Corinth, 1902–03; Sardis, 1910; Pisidian Antioch, 1924; Olynthus, 1928, 1931, 1934, 1938.

PUBLICATIONS

Ancient Synope, Baltimore: The Johns Hopkins Press, 1906; *Sappho and Her Influence* (1924), New York: Cooper Square Publishers, 1963; *The Songs of Sappho, Including the Recent Egyptian Discoveries*, Lexington, Ky.: The Maxwelton Co., 1925; *The Deeds of Augustus as Recorded on the Monumentum Antiochenum Res Gestae divi Augusti*, Baltimore: The Johns Hopkins Press, 1926; *Roman Sculpture from Psidian Antioch*, 1926; *Greek and Latin Inscriptions of Asia Minor*, 1926; *The Greek Vases in the Royal Ontario Museum*, 1930; *Excavations in Olynthus* (14 vols.), Baltimore: The Johns Hopkins Press, 1930–52; *Sardis, Vol. VII: Greek and Latin Inscriptions* (with W. H. Buckler), 1932; *A Short History of Greece*, New York: Huxley House, 1936; *Pindar, a Poet of Eternal Ideas*, Baltimore: The Johns Hopkins Press, 1936; *A Study of Greek Love-Names. Including a Discussion of Paederasty and a Prosopographia* (with E. J. Fluck) (1937), New York: Arno Press, 1979; *Baalbek, Palmyra*, New York: J. J. Augustin, 1946; Joint editor (with G. D. Hadzsits) of "Our Debt to Greece and Rome" series (50 vols.) published in New York by Cooper Union Publishers.

Robinson discovered the site of ancient Olynthus in northern Greece. This site is one of the very few that have provided us with information regarding the forms of Greek domestic architecture from the mid-fifth to mid-fourth centuries B.C.E. as well as providing archaeologists with information regarding many aspects of ancient Greek private life which had hitherto remained unknown.

Olynthus was an important city in antiquity with a population of between thirty and fifty thousand; it was destroyed in 348 B.C.E. by Philip II, father of Alexander the Great. The area uncovered by Robinson over a ten-year period comprised more than one hundred houses including five complete blocks (ten houses per block). The houses were two-storied, with stone foundations and adobe walls, and were laid out according to the Hippodamian grid system. Most had colonnaded court-yards—which contained some of the best examples we have of Greek pebble mosaics—and a portico to the north.

Two cemeteries which were also excavated at the site yielded many vases and terracotta figurines. An aqueduct of approximately nine miles in length was found during the last season of excavation.

Through his expertise and teaching, Robinson helped his department at Johns Hopkins University earn an international reputation in Classical archaeology. He wrote more than thirty books and contributed hundreds of articles to scholarly journals.

SOURCES

Lord, *History of the American School* . . . , 1947; Mylonas, editor, *Studies Presented to David Moore Robinson on his seventieth birthday*, Vol. 1 (1951), Vol. 2 (1953) (vol. 2 edited by Mylonas and Raymond); Butler, *Sardis*, Vol. 1: *The Excavations, Part I: 1910–1914* (1922), reprint, 1969; Stillwell, editor, *PECS*, 1976; Leekley and Efstratiou, *AECNG*, 1980; *NCAB* Vol. A (1930): 221; *WWA* 29 (1956–57); Correspondence with the Dept. of Classics, Johns Hopkins University; *NYT* (January 3, 1958); *TL* (January 4, 1958).

GERHART RODENWALDT

b: October 16, 1886. Berlin, Germany.
d: April 27, 1945. Berlin, Germany.

EDUCATION

University of Berlin.
University of Halle, 1908 (Ph.D.).

APPOINTMENTS AND AWARDS

Univ. of Giessen: Professor of Archaeology (1912–22);
German Archaeological Institute: Director (1922–32); Berlin
University: Senior Professor of Archaeology (beg. 1932).

EXCAVATIONS

Tiryns, 1909.

PUBLICATIONS

Die Komposition der pompejanischen Wandgemälde (1909),
Rome: L'erma di Bretschneider, 1968; *Tiryns, II: Die Fresken
des palastes von Tiryns*, 1912; "Zur begrifflichen und
geschichtlichen Bedeutung des Klassischen in der bildenden
Kunst," 1916; *Der Fries des Megarons von Mykenai*, Halle: M.
Niemeyer, 1921; *Der Sarkophag Caffarelli*, 1923; *Das Relief bei
den Griechen*, Berlin: Schoetz und Parrhysius, 1923; *Propylaeen
Kunsteschichte III: Die Kunst der Antike*, 1927 (1930, 2d. ed.),
(1938, 3d. ed.), (Spanish ed., 1931 [1933, 2d. ed.]); *Die
Akropolis*, Berlin: Deutscher Kunstverlag, 1930 (English edition: *Acropolis of Athens* [1930] Norman, Okla.: Univeristy of
Oklahoma Press, 1958; *Olympia*, New York: B. Westermann

Co., 1936 (trans. by Hinks); "Contributions on art of the Roman Empire," *Cambridge Ancient History*, Vol. 11 (1936), Vol. 12 (1939); "Studi e scoperte Germaniche nell' archeologia l'arte del tardo impero," *Instituto di studi Romani*, 4 (1937); *Altdorische Bildwerke in Korfu*, Berlin: Gebr. Mann, 1938; *Korkyra II, Die Bildwerke des Artemistempels von Korkyra*, 1939; *Korkyra: archaische Bauten und Bildwerke*, Berlin: Gebr. Mann, 1940 (Vol. 1); *Kunst um Augustus*, Berlin: W. de Gruyter, 1942.

Gerhart Rodenwaldt's interests covered a wide range, from Bronze Age Greece to early Christian art. He was considered an expert in a number of areas including ancient wall painting (see 1909 and 1912 publications, above) and Roman art. He produced groundbreaking work on the relationship between the political function of Roman art and its stylistic development, and just before the beginning of World War Two had completed an important opus on the archaic art and architecture of Corfu (see 1938 and 1939, above).

Rodenwaldt was active during a difficult period. German archaeology had enjoyed strong governmental support during the previous century (see ERNST CURTIUS) but this declined after the events of World War One. As director of the German Archaeological Institute immediately after the war, he was credited with having restored the respect of German archaeology throughout the world by reestablishing communications abroad and by expanding the role of the institute to include new centers in Istanbul and Cairo.

SOURCES

Margarete Bieber, "Necrology," *AJA* 50 (1946): 405–406; Adolf H. Borbein, "Gerhart Rodenwaldt: Gedenkworte zur 100. Widerkehr seines Geburtstages," *AA* (1987): 697–700; Lullies and Schiering, *Archäologenbildnisse*, 1988; *IWW*, 1940; Leekley and Noyes, *AEGI*, 1975; Correspondence with the German Archaeological Institute, Berlin.

MICHAEL I(VANOVITCH) ROSTOVTZEFF

b: November 10, 1870. Near Kiev, Russia.
d: October 20, 1952. New Haven, Connecticut.

EDUCATION

First Classical Gymnasium of Kiev, 1888.
University of Kiev, 1890.
University of St. Petersburg, 1892 (M.A.), 1903 (Ph.D.).
German Archaeological Institute at Rome.
University of Vienna, 1898.

APPOINTMENTS AND AWARDS

St. Petersburg College for Women: Professor of Ancient History (1898–1918); Imperial University of St. Petersburg: Lecturer (1898–1903), Professor of Latin (1903–18); The Sorbonne, Paris: Lecturer (1918); Oxford Univ.: Lecturer (1918–20); Univ. of Wisconsin: Professor of Ancient History (1920–25); Yale University: Sterling Professor of Ancient History and Archaeology (1925–39), Director of Archaeological Studies (1939–44), Prof. Emeritus (1939); American Historical Association, President (1935). Member: American Philosophical Society (1935). Hon. Degrees: Leipzig (1910); Oxford Univ. (1919); Univ. of Wisconsin (1925); Cambridge Univ. (1931); Harvard Univ. (1936); Univ. of Athens (1937); Univ. of Chicago (1941). Awards: Legion of Honor (France).

EXCAVATIONS

Dura Europos, 1928–37.

PUBLICATIONS

"Geschichte der Staatspacht in der romischen Kaiserzeit," *Philologus*, Supplement 9, 1904; "Studien zur Geschichte des romischen Kolonats," *Archiv*, Beiheft, 1910; *Iranians and Greeks in South Russia* (1922), New York: Russell and Russell, 1969; *Skythien und der Bosporus*, Berlin: H. Schoetz and Co., 1931; *A Large Estate in Egypt in the Third Century* B.C. (1922), New York: Arno Press, 1979; *Caravan Cities* (1932), New York: AMS Press, 1971; *Dura-Europas and Its Art* (1938), New York: AMS Press, 1978; *History of the Ancient World (Vol. I: The Orient and Greece*, 1926, *Vol. II: Rome*, 1927), Westport, Conn.: Greenwood Press, 1971; *Social and Economic History of the Roman Empire* (1926), Oxford: The Clarendon Press, 1957; *The Animal Style in South Russia and China* (1929), New York: Hacker Art Books, 1973; *Seleucid Babylonia*, 1932; *Social and Economic History of the Hellenistic World* (3 vols.) (1941), Oxford: The Clarendon Press, 1964; contributed chapters to Volumes 7, 8, 9, and 11 of the *Cambridge Ancient History*.

Michael I. Rostovtzeff is remembered primarily as one of the most accomplished of ancient historians but he was also one of the very first to consider archaeological evidence equal to that from literary sources in providing us with an intimate picture of the daily comings and goings of ancient life. He used information gleaned from the analysis of pottery, paintings, and architecture in addition to more traditionally used artifacts such as inscriptions, papyri, coins, and literary sources to compile three of his most famous publications: *A History of the Ancient World*, *A Social and Economic History of the Roman Empire*, and *A Social and Economic History of the Hellenistic World*.

Rostovtzeff is also noted for his work as the excavator of the site of Dura-Europos on the Euphrates River. Before his appointment to the Classics Department of Yale University, he had consulted with James Henry Breasted and the Frenchman Franz Cumont regarding the possibility of launching a large-scale excavation of the site which had been spotted in the desert by pilots during World War One; in 1926 Yale University began what was to become a ten-year campaign led by Rostovtzeff.

Dura-Europos proved to be a site nearly tailor-made to the interests and talents of its excavator. From early on in his career Rostovtzeff had shown a deep interest in studying geographic areas which had become cultural *milieux*, and this site, situated on the Euphrates River and formerly controlled by both Parthians and Romans with close connections to Palmyra, was to provide him with diverse archaeological material including well preserved wall paintings, inscriptions, sculpture, and a variety of buildings including a Mithraeum, an early church, and a synagogue. The excavations also yielded important information regarding cities along the ancient trade routes (see 1932, above).

SOURCES

A. H. M. Jones, "Michael Ivanovitch Rostovtzeff 1870–1952," *PBA* 39 (1953): 345–61; Clarence W. Mendell, "Michael I. Rostovtzeff (1870–1952)," *APSY* (1952): 336–39; Frank E. Brown, "Necrology," *AJA* 58 (1954): 55; *NYT* (October 21, 1952); *TL* (October 22, 1952).

HEINRICH SCHLIEMANN

b: January 6, 1822. Neubuckow,
Mecklenburg-Schwerin, Germany.
d: December 26, 1890. Naples, Italy.

APPOINTMENTS AND AWARDS

Hon. Fellow: Queen's College, Oxford Univ. (1883). Hon. Degree: D.C.L., Oxford Univ. Award: Gold Medal, Royal Institute of British Architects.

EXCAVATIONS

Burnarbashi, 1868, 1871; Troy, 1871–73, 1878–79, 1882, 1890; Mycenae, 1876; Ithaca, 1878; Orchomenos, 1880–81, 1886; Tiryns, 1884; Thermopylae; Marathon, 1884; Cythera, 1888; Egypt, 1886–87, 1887–88 (with Virchow).

PUBLICATIONS

La Chine et le Japon au temps présent, Paris: Librairie centrale, 1867; *Ithaka, der Peloponnes und Troja: archäologische Forschungen* (1869), Darmstadt: Wissenschaftliche Buchgesellschaft, 1973; *Troy and Its Remains* (1875), New York: Dover Publishers, 1994; *Mycenae: A Narrative of Researches and Discoveries at Mycenae and Tiryns* (1878), New York: B. Blom, 1967; *Ilios: The City and Country of the Trojans* (1880), New York: B. Blom, 1968; "Exploration of the Boeotian Orchomenos," *JHS* 2 (1881): 122–163; *Troja: Results of the Latest Researches*, 1884; *Tiryns: The Prehistoric Palace of the King of Tiryns* (1886), New York: B. Blom, 1967.

Heinrich Schliemann remains the most controversial figure in the field of Classical archaeology. Past and current controversy notwithstanding, through his discoveries at Troy, Mycenae, and Tiryns Schliemann undeniably earned the right to be named the "father" of prehistoric Greek archaeology.

After an unhappy early childhood (his mother died when he was only nine years of age and he was subsequently separated from his father for five years), poor financial circumstances forced him to give up all hope of a formal education. At the age of fourteen the young Schliemann found himself apprenticed to the owner of a small grocer's shop in Fürstenberg. Displaying an innate practical intelligence and determination which were to become hallmarks of his mature character, Schliemann set about teaching himself a number of foreign languages and quickly acquainted himself with the ways of the business world. He subsequently became a merchant in indigo, moved to St. Petersburg and, just when events were leading to the Crimean War, speculated in an ingredient of gun powder (saltpetre) and became a millionaire by the age of forty.

Finding himself bored with the routine of running his various businesses, Schliemann retired in 1863 and looked to archaeology and to Greece for a new vocation. He had been raised listening to and reading the poems of Homer, and according to his own account had determined, at the ripe age of eight, someday to discover Homer's Troy. Despite this childhood conviction, however, he did not go to Greece until he was forty-eight when he visited Corfu, Kephallenia, Ithaca, and Athens, as well as Asia Minor.

At this time it was commonly held by those few scholars who believed Homer's Troy to have in fact existed that the ancient city must have stood on the site of Pinarbasi (Bunarbashi) in northwestern Turkey. This had been determined by a number of earlier European travelers (see WILLIAM GELL) who had based their opinions upon considerations of topographical similarities to Homer's descriptions of Troy. However, when Schliemann visited the site and carried out preliminary excavations, he could not reconcile the site's lack of a hot and a cold spring (as had been mentioned by Homer[1]) and later proclaimed that he had intuitively felt that Bunarbashi was not the site of ancient Troy. Soon after, he met Frank Calvert, an Englishman (born in Malta) who owned a large tract of land in northwest Turkey, including the mound of Hissarlik. After years of investigation in the area, Calvert had determined that Homer's Troy lay within this unnaturally formed mound of earth, but he had not personal money with which to carry out large-scale excavations and had been unable to convince CHARLES NEWTON (the British Vice Consul at Mytilene) to procure funds from the British Museum for such an expedition. Calvert met with Schliemann in 1868 and, largely due to the vehemence of Calvert's belief in Hissarlik being the site of ancient Troy, Schliemann was also convinced.

Due to his total lack of experience in field archaeology, Schliemann assumed that the Homeric city of Troy would lie at the lowest level of the mound, and so he began his first season of excavation at Hissarlik in 1871 (accompanied by his Greek bride, Sofia) by digging a large trench running north to south across the center of the mound with the intention of eventually clearing everything off from either side of it. In the process of digging this mound he blundered his way through many levels of the ancient city, casting aside the stones from its walls and taking little note of where certain structures had been located. After the 1871 season he continued excavations at the site and in 1873 discovered the now famous "Treasure of Priam" which was comprised of gold, silver, and bronze objects, including a large amount of jewelry. This rich find served to convince Schliemann that he had reached the Troy of Homer's poem and that it had occupied the second lowest level of the mound rather than the first as he had originally assumed.

After satisfying himself that he had discovered Homeric Troy, he set about publishing his findings as well as lecturing extensively before scholarly institutes throughout Europe. His publications and lectures were well received in Britain (especially due to the enthusiasm of CHARLES NEWTON, then keeper of Greek and Roman antiquities at the British Museum) but he was often ridiculed by his own countrymen. Undaunted, he next determined to excavate the other major city mentioned in Homer, Mycenae.

Schliemann began excavating at Mycenae in 1876 under the same agreement with the Greek government that ERNST CURTIUS had just drawn up for the excavation of Olympia, that is, that all expenses for the excavation would be borne by Schliemann and that all finds were to become the property of the Greek government.

Following the observations of Pausanias, he began his search for the royal graves just inside the massive Cyclopean walls, to the right of the monumental entrance gate. Within a very short time he uncovered the famous shaft graves and their contents of gold, silver, and bronze objects. This discovery constituted the largest find of ancient artifacts ever recovered from a single site and were certainly the most impressive. Having published his findings and still haunted by questions regarding the identification of Hissarlik as being Troy, he returned to Asia Minor in 1878. This time however, due to the previous criticism of his methods and conclusions, he sought out the experience and opinions of other scholars including A. H. Sayce, J. P. Mahaffy, Max Müller, and Frank Calvert. With the help of these specialists, Schliemann was able to identify seven levels of occupation at Troy.

For the 1882 season he brought in one of the brightest scholars in the field, WILHELM DÖRPFELD, the young German architect/archaeologist who had learned a scientific approach to field archaeology at Olympia under ERNST CURTIUS. It was Dörpfeld who taught Schliemann the value of precise measurements and stratigraphy, as well as patience. Together, they determined that there were in fact nine levels of occupation at Troy, and in Schliemann's last season at the site (1890) he was finally able to establish a link between Troy and the other palace sites of Mycenae and Tiryns (which he and Dörpfeld had excavated together in 1884) when a megaron-type structure, together with unmistakably Mycenaean pottery, was found. These were located in Level VI, and so Schliemann realized that Level II (the level of "Priam's Treasure") had in fact belonged to a much earlier date than Homer's Troy, and that Level VI was the city of Homer's Ilion (see CARL BLEGEN for modifications of this theory).

Schliemann and his publications were the recipients of much criticism and ridicule and it is to his credit that he was able to stave off the self-doubt with which he must have been afflicted when most of the scholarly world denounced him as a gold-digger, a charlatan, and a fool. While it is true that he did immeasurable damage to the stratigraphy, particularly at the site of Troy, one needs to view Schliemann's career in the correct perspective. Schliemann was completely self-taught and had had no formal training or education in archaeological method. Indeed, at this time in history there was no established methodology in archaeology. In the mid-nineteenth-century "archaeology" most often denoted the practice of digging at ancient sites and preserving only the most beautiful objects (preferably of gold or silver), with no awareness of the value of sketches, measurements, or stratigraphy. The aim of the mid-nineteenth-century excavator (with only a few exceptions) was to collect as many precious objects as possible and to sell them to private collectors or to museums for the highest price (see CESNOLA).

While it is true that one of Schliemann's intentions had been to find cities "rich in gold," his overriding motive for carrying out excavations was to establish the verisimilitude of Homeric literature. He had no wish to sell the precious finds (although it is true that he often used them as "bargaining chips" to procure new excavation permits). He displayed an honest interest in furthering knowledge and scholarship regarding the Homeric Age; from the very beginning of his excavations, he was careful to preserve and record every artifact that he found, whether it was a gold sauceboat or a pottery sherd. He was very prompt in the publication of his findings, and in this and in his use of a team approach to archaeological investigation (he often sent out metal samples to laboratories for scientific analysis, and, as previously mentioned, brought in experts from other fields) he anticipated many features of the methodology of modern field archaeology. Despite having begun his career in a singularly unscientific manner and although he often displayed an egotistical and stubborn personality, Schliemann learned from his mistakes and does not seem to have sacrificed knowledge for fear of losing face. It is to his credit that on several occasions he openly admitted having made irreparable errors. In recent years Schliemann has been the focus of criticism concerning the truthfulness of his statements regarding his life and his archaeological discoveries (see Traill, below), but while Schliemann may have been found guilty of embellishing some aspects of his childhood and exaggerating the circumstances of some of his discoveries, these criticisms have largely been found to have no basis.[2] In the end, in spite of the controversy both in his day and in the present, whether the criticism is fair or true, no one can deny the fact that Heinrich Schliemann, through his determination, faith, and single-mindedness of purpose, discovered a whole historical epoch which served to rewrite history and which gave birth to a new field in Classical archaeology, the study of the Greek Bronze Age.

SOURCES

Michaelis, *A Century of Archaeology*, 1908; Ludwig, *Schliemann*, 1931; Moncune, *RGEHB*, Vol. 8, 1992; Schuchhardt, *Schliemann's Discoveries of the Ancient World* (1891), reprint, 1979; Frazer, *Pausanias's Description of Greece*, reprint, 1965; Daniel and Renfrew, *The Idea of Prehistory*, 1988; McDonald, *The Discovery of Homeric Greece*, 1967; Fitton, *The Discovery of the Greek Bronze Age*, 1995; Miller, *Greece Through the Ages*, 1972; Vermeule, *Greece in the Bronze Age*, 1972; Fitton, "Charles Newton and the Discovery of the Greek Bronze Age," in Christine Morris, *Klados: Essays in Honor of J. N. Coldstream*, 1995: 73–78; Leekley and Noyes, *AESG*, 1976; Leekley and Efstratiou, *AECNG*, 1980; Marcelle Robinson, "Pioneer, Scholar and Victim: An Appreciation of Frank Calvert (1828–1908)," *AS* 44 (1994): 153–68; Susan Heuck Allen, "In Schliemann's Shadow: Frank Calvert; The Unheralded Discoverer of Troy," *Archaeology* May/June (1995): 50–57; David A. Traill, "Schliemann's 'Dream of Troy': The Making of A Legend," *CJ* 81 (1985): 13–24; Traill, editor, *Excavating Schliemann*, 1993.

NOTES

1. *Iliad*, 22, pp. 147–52.
2. Meyers, *OEANE*, 1996.

T(HEODORE) LESLIE SHEAR

b: August 11, 1880. New London, New Hampshire.
d: July 3, 1945. Lake Sunapee, New Hampshire.

EDUCATION

New York University, 1900 (A.B.), 1903 (A.M.).
Johns Hopkins University, 1904 (Ph.D.).
American School of Classical Studies at Athens, 1904–05.
University of Bonn, 1905–06.

APPOINTMENTS AND AWARDS

Barnard College: Instructor, Greek and Latin (1906–10); Columbia Univ.: Assoc. Professor of Greek (1911–23); Princeton Univ.: Lecturer, Art and Archaeology (1920–27), Professor of Classical Archaeology (1928–45); American School of Classical Studies at Athens: Field Director (beg. 1929), Trustee (1936–42). Member: American Philosophical Society; American Numismatic Society; American Academy of Arts and Sciences. Hon. Member: Greek Archaeological Society, Athens.

EXCAVATIONS

Cnidus, S.W. Turkey, 1911; Sardis, 1922; Corinth, 1925–31; Athens, 1931–39 (Field Director, Agora excavations).

PUBLICATIONS

The Influence of Plato on St. Basil, Baltimore: J. H. Furst Co., 1906; *Sardis*: "Architectural Terracottas," 1925; *Corinth*, Vol. 5: "The Roman Villa," 1930.

A student of GEORG LOESCHCKE, T. Leslie Shear directed excavations at a number of key sites including those at ancient Corinth where he uncovered the Roman villa, the theater, and part of the North Cemetery. He will always be best remembered, however, for his work as field director of the Agora excavations begun by the American School of Classical Studies at Athens in 1931. This dig is widely regarded as being the school's greatest achievement to date.

The Athenian Agora had been inhabited from the Bronze Age down to the early part of the twentieth century but it is as the center of Athens during the Classical period that it holds the most interest. It was here that the day-to-day political, commercial, and social activities of the city took place, where many commemorative monuments were set up, the practice of ostracism carried out, and where Socrates spoke with his followers. The Agora excavations initially covered a sixteen acre area and have yielded a diverse selection of ancient fragments including terracotta figurines, tens of thousands of ancient coins (mainly bronze), fragments of sculpture, architectural foundations and inscriptions. In fact, the Agora excavations have yielded more information about ancient Greece than any other single source. Shear was regarded by his colleagues as possessing a special genius for practical administration, and the subsequent success of these excavations falls largely to the solid organization that he provided in their initial stages of development.

SOURCES

Edward Capps, "Theodore Leslie Shear (1880–1945)," *APSY* (1945): 414–16; *CB*, 1945; Dow, *A Century of Humane Archaeology*, 1979; Lord, *History of the American School . . .*, 1947; *WWWA*, 1940–41; *Hesperia*, Supplement 8, 1949 (Volume dedicated to T. Leslie Shear); *NYT* (July 5, 1945).

ERIK SJÖQVIST

b: July 15, 1903. Ronneby, Sweden.
d: July 16, 1975. Sweden.

EDUCATION

Uppsala University, 1924 (A.B.), 1926 (M.A.), 1940 (Ph.D.).

APPOINTMENTS AND AWARDS

Swedish Cyprus Expedition: Field Director (1927–31); Royal Library, Stockholm: Librarian (1932–39); Swedish Institute in Rome: Director (1940–48); Princeton Univ.: Visiting Prof. of Archaeology (1948–49); Private Secretary, Crown Prince of Sweden (later King Gustaf VI Adolf) (1949–51); Princeton Univ.: Professor of Classical Archaeology (1951–71), Emeritus Professor (1971); Univ. of Cincinnati: Taft-Semple Lecturer (1966); Univ. of Michigan and American Academy of Rome: Jerome Lecturer (1966–67).

EXCAVATIONS

The Argolid (under AXEL PERSSON); Agia Irini, Cyprus; Morgantina, Sicily (with RICHARD STILLWELL) beg. 1955.

PUBLICATIONS

Co-contributor to volumes in the *Swedish Cyprus Expedition* series; *Sicily and the Greeks: Studies in the Interrelationship Between the Indigenous Populations and the Greek Colonists*, Ann Arbor: University of Michigan Press, 1973; Excavation reports on Morgantina authored by Sjöqvist and/or R. Stillwell appeared in *AJA* vols. 61–68 (1957–64).

Erik Sjöqvist was the field director of the highly successful Swedish Cyprus Expedition from 1927 to 1931 (see EINAR GJERSTAD); he also carried out important excavations in Sicily at the ancient city of Morgantina.

Sjöqvist's Cyprus Expedition supervisor, Einar Gjerstad, has called him "a born field archaeologist"[1]; his skill was put to the test when he excavated a temple area on Cyprus near the village of Agia Irini. While other members of the Swedish team were occupied elsewhere on the island, Sjöqvist excavated the site and uncovered two thousand statues. This was one of the most interesting and rewarding finds that the team was going to make; the statues (mainly terracotta but some sculpted) ranged from a few inches to life-size and were found arranged in a semicircle according to height, facing an ancient stone altar. Through his careful and precise measuring and recording of exactly where and at what depth each object had been found, Sjöqvist was able to work out a solid framework for the chronological development of Cypriot sculpture during the Archaic period. Through further excavation of the site it was established that the cult at Agia Irini dated originally to c. 1200 B.C.E. and that it had continued through various stages to the sixth century B.C.E.

After joining the faculty of Princeton University, Sjöqvist turned his attention to the history of ancient Sicily and the city of Morgantina. This city had been home to Greek colonists from the Late Bronze Age through the early Hellenistic period, and it was during the latter that it enjoyed its greatest prosperity. Sjöqvist's interest in Morgantina centered upon the relationship between the island's indigenous population and its Greek colonists.

SOURCES

Einar Gjerstad, "The Born Field Archaeologist," in Åström, et al., *"The Fantastic Years on Cyprus" The Swedish Cyprus Expedition and its Members*, SIMA-PB 79 (1983): 33–35; Gjerstad, *Ages and Days in Cyprus*, 1980; Åström, et al., "Who's Who in Cypriote Archaeology: Biographical and Bibliographical Notes," 23, *SIMA*, 1971; Holloway, *The Archaeology of Ancient Sicily*, 1991; *DAB*, Vol. 1, 1974; Correspondence with Uppsala University.

NOTE

1. See Gjerstad article, above.

A(RTHUR) H(AMILTON) SMITH

b: October 2, 1860. London, England.
d: September 28, 1941. Weybridge, England.

EDUCATION

Trinity College, Cambridge University, 1883.

APPOINTMENTS AND AWARDS

Dept. of Greek and Roman Antiquities, British Museum: Assistant (1886–1904), Asst. Keeper (1904–09), Keeper (1909–25); Society for the Promotion of Hellenic Studies: President (1924–29); British School at Rome: Director (1928–30, 1932). Fellow: British Academy (1924); Society of Antiquaries. Award: C.B.E. (Commander of the British Empire, 1925).

EXCAVATIONS

Exploratory tour of Asia Minor, 1884 (with W. M. Ramsay); Amathus, Curium, and Enkomi, Cyprus, 1893–94, 1896 (British Museum excavations).

PUBLICATIONS

Catalogue of Engraved Gems in the Department of Greek and Roman Antiquities, British Museum, 1888 (1926, 2d. ed.); *Catalogue of Sculpture in the Department of Greek and Roman Antiquities* (3 vols.), London: Trustees of the British Museum, 1892–1904; *White Athenian Vases in the British Museum* (with A. S. Murray), London: Trustees of the British Museum, 1896; *A Guide to the Department of Greek and Roman Antiquities in the*

276

British Museum (1899), London: Trustees of the British Museum, 1912; *Excavations in Cyprus*, 1900; *The Archaic Artemisia*, by DAVID G. HOGARTH (with chapters by A. H. Smith et al.), London: Trustees of the British Museum, 1908; *Catalogue of the Engraved Gems and Cameos: Greek, Etruscan and Roman in the British Museum*, by H. B. Walters, London: Trustees of the British Museum, 1926 (revised ed.), *Corpus Vasorum Antiquorum*, Fascicle 1 (1930), Fascicle 2 (1936).

Smith produced the first comprehensive catalogs of engraved gems and Greek sculpture from the Department of Greek and Roman Antiquities of the British Museum. The work on sculpture was an especially large undertaking, as the museum's collections at this time included the Elgin and Phigaleian marbles, the Lycian sculptures (including the Harpy Tomb and Nereid Monument), the sculptures of Cnidus and Cyrene, and the remains of the Mausoleum and temples at Ephesus. These collections had been completely rearranged by the then keeper, A. S. Murray, but their cataloging was carried out solely by Smith.

Of interest is an invention of Smith's called a cyclograph. This apparatus enabled a single photograph to be taken of a representation on a cylindrical surface, and he used this invention to provide plates for his 1896 publication, above.

SOURCES

F. G. Kenyon, "Arthur Hamilton Smith 1860–1941," *PBA* 27 (1941): 393–404; *TL* (August 30, 1941).

RICHARD STILLWELL

b: February 16, 1899. Niagara Falls, New York.
d: July 27, 1982. Providence, Rhode Island.

EDUCATION

Pomfret School, Connecticut.
Princeton University, 1921 (B.A.), 1924 (M.F.A.).

APPOINTMENTS AND AWARDS

American School of Classical Studies at Athens: Fellow in Architecture (1924–26); Princeton University: Instructor (beg. 1926), Professor of Art and Archaeology, Howard Crosby Butler Memorial Professor of the History of Architecture (1959–67), Professor Emeritus (1967); American School of Classical Studies at Athens: Asst. Professor of Architecture (1928–31), Asst. Director (1931–32), Director (1932–35); Corinth Excavations: Field Director; Athenian Agora Excavations: Supervising Architect (1932–35); American School of Classical Studies at Athens: Annual Professor of Architecture (1947–48); *American Journal of Archaeology*: Editor-in-Chief (1954–73); American School of Classical Studies at Athens: Acting Director (1975).

EXCAVATIONS

Corinth; Antioch; Morgantina.

PUBLICATIONS

Corinth: Vol. 1.1 *Introduction, Topography, Architecture* (1932), Vol. 1.2 *Architecture* (1941), Vol. 2 *The Theater* (1952),

278

Vol. 3.1 *Acrocorinth* (1930) (contributor); *Antioch-on-the-Orontes*, editor, Vol. 2 (1938), Vol. 3 (1941), Vol. 5 (1972), Princeton, N.J.: Princeton University Press; *The Chapel of Princeton University*, Princeton, N.J.: Princeton University Press, 1971; *Princeton Encyclopaedia of Classical Sites* (editor), Princeton, N.J.: Princeton University Press, 1976; Excavation reports on Morgantina were authored by Stillwell and/or ERIK SJÖQVIST and appeared in *AJA* Vols. 61–68 (1957–64).

Stillwell took part in a number of important archaeological excavations including those at Corinth (with T. L. SHEAR and OSCAR BRONEER), Antioch, and Morgantina in Sicily. Work at the latter site was begun in 1955 by Stillwell and ERIK SJÖQVIST; it was located at present-day Serra Orlando but was not recognized as being the ancient city of Morgantina until 1958 when it was identified by KENAN ERIM, then a graduate student. This strategically located Greek city is unique among Classical sites because it initially blended elements of the surrounding indigenous culture into its make-up.

During his twenty years as editor-in-chief of the *American Journal of Archaeology*, Stillwell worked hard to ensure that the journal kept pace with a rapidly expanding field. Upon his retirement from teaching he undertook a massive project: the editing of the one-thousand-plus *Princeton Encyclopedia of Classical Sites* which was published in 1976. In this much needed reference work can be found the descriptions of two thousand Classical sites located throughout the Mediterranean area together with a bibliography for each.

Stillwell died while on a visit to Providence, Rhode Island.

SOURCES

Lord, *History of the American School . . .* , 1947; T. Lesley Shear Jr., "Richard Stillwell (1899–1982)," *AJA* 87 (1983): 423–25; Dow, *A Century of Humane Archaeology*, 1979; Stillwell, editor, *PECS*, 1976; *NYT* (August 3, 1982).

EUGÉNIE SELLERS STRONG

b: March 25, 1860. London, England.
d: September 16, 1943. Rome, Italy.

EDUCATION

Convent of St. Paul, Dourdan, France.
Girton College, Cambridge University, 1882.
British School at Athens.

APPOINTMENTS AND AWARDS

British Museum: Occasional Lecturer in Archaeology; Librarian to the Duke of Devonshire, Chatsworth (1904–09); British School at Rome: Asst. Director (1909–25); Archaeological Institute of America: Norton Lecturer (1913); Rhind Lecturer (1920). Fellow: Girton College, Cambridge Univ.; Society of Antiquaries, 1920. Hon. Member: Archaeological Society of Athens; AIA. Hon. Degrees: LL.D., Univ. of St. Andrews (1897); Litt.D., Univ. of Dublin (1907); Litt.D., Manchester Univ., 1923. Awards: C.B.E. (Commander of the British Empire, 1927); Serena Gold Medal (for Italian Studies), British Academy (1938); Gold Medal of the City of Rome (1938).

PUBLICATIONS

English translation of Carl Schuchhardt's *Schliemann's Discoveries of the Ancient World*, London: Macmillan and Co., 1891; English translation of Adolf Furtwängler's *Meisterwerke der Griechischen Plastik*, 1895; *The Elder Pliny's Chapters on the History of Art* (trans. by K. Jex-Blake, commentary by E. Strong) (1896), Chicago: Argonaut Publisher, 1968; English translation of F. Wickhoff's *Roman Art*, 1900; *Roman Sculpture from Augustus*

280

to Constantine (1907), New York: Hacker Art Books, 1971; *Apotheosis and Afterlife: Three Lectures on Certain Phases of Art and Religion in the Roman Empire* (1915), Freeport, N.Y.: Books for Libraries Press, 1969; *La Chiesa Nuova* (with Piero Misciattelli), Rome: Scietà editrice d'arte illustrata, 1923; *Art in Ancient Rome from the Earliest Times to Justinian* (1929, 2 vols., published simultaneously in English, French, and Italian), Westport, Conn.: Greenwood Press, 1970; Contributions on Roman art in *Cambridge Ancient History* (Vol. 9, 1932; Vol. 10, 1934;) " 'Romanita' Throughout the Ages," *JRS* 29 (1939): 137–66.

Eugénie Strong (*née* Sellers) was regarded as one of the most distinguished British archaeologists and art historians of her day. Her initial interest was in Greek art and she became the first female student to be admitted to the British School of Archaeology in Athens. After completing her studies there she came under the tutelage of WILHELM DÖRPFELD and later ADOLF FURTWÄNGLER and, while working on a book on Pliny, she became interested in Roman culture. Her subsequent translation of F. Wickhoff's *Roman Art* marked a significant turning point in her career.

From the time of J. J. WINCKELMANN Roman art had been regarded as merely an outgrowth of Greek, and an inferior one at that. In her subsequent publications Strong worked hard to establish the idea that Roman art is worthy of scholarly attention in its own right. She emphasized its native roots, and suggested that Roman artists and artisans had consciously worked to retain the integrity of the genre against the onslaught of Hellenism which occurred as the Roman Empire expanded eastward.

Her 1907 publication was the first comprehensive treatment of the subject and remains the standard text. Strong was also intensely interested in post-Classical art, especially baroque architecture.

SOURCES

J. M. C. Toynbee, *DNB* 1941–50; Brendel, *Prolegomena to the Study of Roman Art*, 1979; Jocelyn M. C. Toynbee, "Mrs. Arthur Strong," *AntJ* 23 (1943): 188–89; Waterhouse, *British School at Athens*, 1986; *WW*, 1940; *TL* (September 21, 1943).

JAMES STUART

b: 1713. London, England.
d: February 2, 1788. London, England.

EDUCATION

College de Fide Propaganda, Rome.

APPOINTMENTS AND AWARDS

Society of Dilettanti: Painter (1763–69); Greenwich Hospital: Surveyor; Independent Architect. Fellow: Royal Society; Society of Antiquaries. Member: Society of Dilettanti (1751).

PUBLICATIONS

De Obelesco Caesaris Augusti, Campo Martio Nuperrime Effoso, Epistola Jacobi Stuart Angli, ad Carolun Wentworth, Comitem de Malton, 1750; *The Antiquities of Athens measured and delineated by James Stuart, F.R.S. and F.S.A., and Nicholas Revett, Painters and Architects* (Volume 1; Volume 2, 1789 [posthumously published by Mrs. Stuart, edited by William Newton]; Volume 3, 1795 [edited by Willey Reveley]; Volume 4, 1814 [edited by Joseph Woods; also contained material on Pola, Dalmatia which Stuart and Revett visited in 1750]), New York: B. Blom, 1968.

The publication of James Stuart and NICHOLAS REVETT's *Antiquities of Athens* in 1762 had a powerful effect upon western Europe's awareness of both Greece and its antiquities. This work almost single-handedly gave birth to the adoption of the Classical style in architecture throughout Britain (see J. J. WINCKELMANN) and its provinces (Stuart designed the earliest Classical building in London) and in this regard Stuart and Revett have been hailed as the pioneers of Classical archaeology. Stuart became known as "Athenian Stuart" and was regarded as the authority on the various orders of Classical architecture.

Born into a poor family, James Stuart left Britain for Italy in 1741, traveling most of the way on foot. It was in Rome that he first made the acquaintance of Nicholas Revett. Stuart, who had studied Greek and Latin at a university in Rome, was taken by Revett's idea to go to Athens to take close account of its ancient buildings, and to obtain their exact measurements.

The two acquired financial backing for the proposed trip from a number of wealthy British residents in Italy and from the Society of Dilettanti in London, setting out for Greece from Rome in 1751. They were detained in Venice (during which time they visited Pola in Dalmatia, see 1814 publication, above) but finally arrived in Greece in March of that year. After spending two years in Athens, they were forced to leave due to the political unrest which Greece was experiencing at that time and took a circuitous route back to England via some of the Greek islands and western Asia Minor, arriving in Britain in 1755.

The first volume of *Antiquities of Athens* was not published until 1762; the two friends then had a falling out and Stuart purchased Revett's rights to the material which they had both collected in Greece. He then continued to prepare material for future volumes. Unfortunately Stuart died before the second volume could be completed, and this was later seen through the press by his wife, Elizabeth.

A few publications on Athens had appeared previous to the 1762 work but the information contained in them had not been scholarly and the illustrations were poor and erroneous. Stuart and Revett had wanted to set the study of Classical architecture on a serious and scholarly foundation and in this they succeeded, as volume one of *The Antiquities of Athens* provided a standard to which all later archaeological works could aspire.

Upon his return to Britain Stuart was briefly employed as an artist but found his true vocation as an architect, a profession in which he was to become quite successful. He had won more public acclaim for his work than had Revett (thought to be a possible reason for their later estrangement) and upon his death was interred in St. Martin-in-the-Fields Church in London.

SOURCES

DNB, Vol. 19; Clarke, *Greek Studies in England, 1700–1830*, 1945; Edwards, *Lives of the Founders of the British Museum* (1870), reprint, 1969; Stuart and Revett, *The Antiquities of Athens*, Vol. 1, 1825; Michaelis, *Ancient Marbles in Great Britain*, 1882; Cust, *History of the Society of Dilettanti*, 1914; Miller, *Greece Through the Ages*, 1972; Weber, *Voyages and Travels . . .* , 1953.

MARY HAMILTON SWINDLER

b: January 3, 1884. Bloomington, Indiana.
d: January 16, 1967. Haverford, Pennsylvania.

EDUCATION

Indiana University, 1905 (A.B.), 1906 (A.M.).
American School of Classical Studies at Athens.
Bryn Mawr College, 1912 (Ph.D.).

APPOINTMENTS AND AWARDS

Bryn Mawr College: Reader in Greek Archaeology (1912), Professor of Classical Archaeology (1931–49); *American Journal of Archaeology*: Editor (1932–46); American School of Classical Studies at Athens: Visiting Professor (1938); Univ. of Pennsylvania: Visiting Professor of Archaeology and Visiting Curator of the University Museum (1949–50); Univ. of Michigan: Visiting Professor (1950–53); Bryn Mawr College: Professor of Classical Archaeology (1953–56). Fellow: Royal Society of Arts, German Archaeological Institute. Hon. Degree: LL.D., Indiana Univ. (1941). Award: Achievement Award of the American Association of University Women (1951).

PUBLICATIONS

"Another Vase by the Master of the Penthesilea Cylix," *AJA* 13 (1909): 142–50; *Cretan Elements in the Cults and Ritual of Apollo*, Pennsylvania: Bryn Mawr College, 1913; "The Penthesilea Master," *AJA* 19 (1915): 398–417; "The Bryn Mawr Collection of Greek Vases," *AJA* 20 (1916): 308–45; *Ancient Painting* (1929), New York: AMS Press, 1979.

Mary Hamilton Swindler achieved early recognition with her article published in the *AJA* in 1909 (above) in which she identified a pot as being the work of the Penthesilea Painter, and she later won international acclaim with her major publication, *Ancient Painting*.

In this work she surveyed vast and far-ranging material beginning with Palaeolithic cave paintings, on through Egyptian, Greek, and Roman painting, and ending with early Christian art. This was the first work of its type and has become the standard volume in English on the subject.

In addition, as the long-time editor of the *American Journal of Archaeology*, Swindler had a major influence on the development of Classical archaeological studies in America.

She was instrumental in bringing about the important excavation of Tarsus in Cilicia which was carried out under the auspices of Bryn Mawr College, Harvard University, and the Archaeological Institute of America during the years 1934–49. These excavations were led by HETTY GOLDMAN, also a graduate of Bryn Mawr College.

Swindler founded the Ella Riegel Memorial Museum at Bryn Mawr College in 1941 and was the consulting editor on Classical archaeology for the *Encyclopaedia Britannica*.

SOURCES

Emily Vermeule and Sara Anderson Immerwahr, *NAW*; "Mary Hamilton Swindler," *AJA* 54 (1950): 292–93; *NYT* (January 18, 1967).

CHARLES TOWNELEY
(SOMETIMES SPELLED TOWNLEY)

b: October 1, 1737. Towneley, Lancashire, England.
d: January 3, 1805. London, England.

EDUCATION

College of Douay, France.

APPOINTMENTS AND AWARDS

Member: Society of Dilettanti (1786); Trustee, British Museum (1791).

Kept out of British public life because he was a Catholic, Charles Towneley remained a country gentleman in England until he visited Rome and Florence in 1765. There he was smitten by the sight of ancient Greek and Roman art and in 1768 began to accumulate his own pieces. He encouraged the excavation of ancient sites in order to procure more artifacts and eventually possessed one of the largest and finest collections in all of Britain.

When he returned to Britain in 1772 he continued to collect from European dealers and from his previous connections in Italy. He bought and renovated a house in Westminster, London, in order to display his collection to best advantage, and there Towneley welcomed a broad spectrum of visitors; he was regarded as one of the country's authorities on works of Classical art.

His collection of ancient marbles and terracottas was purchased by the British Museum after his death for £20,000 (a figure thought to be well below their actual worth) and a new gallery was built in the museum to accommodate them; the gallery was opened to the public in 1808. Towneley's collection of bronzes, coins, gems, and drawings was purchased by the

British Museum in 1814 and, combined with his other collection purchased earlier, formed one of the cornerstones of the British Museum's Department of Greek and Roman Antiquities.

SOURCES

Edwards, *Lives of the Founders of the British Museum* (1870), reprint, 1969; Michaelis, *Ancient Marbles in Great Britain*, 1882; Cust, *History of the Society of Dilettanti*, 1914; Clarke, *Greek Studies in England, 1700–1830*, 1945; *DNB*, Vol. 19.

JOHN (IOHANNES) TRAVLOS

b: 1908. Rostov, Russia.
d: October 28, 1985. Athens, Greece.

EDUCATION

School of Architecture of the National Metsovian Polytechneion, 1931 (B.A.), 1935 (Ph.D.).

APPOINTMENTS AND AWARDS

American School of Classical Studies at Athens: Architect, Agora Excavations, Athens (1935–40), Architect, Excavations (1940–73), Hon. Architect (1973); Institute for Advanced Study, Princeton Univ.: Visiting Member (1952–53, 1967–68). Member: Archaeological Society of Athens.

EXCAVATIONS

Athens; Eleusis; Corinth; Eretria; Gla; Pylos.

PUBLICATIONS

Πολεδομικὴ ἐξέλιξις τῶν Ἀθηνῶν (*The Urban Development of Athens*), 1960; *Neo-Classical Architecture in Greece*, 1967; *Pictorial Dictionary of Ancient Athens*, New York: Praeger Publishers, 1971 (published simultaneously in German as *Bildlexikon zur Topographie des Antiken Athen* [1971], Tübingen: Wasmuth, 1988).

A Classical architect, Travlos produced two publications on the city of Athens. His earlier work (1960) provided a discussion of the urban development of the city at key points in its history, a survey which spanned a five-thousand-year period up to 1959 C.E. His 1971 opus, on the other hand, was more focused; he narrowed the timespan to cover from the beginning of the Archaic period down to the Roman epoch, and within this shorter time frame he provided detailed architectural accounts of the many ancient buildings and monuments which occupied the city.

Travlos's success with these publications stemmed from his first-hand knowledge of the sites, a familiarity which he gained from his close association with the American School of Classical Studies at Athens. He was a gifted draughtsman and provided many of the illustrations for this organization's publications as well as for his own.

He also had a special interest in restoration; he supervised the reconstruction of the Stoa of Attalos which borders the ancient Agora in Athens, assisted the Cypriot authorities in partially restoring the ancient theaters at Salamis and Kourion and the odeion at Paphos, and (with Alison Frantz) restored the Byzantine Church of the Holy Apostles in Athens (c. 1000 C.E.) to its original state.

SOURCES

Homer A. Thompson, "John Travlos, 1908–1985," *AJA* 90 (1986): 343–45; Travlos, *Pictorial Dictionary of Ancient Athens*, (1971), reprint, 1980; *TL* (November 2, 1985).

CHRISTOS TSOUNTAS

b: 1857. Stenimachos, Thrace, Greece.
d: June 9, 1934. Athens, Greece.

EDUCATION

University of Athens.

APPOINTMENTS AND AWARDS

Greek Archaeological Service: Supervisor of Antiquities (1883–1904); Univ. of Athens: Professor of Archaeology (1904–25); New Univ. of Thessalonica (1926). Member: Greek Academy. Hon. Member: Society for the Promotion of Hellenic Studies, London.

EXCAVATIONS

Sesklo, 1901–02; Mycenae, 1886–93; Naxos; Paros; Syros; Vaphio; Amyklai, 1889–90.

PUBLICATIONS

"ΚΥΚΛΑΔΙΚΑ (ΙΙιν. 8–12)" ΕΦΗΜΕΠΕΣ ΑΡΧΑΙΟΛΟΓΙΚΗ (1898): 137–212; "ΚΥΚΛΑΔΙΚΑ ΙΙ," Ibid. (1899): 73–134; αἱ Προϊστορικαὶ ἀκροπόλεις Διμηνίου καὶ Σέσκλου, 1908; *The Mycenaean Age: A Study of the Monuments and Culture of Pre-Homeric Greece* (J. Irving Manatt, trans.) (1897), Chicago: Argonaut Publishers, 1969; Ἰστορια της αρχαιας Ἑλληνικης τεχνης (2 vols.) 1928.

Tsountas is considered one of the pioneers of modern archaeology and one of the most eminent of the Greek archae-

291

ologists; he dug at a number of key sites in Greece including prehistoric Sesklo, Mycenae, and in the Cycladic Islands. His work contributed greatly to the clarification of Aegean Bronze Age chronology and his synthesis and systematization of available data assisted in the expansion of our knowledge of Bronze Age civilization in general.

At Mycenae he continued the work of HEINRICH SCHLIEMANN and uncovered the remains of the palace which sits atop the citadel; he discovered the subterranean reservoir located at the eastern end of the acropolis and furthered our knowledge of Bronze Age burial customs by his excavation of more than seventy chamber tombs. Tsountas brought all of his accumulated knowledge to bear in his 1893 publication (above) in which he provided a comprehensive and integrated picture of Mycenaean culture.

He established some important chronological boundaries at Mycenae by outlining synchronisms between Mycenaean pottery and pottery and frescoes from Egypt. He was then able to set the sixteenth century B.C.E. as the upper limit of Mycenaean civilization and placed its destruction at approximately the twelfth century B.C.E., dates which are still generally accepted today. He was also the first to suggest that the shaft graves discovered by Schliemann predated the *tholos* tombs.

After his work at Mycenae, Tsountas turned his attention to the Cyclades. Apart from the early work of JAMES THEODORE BENT, little attention had previously been paid to the history of these islands. It was Tsountas who was the first to recognize that the remains of the Early Bronze Age inhabitants of the islands constituted a homogeneous culture that was very old and was quite distinct from those found on Crete and the Greek mainland. Two of his articles published in *Archaiologike Ephemeris* (1898, 1899, above) are still considered to be fundamental reading for anyone studying the archaeology of these islands.

His work at Sesklo laid the foundation for later work at this important Neolithic site. Tsountas also earned fame by his discovery of the famous Mycenaean gold "Vapheio Cups" in a pit in a previously rifled *tholos* tomb at Vapheio near Sparta in the Peloponnese.

SOURCES

"Necrology," *AJA* (1935): 379 (no author stated); Leekley and Noyes, *AESG*, 1976; Leekley and Efstratiou, *AECNG*, 1980; McDonald, *Discovery of Homeric Greece*, 1967; Frazer, *Pausanias's Description of Greece*, reprint, 1965; Renfrew, *The Emergence of Civilisation*, 1972; Barber, *The Cyclades in the Bronze Age*, 1987; Fitton, *The Discovery of the Greek Bronze Age*, 1995; *IWW*, 1935; Correspondence with the Archaeological Society of Athens.

ESTHER BOISE VAN DEMAN

b: October 1, 1862. South Salem, Ohio.
d: May 3, 1937. Rome, Italy.

EDUCATION

South Salem Academy, Ohio.
University of Michigan, 1891 (B.A.), 1892 (M.A.).
Bryn Mawr College, 1893.
University of Chicago, 1898 (Ph.D.).
American Academy at Rome, 1901–03.

APPOINTMENTS AND AWARDS

Wellesley College: Instructor in Latin (1893–95); Bryn Mawr School, Baltimore: Instructor in Latin (1895–96); Mt. Holyoke College: Acting Professor in Latin (1898–99), Assoc. Professor of Latin (1899–1901); Goucher College: Assoc. Professor of Latin and Archaeology (1903–06); American Academy at Rome: Carnegie Fellow, 1906–10; Carnegie Institute: Associate (1910–25); Univ. of Michigan: Carnegie Research Professor in Roman Archaeology (1925–30); Carnegie Institute: Staff Member (retired, beg. 1930); Archaeological Institute of America: Charles Eliot B. Norton Lecturer (1924–25). Hon. Degree: Univ. of Michigan (1936).

PUBLICATIONS

The Atrium Vestae, Washington, D.C.: Carnegie Institution, 1909; "Methods of Determining the Date of Roman Concrete Monuments," *AJA* 16 (1912): 230–51; "The Sullan Forum," *JRS* 12 (1922): 1–31; "The Neronian Sacra Via," *AJA* 27 (1923): 383–424; "The House of Caligula," *AJA* 28 (1924):

368–98; *The Building of the Roman Aqueducts* (1934), Washington: McGrath Publishing Co., 1973; *Ancient Roman Construction in Italy from the Prehistoric Era to Augustus*, Washington, D.C.: Carnegie Institution, 1947 (prepared for press and published posthumously by Marion E. Blake).

Esther Boise Van Deman, who spent most of her career living in Rome, was instrumental in developing the modern study of Roman architecture. She was considered one of America's leading Roman archaeologists and was one of the best known female archaeologists of her day.

Van Deman was a pioneer in the study of the chronology of Roman brick and concrete construction. She carefully examined the different types of building materials used by the Romans and was able to establish a set of criteria for their chronological dating, criteria which for the most part are still adhered to today within Italy.

She brought the breadth of her knowledge to bear in a landmark work on Roman aqueducts and their builders. This volume included the period beginning with the fourth century B.C.E. and ended with the edifices of Severus Alexander in the third century C.E. It remains the most scholarly work on the subject.

SOURCES

David M. Robinson, "Necrology," *AJA* 41 (1937): 315–16; Correspondence and material provided by the Carnegie Institution of Washington, D.C.; Lucy Shoe Meritt, *NAW* 3 (1971); John C. Rolfe, *AJA* 39 (1935): 633; *NYT* (May 5, 1937).

EUGENE VANDERPOOL

b: August 3, 1906. Morristown, New Jersey.
d: August 1, 1989. Athens, Greece.

EDUCATION

Princeton University, 1929 (B.A.).
American School of Classical Studies at Athens, 1929–30.

APPOINTMENTS AND AWARDS

American School of Classical Studies at Athens: Professor
of Archaeology (1949–71); Archaeological Society of Athens:
Hon. Vice President. Award: Gold Medal, Archaeological
Institute of America (1975).

EXCAVATIONS

The Agora, Athens, 1932–47; The Agora, Athens, 1947–67
(Deputy Director); Koroni, Attica, 1960.

PUBLICATIONS

"The Rectangular Rock-Cut Shaft," *Hesperia* 7 (1938):
363–411; "An Archaic Inscribed Stele from Marathon," *Hesperia* 11 (1942): 329–37; "Some Ostraka from the Athenian
Agora," *Hesperia* Suppl. 8 (1949): 394–412; "Excavations at
Koroni (Porto Raphti), Attica, 1960," *Klio* 39 (1961): 271–75;
Ostracism at Athens, Cincinnati: University of Cincinnati, 1970;
"The Prison of Socrates," *ILN* 264 (June 1976): 87–88.

An authority on Attic topography and Greek epigraphy,
Vanderpool wrote a total of ninety-eight articles for scholarly

journals. Much of his work was carried out in the vicinity of Athens and in various outlying areas of Attica. He made major contributions with his work on *ostraka*, and in 1976 published an article in which he identified the remains of a building in the southwest corner of the Agora as being the prison where Socrates was held and put to death in 399 B.C.E. He also discovered the marble *stele* which was set up by the Athenians to commemorate the victory at Marathon in 490 B.C.E.

His work at Koroni in eastern Attica shed light on the history of Athens in the third century B.C.E. and added to our understanding of the chronology of Hellenistic pottery. He was awarded the Archaeological Institute of America's Gold Medal for Distinguished Achievement in 1975.

SOURCES

John McKesson Camp II, "Eugene Vanderpool, 1906–1989," *AJA* (1990): 291–92; "Bibliography of Eugene Vanderpool," *Hesperia* Suppl. 19 (1981): vii-xii; *NYT* (August 3, 1989).

MICHAEL (GEORGE FRANCIS) VENTRIS

b: July 12, 1922. Wheathampstead, Hertfordshire, England.
d: September 6, 1956. London, England.

EDUCATION

Early years in Switzerland (to 1930).
Bickley, Kent, England (preparatory school).
Stowe School, England, 1939.
Architectural Association School, London, 1940–42 and 1946–48 (with honors).

APPOINTMENTS AND AWARDS

Ministry of Education, Architects's Branch (1949–52); Dept. of Greek, University College, London: Hon. Research Assoc. (1954). Fellow: Society of Antiquaries; Fellowship, *Architects' Journal* (1956). Hon. Degree: Ph.D., Uppsala University (1954). Awards: Order of the British Empire (1955); Kenyon Medal, British Academy (awarded posthumously).

PUBLICATIONS

"Evidence for Greek Dialect in the Mycenaean Archives," (with J. Chadwick) *JHS* 73 (1953): 84–103; "King Nestor's Four-Handled Cups: Greek Inventories in the Minoan Script," *Archaeology* 7, no. 1 (1954): 15–21; *Documents in Mycenaean Greek* (with J. Chadwick) (1956), Cambridge: Cambridge University Press, 1973 (revised ed.); *The Knossos Tablets: A Revised Transliteration of All the Texts in Mycenaean Greek Recoverable from Evans' Excavations of 1900–1904 Based on Independent Examination* (with M. Ventris et al.); *Work Notes on Minoan Language Research and*

298

Other Unedited Papers (edited by Anna Sacconi), Rome: Edizioni dell'Ateneo, 1988.

Michael Ventris became a pivotal figure in Classical archaeology with his decipherment of the ancient script, Linear B. As a schoolboy, Ventris attended a lecture given by SIR ARTHUR EVANS at which the latter discussed the discovery of the Minoan palace of Knossos and the nearly two thousand baked clay tablets that contained the as yet undeciphered ancient scripts which Evans called Linear A and Linear B. Ventris later recollected that it was at this lecture that he determined, one day, to unravel the mystery of these "Minoan" tablets.

At the age of eighteen he published an article in the *American Journal of Archaeology* (1940) in which he proposed that the scripts (Linear A and Linear B) were related to Etruscan but he was eventually forced to abandon this idea. After establishing a career in architecture, Ventris returned to the problem and in 1949 began a painstaking analysis.

In 1939 CARL W. BLEGEN had discovered more Linear B tablets (this time at Pylos on the Greek mainland), but because of the war the tablets remained unpublished until 1951. However, with their publication the amount of material available was increased tremendously, and in 1952 Ventris was able to form a basis for the decipherment of the script and proposed that Linear B was possibly an early form of Greek. At this point he sought the aid of John Chadwick with whom he developed his theory and the two published their findings for the first time in *JHS* in 1953 (above).

Ventris's claim that the Linear B script was an early form of Greek had major ramifications in several areas. Firstly, history books literally had to be rewritten because up to this time the Mycenaeans had been believed to be a pre-Greek people with no connection to the later Classical Greeks. Secondly, Ventris's findings supported HEINRICH SCHLIEMANN'S contention that the opulent (Greek) Homeric culture of the *Iliad* and *Odyssey* was indeed the very same Mycenaean culture that he had discovered. Scholars had opposed this idea while it had been widely held that the Mycenaeans were not Greeks. Thirdly, his findings clarified the events which occurred on Minoan Crete in the Late Bronze Age, for the prevalence of Linear B tablets at Knossos in the final phase of the palace indicated that the Mycenaeans had eventually gained control of the former Minoan residence (see Arthur Evans, Carl W. Blegen, ARNE FURUMARK).

Michael Ventris was killed on the outskirts of London when his car collided with a lorry. He was thirty-four years old.

SOURCES

Emmett L. Bennett Jr. and A. J. B. Wace, "Tributes to Michael Ventris," *Archaeology* 9, no. 4 (1956) 279–80; John Chadwick, *DNB* 1951–60; *CB* (January 1957): 566–67; *AF* November 1956; Ventris, "King Nestor's Four-Handled Cups: Greek Inventories in the Minoan Script," *Archaeology* 7, no. 1 (1954): 15–21; *TL* (September 8, 1956), (September 10, 1956), (September 17, 1956), (September 20, 1956).

A(LAN) J(OHN) B(AYARD) WACE

b: July 13, 1879. Cambridge, England.
d: November 9, 1957. Athens, Greece.

EDUCATION

Shrewsbury School, England.
Pembroke College, Cambridge, 1901 (B.A.).

APPOINTMENTS AND AWARDS

Univ. of St. Andrews: Lecturer (1912–14); British School at Athens: Director (1914–23); Victoria and Albert Museum, London: Deputy Keeper in charge of Textiles (1924–34); Cambridge Univ.: Lawrence Professor (1934–44); Farouk I University at Alexandria: Chair, Classics and Archaeology (1944–52). Fellow: British Academy (1947); Society of Antiquaries. Hon. Fellow: Pembroke College, Cambridge University. Member: Institute for Advanced Study, Princeton Univ.; American Philosophical Society; German Archaeological Institute. Hon. Member: Archaeological Institute of America; Greek Archaeological Society. Hon. Degrees: LL.D., Univ. of Liverpool; D.Litt., Univ. of Amsterdam.

EXCAVATIONS

Geraki (Lakonia); Volo; Dimini; Zerelia (Thessaly), 1908; Halos (Phthiotis), 1912; Korakou (with CARL W. BLEGEN); Zygouries (with Carl W. Blegen); Mycenae, 1920–23; 1939; 1950–55.

PUBLICATIONS

Prehistoric Thessaly (with M. S. Thompson) (1912), New York: AMS Press, 1979; *The Nomads of the Balkans* (with M. S. Thompson) (1914), Freeport, N.Y.: Books for Libraries Press, 1971; "The Pre-Mycenaean Pottery of the Mainland," (with CARL W. BLEGEN) *BSA* 22 (1916–18): 175–89; "Chamber Tombs at Mycenae," *Archaeologia* 82, 1932; *Studies in Civilization* (contributor) (1941), Port Washington, N.Y.: Kennikat Press, 1969; *Mycenae: An Archaeological History and Guide* (1949), New York: Biblo and Tannen, 1964; *Hermopolis Magna, Ashmunein: The Ptolemaic Sanctuary and the Basilica* (by A. J. B. Wace et al.), Alexandria: Alexandria University Press, 1959; *A Companion to Homer* (with Frank H. Stubbings), London: Macmillan and Co., 1962 (published posthumously); *Excavations at Mycenae, 1939–1955*, by A. J. B. Wace et al. (edited and indexed by Elizabeth French), London: British School of Archaeology at Athens: Thames and Hudson, 1979.

At Cambridge Wace was a fellow student of the older R. M. DAWKINS with whom he later traveled extensively in Greece. His first scholarly interest was in the Hellenistic period but this changed when he "fell in love with Neolithic pottery."[1]

While Wace was its director (and with ARTHUR EVANS's discoveries continuing on Crete), the British School at Athens began to focus on the site of Mycenae during the early 1920s. At this time it seemed to many that Mycenae was both politically and culturally an extension of the Bronze Age Minoan culture. However, Wace's exploration of Thessaly had led him to believe that the culture of mainland Greece had played a more major role in the shaping of Mycenaean civilization.

Wace met CARL W. BLEGEN in Athens in the early 1900s. Based upon Wace's experience in Thessaly and Blegen's work at Korakou, the two published an article (see 1916–18, above) in which they proposed the division of Bronze Age mainland Greece into three parts—Early, Middle, and Late Helladic. This article supported Wace's contention that mainland Greek culture actually controlled the Minoan elements found at Mycenae and not vice versa. It also pushed back the roots of Classical Greek civilization to the Middle Bronze Age period (Middle Helladic) and to the makers of Minyan ware pottery.

Previously it had been believed that the Greeks had not

entered mainland Greece until the time of the Dorian invasions, and for many this was still held to be the case. And yet with Blegen's 1939 discovery of the Linear B tablets at Pylos and with MICHAEL VENTRIS's confirmation that this script was indeed Greek, Wace's early contention that influence between the Mycenaean and Minoan cultures went in both directions was upheld. Moreover, Wace was shown to be correct in believing that the Mycenaeans were in fact Greeks and that, in the end, it was these very same Greeks of the mainland who had prevailed.

SOURCES

F. H. Stubbings, "Alan John Bayard Wace 1879–1957," *PBA* 44 (1958): 263–80; Wace and Blegen, "The Pre-Mycenaean Pottery of the Mainland," *BSA* 22 (1916–18): 175–89; Waterhouse, *British School at Athens*, 1986; Leekley and Efstratiou, *AECNG*, 1980; Leekley and Noyes, *AESG* 1976; *TL* (November 11, 1957).

NOTE

1. Waterhouse, *British School at Athens*, p. 126.

J(OHN) B(RYAN) WARD-PERKINS

b: February 3, 1912. Kent, England.
d: May 28, 1981. Cirencester, England.

EDUCATION

Winchester School, England.
New College, Oxford University, 1934.

APPOINTMENTS AND AWARDS

London Museum: Assistant (1936–39); Royal University of
Malta: Chair of Archaeology (1939); British School at Rome:
Director (1945–74); Fine Arts Institute, New York Univ.: Visiting Professor (1957); Rhind Lecturer (1960); Jerome Lecturer (1969). Member: British Academy (1951). Hon. Degrees:
D. Litt., Birmingham Univ. (1969); LL.D., Univ. of Alberta
(1969). Awards: Serena Medal, British Academy (1962);
C.B.E. (Commander of the British Empire); Medaglia d'oro
per I Benemeriti della Cultura.

EXCAVATIONS

Buttley Priory, Suffolk, England, 1933; Gergovia, France
(with Olwen Brogan and Emil Desforges), 1934; Oldbury,
Kent, 1938; Lockleys, Herts, 1937; Leptis Magna, Tripolitania, Cyrenaica (1940s and early 1950s); Sabratha, North
Africa, 1948 (with Kathleen Kenyon); southern Etruria, beg.
1954; Veii, Italy.

PUBLICATIONS

"Visigothic France," *Archaeologia* 87 (1938); "Severan Art
and Architecture at Leptis Magna," *JRS* 38 (1948): 59–80;

Inscriptions of Roman Tripolitania (with Joyce Reynolds), 1952; "Limes Tripolitanus," (with Richard Goodchild) *JRS* (1949): 59–80; "The Hunting Baths at Leptis Magna," (with J.M.C. Toynbee) *Archaeologia* 93 (1949): 165–195; *The Shrine of St. Peter and the Vatican Excavation* (with J.M.C. Toynbee), New York: Parthenon Books, 1957; *The Great Palace of the Byzantine Emperors*, 1958 (contributor, edited by David Talbot-Rice); *Veii: The Historical Topography of the Ancient City*, London: British School at Rome, 1961; *Etruscan and Roman Architecture* (with AXEL BOËTHIUS) (1970, 1978, 2d. ed.); *Cities of Ancient Greece and Italy: Planning in Classical Antiquity*, New York: G. Braziller, 1974; *Pompeii, AD 79: Essay and Catalogue* (with Amanda Claridge), New York: Knopf, 1978; *Justinianic Mosaic Pavements in Cyrenaican Churches* (with Elisabeth Alföldi-Rosenbaum), Rome: "L'Erma" di Bretschneider, 1980; *Roman Imperial Architecture*, 1981 (originally published as Parts 2–4 of 1970 publication above).

Ward-Perkins's early interest was in pre-Roman Iron Age Britain and France. During World War Two he was posted to North Africa (under the command of Sir MORTIMER WHEELER) and there became familiar with the ruins of Roman Tripolitania. After the war he became director of the British School at Rome but, because excavation work in post-war Italy was at a standstill, he focused his attention on the Roman remains in North Africa. During the decade after the war he produced some thirty articles on the excavation work carried out in this area (some coauthors being R. Goodchild, J. M. C. Toynbee, and J. Reynolds). Subjects ranged from topography to epigraphy.

Beyond his excavations in North Africa and later at Veii, Ward-Perkins is best known for his work on the topography of southern Etruria (it has been likened to THOMAS ASHBY's work on the Roman Campagna). He directed topographical studies which defined three successive periods of history in the area (pre-Roman, Roman, and Medieval). This survey of southern Etruria resulted in the formulation of new recording and mapping techniques, and these methods have since been used in other areas of Italy as well as in other countries.

He was also responsible for reviving two projects that had been planned but never finished, these being the publication of the sculpture of the Roman Empire (*Corpus signorum imperii Romani*) and the mapping of the Roman Empire (*Tabula imperrii Romani*) which had been begun by O. G. S. Crawford in 1928 with only five sheets having been produced by 1965.

SOURCES

J. J. Wilkes, "John Bryan Ward-Perkins 1912–1981," *PBA* 69 (1983): 631–55; *TL* (June 5, 1981).

(Sir Robert Eric) Mortimer Wheeler

b: September 10, 1890. Glasgow, Scotland.
d: July 22, 1976. Surrey, England.

EDUCATION

University College, London, 1912 (M.A.).

APPOINTMENTS AND AWARDS

National Museum of Wales, Cardiff: Keeper of Archaeology (1920–24), Director (1924–26); Univ. College at Cardiff: Lecturer in Archaeology (1920–24); London Museum: Director (beg. 1926); Univ. of London: Lecturer in British Archaeology (1934–55); Institute of Archaeology, London Univ.: Hon. Director (beg. 1937); Director General of Archaeology in India (1944–49); Secretary, British Academy (1949–68). Member: British Academy; Society of Antiquaries. Award: K.C.B. (Knight Commander of the Bath, 1952).

EXCAVATIONS

Wroxeter, 1913; Caerleon, Segontium, and Brecon Gaer (Wales), 1920–26; Lydney, 1928–29; St. Albans (Roman Verulamium), 1931–35; Maiden Castle, Dorset, 1934–36; Taxila and Harappa, India, 1946; Mohenjodoro, India, 1949–50; Arikamedu, India, 1944–45; Charsada, Pakistan, 1958; Stanwick, North Yorkshire, 1951–52.

PUBLICATIONS

Prehistoric and Roman Wales, Oxford: The Clarendon Press, 1925; *London in Roman Times*, London: W. Clowes and Sons,

1930; *London and the Saxons*, London: London Museum, 1935; *Verulamium, a Belgic and Two Roman Cities* (with Tessa Verney Wheeler), 1936; *Maiden Castle, Dorset*, 1943; *Stanwick Fortifications*, 1954; *Rome Beyond the Imperial Frontiers* (1954), Westport, Conn.: Greenwood Press, 1971; *Still Digging*, New York: Dutton, 1955; *Impact and Imprint: Greeks and Romans Beyond the Himalayas*, Newcastle-Upon-Tyne: King's College, 1959; *Charsada: A Metropolis of the North-west Frontier, Being a Report on the Excavations of 1958*, Oxford: Oxford University Press, 1962; *Roman Art and Architecture* (1964), New York: Thames and Hudson, 1985; *Roman Africa in Color*, London: Thames and Hudson, 1966; *Flames Over Persepolis* (1968), Westport, Conn.: Greenwood Press, 1979; *Archaeology from the Earth* (1954), Oxford: The Clarendon Press, 1970; *Caerleon Roman Amphitheatre and Prysg Field Barrack Buildings, Monmouthshire and Caerlion, Sir Fynwy* (with the late V. E. Nash Williams), London: Her Majesty's Stationery Office, 1970; *My Archaeological Mission to India and Pakistan*, London: Thames and Hudson, 1976.

A man of extraordinary energy, Wheeler was early on deeply influenced by the work of General Augustus Pitt-Rivers. Pitt-Rivers's more systematic and scientific approach to archaeology appealed to Wheeler—his focus on typology, meticulous excavation of everyday finds regardless of their aesthetic value, and his efforts to learn more of the culture from which the artifacts originated. After the death of Pitt-Rivers, this approach was practiced by only a few British archaeologists; it became Wheeler's mission to revitalize his method and with it, to fill in the large gaps that existed in our knowledge of prehistoric and Roman Britain.

One of his greatest contributions in regard to methodology was his development of what has been called the grid-system. This was based on finding and following the natural stratigraphy of a site. After a site was surveyed, a grid would be placed over it, and the squares (about five meters square) were separated by balks (unexcavated walls). Each layer of the square was carefully taken off while the balks were used to enable the excavator to check the strata that he was working in, and to provide a stratigraphy for the area after the excavated ground had been taken down to its lowest level. Such meticulous mapping, excavation, and recording of a dig required that an archaeologist supervise an area covering no more than two or three squares at a time; this was in sharp contrast to the excavation practices of the day, where large areas were often dug by hundreds of workers with very little supervision.

Wheeler's early interest was in the Roman occupation of Wales, and he worked at key sites including Caerleon (Roman Isca) where the remains of a large Roman fortress (of the Second Augustan Legion) and an amphitheater were uncovered.

He then moved on to English sites and excavated at Verulamium, a site that shed light on the history of Britain during the century prior to the Roman occupation. At the next major site, Maiden Castle in Dorset, Wheeler excavated an area whose history could be traced from the Neolithic period to its capture by the Second Legion under the command of the Roman emperor Vespasian.

During World War One Wheeler was stationed in North Africa and while there worked with one of his subordinates, J. WARD-PERKINS, to protect the ancient sites of Leptis Magna and Sabratha.

Toward the end of the war Wheeler was appointed director general of archaeology in India and spent some years there. At Taxila he shed light on the Achaemenid period and on the impact of the conquests of Alexander the Great. His excavations of 1944 established the existence of a Roman trading port at Arikamedu. Wheeler was able to secure dates for ancient Indian history by correlating Indian artifacts with Roman imported goods found at the same levels. His identification of strong fortification walls in the Indus Valley enabled V. GORDON CHILDE to modify some of his assumptions with regard to the character of that primitive culture. In addition to his work in Britain, North Africa, and India, Wheeler is remembered for his accomplished students who include J. Ward-Perkins, V. Nash Williams, and Kathleen Kenyon.

SOURCES

Jacquetta Hawkes, "Robert Eric Mortimer Wheeler 1890–1976," *PBA* 63 (1977): 483–507; Houlder, *Wales: An Archaeological Guide*, 1978; Stiebing Jr., *Uncovering the Past: A History of Archaeology*, 1993; Daniel, *A Hundred and Fifty Years of Archaeology*, 1975, 2d. ed.; *NYT* (July 23, 1976); *TL* (July 23, 1976).

(Sir) George Wheler

b: 1650. Breda, Holland.
d: January 15, 1723. Durham, England.

EDUCATION

Wye School, Kent, England.
Lincoln College, Oxford University, 1666, 1683 (M.A.),
1702 (D.D.).

APPOINTMENTS AND AWARDS

Clergyman, Basingstoke, Hampshire (1685–1702), Winston (1706–09); Canon, Rector, Houghton-le-Spring, Durham (1709–23). Award: K.C.B. (Knight Commander of the Bath, 1682).

PUBLICATIONS

A Journey into Greece, London: W. Cademan, 1682; *Account of Churches and Places of Assembly of the Primitive Christians*, London: S. Roycroft, 1689; *The Protestant Monastery; or Christian Oeconomicks, containing Directions for the Religious Conduct of a Family*, 1698.

George Wheler's journey through Greece proved to be of great importance particularly with regard to the buildings on the acropolis in Athens.

Wheler and a friend (James Spon, a German living in Lyons, France) traveled to Greece in 1675. They were two of the earliest Europeans to visit the area and most importantly, were among the last to view the buildings on the acropolis prior to the great destruction of 1687 when a Venetian shell hit the Parthenon (which the Turks were using to store gunpowder) causing an explosion which blew off the roof of the building, taking with it much of the *cella* and the central parts of the pediments.

Today Wheler's account is useful, then, not for the conclusions that he drew (e.g., he believed that the pedimental sculptures on the Parthenon had been commissioned by the Emperor Hadrian) but for his descriptions, both written and sketched.

When he viewed the buildings on the acropolis only the Propylaea was in a ruinous state; the Athena Nike temple, the Erechtheum, and the Temple of Athena Parthenos were all in a fairly good state of preservation. By the time STUART and REVETT visited the site in 1750, the center and roof of the Parthenon had been blown out and there was no sign of the Athena Nike temple. After fragments of the latter had been found by the Greeks in 1835 among the old Turkish fortification walls, the temple was reconstructed largely due to the descriptions given in the works of Wheler and Spon.[1]

The descriptions of the pedimental statuary on the Parthenon have also proved invaluable, though the central statues of the east pediment were already missing by the time of their visit. In addition, Wheler and Spon provided descriptions and sketches of other ancient sites in Greece including Eleusis, Sounion, Aegina, Delphi, and Corinth. They also visited Constantinople and Ephesus.

Wheler brought back a number of ancient fragments including some inscriptions, all of which he presented to Oxford University in 1683. He was knighted in 1682 and is buried in the galilee of Durham Cathedral.

SOURCES

DNB 20, 1909; *Art and Archaeology* 10, no. 4 (October 1920): 131–41; Miller, *Greece Through the Ages*, 1972; Cook, *The Elgin Marbles*, 1984.

NOTE

1. Spon published his memoirs of the journey in *Voyage d'Italie, de Dalmatie, de Gréce, et du Levant, fait aux annés 1675, 1676*, 1678.

J(OHANN) J(OACHIM) WINCKELMANN

b: December 9, 1717. Stendal, Prussia.
d: June 8, 1768. Trieste, Italy.

EDUCATION

Cologne Gymnasium.
University of Halle.

APPOINTMENTS AND AWARDS

Seehausen, Prussia: Schoolmaster; Papal Librarian, Secretary of State; Librarian (to Cardinal Albani) (beg. 1759); Chief Supervisor of Antiquities, Rome (beg. 1763).

PUBLICATIONS

Geschichte der Kunst des Alterhums (*History of the Art of Antiquity*), 1764 (1776, 2d. ed.) (published posthumously), Darmstadt: Wissenschaftliche Buchgesellschaft, 1972; *Versuch einer Allegorie, besonders für die Kunst* (*Attempt at an Allegory, Particulary for Art*), 1766; *Anmerkungen über die Geschichte der Kunst des Alterthums* (*Remarks on the History of the Art of Antiquity*), 1767; *Monumenti Antichi Inediti* (*Unpublished Antique Monuments*) (1767), Baden-Baden: Strasbourg, Heitz, 1967.

Johann Joachim Winckelmann was born in Prussia, the son of a cobbler, and went on to become one of the most influential figures in the history of art, specifically Classical archaeology. His most famous work was the *History of the Art of Antiquity*; in this book he formulated a theoretical structure and established a focus for the study of the history of art which survives in large part to the present day. In addition, Winckelmann's work stimulated interest in Classical antiquities throughout Europe, and he subsequently became the hero of the Neo-Classical movement during the late eighteenth century.

While visiting the sites of Herculaneum (which had been discovered in 1709) and Pompeii (discovered in 1748) he was struck by the beauty of the objects that he saw and began to formulate his *History*. Prior to Winckelmann's time the study of art and antiquities had been conceptualized very differently; traditionally, histories of art had been conceived as biographies of single artists, studies in antiquity had concentrated on the study of texts, and ancient artifacts were examined chiefly with regard to the iconographical meaning of their motifs. Winckelmann's work would revolutionize these practices by establishing new foundations both for the study of the history of art and of antiquities: a history of art would now envelop a culture from its beginning through its flowering to its eventual decline. Winckelmann also sought to explain the underlying reasons for these various stages of development. In his *History* he discussed in detail the art (especially sculpture) of Egypt, Greece, Etruria, and Rome but centered upon the study of Greek art, setting out a historical and theoretical framework of its development. Prior to Winckelmann, all art from Greece (known largely in the form of Roman copies at that time) and Rome had been lumped together under the one heading, "Classical antiquities"; from his time on, however, Greek and Roman art began to be separated. He classified Greek art as having gone through four stages of development: Archaic, Early Classical (including the work of Pheidias), Later Classical (including the work of Praxiteles), and Hellenistic and Late Antique (which included Roman art). From this detailed discussion of the development of Greek art he set into motion a trend which has survived to the present day, for Greek art emerged as the ideal by which all art should be measured. Winckelmann emphasized the superiority of Greek art over the art of Rome (which he saw as a breakdown of the Classical ideal), and stressed the pivotal importance of the best examples of Greek sculpture which were produced during the fifth and fourth centuries B.C.E. Although today this viewpoint is seen as a value judgment, it is important because Winckelmann was the first scholar to separate Greek art from Roman, even if he perceived Roman art as simply a degenerated form of the Greek.

In addition to these contributions, Winckelmann stands out as the individual who first expounded the notion that to truly know the Greeks one not only had to study their philology, philosophy, and literature, but also other aspects of their lives including their art, architecture, and numismatics. This opinion, novel at the time, opened up completely new avenues of scholarship and helped change the course of antiquarian studies.

SOURCES

Potts, *Flesh and the Ideal: Winckelmann and the Origins of Art History*, 1994; Leppman, *Winckelmann*, 1970; Michaelis, *A Century of Archaeological Discoveries*, 1908; Parslow, *Rediscovering Antiquity . . .* , 1995; Gilbert Bagnani, "Winckelmann and the Second Renascence, 1755–1955," *AJA* 59 (1955): 107–18; Miller, *Greece Through the Ages*, 1972; Hibbert, *Rome: Biography of a City*, 1985; Stiebing Jr., *Uncovering the Past: A History of Archaeology*, 1993.

J(OHN) T(URTLE) WOOD

b: February 13, 1821. London, England.
d: March 25, 1890. Worthing, England.

EDUCATION

Rossall Hall School.
Cambridge University.

APPOINTMENTS AND AWARDS

Private architect; Smyrna and Aidin Railway (western Turkey): Architect (1858–63). Fellow: Society of Antiquaries (1875); Royal Institute of British Architects (1874; Hon. Fellow, 1878).

EXCAVATIONS

Ephesus, 1860s.

PUBLICATIONS

Discoveries at Ephesus, Including the Site and Remains of the Great Temple of Diana (1822), London: Longmans, Green, 1877; *Discoveries on the Site of Ancient Ephesus*, 1890 (published posthumously).

J. T. Wood was an architect who, possibly due to his early studies in the Classics, had a driving ambition to discover the Temple of Artemis at Ephesus, the Late Classical temple that was considered one of the seven wonders of the ancient world. Wood took the position of architect with the Smyrna and Aidin Railway specifically with the idea that he could spend a good deal of his time in Turkey in search of the temple which had "disappeared" during the Middle Ages.

While excavating in the theater at Ephesus he discovered a Greek inscription which referred to a traditional procession during which objects were carried from the Temple of Artemis through the Magnesian Gate to the theater. Wood reasoned that if he could locate this gate there was probably a paved way which would lead to the great temple. He continued his excavation and in 1867 unearthed the Magnesian Gate and indeed, there was a paved road; he excavated along this road and on May 2, 1869 he discovered the *temenos* wall of the Sanctuary of Artemis. The work continued and on December 31, 1869 he found the temple itself lying beneath twenty feet of wet sand. The excavation proved to be a very long, slow ordeal, and its waterlogged condition required constant pumping. After eleven years Wood and his wife departed for Britain in 1874; he returned to the site for a brief visit in 1883 but was unable to accomplish anything more due to the wet terrain.

The Temple of Artemis has been called one of the seven wonders of the ancient world due to its sheer size and elaborate sculptural elements. According to Pliny the columns of the double colonnade which surrounded the *cella* rose sixty feet and were topped off by enormous Ionic capitals. The bases of these columns featured relief sculptures of human figures (unusual but not unknown in other temples in Ionia); Wood was able to procure examples of these and had them conveyed to London for installation in the British Museum, which had sponsored the excavations.

SOURCES

St. John Irvine, *TL-Literary Supplement*, March 13, 1937; R. A. Higgins, *DNB* "Missing Persons" volume, 1993; Michaelis, *A Century of Archeological Discoveries*, 1908; Clayton and Price, editors, *The Seven Wonders of the Ancient World*, 1988.

ROBERT WOOD

b: c. 1717.[1] Riverstown Castle, Near Trim, Ireland.
d: September 9, 1771. Putney, England.

APPOINTMENTS AND AWARDS

Under Secretary of State (1756–63); Archaeological Expeditions, Society of Dilettanti: Director. Member: Society of Dilettanti (1763).

PUBLICATIONS

The Ruins of Palmyra, otherwise Tedmore in the Desart, London: s.n., 1753 (French translation 1753, 1819 and 1829); *The Ruins of Balbec, otherwise Heliopolis in Coelosyria*, London: s.n., 1757; *A Comparative View of the Antient and present State of the Troade to which is prefixed an Essay on the Original Genius of Homer*, 1767; *An Essay on the Original Genius of Homer, with a Comparative View of the Ancient and Present State of the Troade* (1769) (enlarged edition of essay of 1767, above), Washington: McGrath Pub. Co., 1973; Preface to CHANDLER and REVETT'S *Ionian Antiquities*, 1769.

As a young man Robert Wood traveled throughout western Asia Minor and Greece (as well as to Italy), spurred on by a love of Homer's poems and a wish to read them in the surroundings in which they were set. Upon his return he was asked by two Oxford graduates, James Dawkins and John Bouverie, to accompany them on a journey to these very same areas which they had never seen. The party left Rome in 1750 and, having visited a few of the Greek Islands, traveled on to the Propontis and Bosphorus, the coast of western Asia Minor, Syria, Palestine, and Egypt. Unfortunately, John

Bouverie died while visiting Magnesia and was buried at Smyrna (present day Izmir).

Wood was not a great admirer of Greek architecture (favoring Roman) and so he had a special interest in seeing the ruins of Palmyra and Baalbek. Palmyra was known to have been an important Roman site being situated along the ancient trade route halfway between the valley of the Euphrates and the coast of Syria. Inhabited since the Neolithic period but not becoming urbanized until late Hellenistic times, the city really developed under Roman rule[2] and, being a vital link in ancient trade between East and West, flourished for about two hundred years from the second to third centuries C.E. At this time its ruler, Queen Zenobia, rebelled against Roman authority and the city was subsequently partly razed by the emperor Aurelian. New trade routes then developed to the north and the city never regained its former prominence.

The first Europeans to see Palmyra in modern times were a party of English traders led by a Dr. Halifax. His group visited the site in 1691 and Halifax related how impressive and sumptuous were the remains of the ancient city. Wood and Dawkins reached Palmyra in March of 1751 but were able to stay for only two weeks, having been advised to leave because of the imminent danger of attack by bandits who freely roamed the surrounding desert. Despite the short period of their stay, they were able to record a great deal of information about the ruins of this once great city. Like STUART and REVETT (who were in Athens at the same time that Wood and Dawkins were at Palmyra and Baalbek), they took meticulous measurements of the buildings and, having hired an Italian architect and draughtsman (Giovanni Batista Borra) to produce drawings of the architectural remains, they were able to come away with many excellent detailed sketches. Wood and Dawkins also made copies of many of the inscriptions that they found and removed as many as seemed safe. On their outward journey they stopped at ancient Baalbek, measuring and sketching its ruins.

Wood produced two scholarly volumes on these two sites and, although these proved popular and were met with critical acclaim, they were never able to capture the public's imagination as would the work of Stuart and Revett on the antiquities of Athens. This was due to the fact that Stuart and Revett's publication put Britain "in the grip of Grecian Gusto"[3] soon after the publication of Wood's works and as a result there was little enthusiasm among the public for Roman antiquities.

Wood was a prominent member of the Society of Dilettanti in London and it was he who recommended RICHARD CHANDLER to be the leader of the society's expedition to Asia Minor in 1764. He also drew up the exacting instructions to the participants of that project, a fact which later proved to ensure its success.

SOURCES

DNB 21; Cust, *History of the Society of Dilettanti*, 1914; Wood, *The Ruins of Palmyra, otherwise Tedmor, in the Desart* (1753), reprint, 1971; Wood, *The Ruins of Balbec, otherwise Heliopolis in Coelosyria* (1757), reprint, 1971; Browning, *Palmyra*, 1979; Cox, *Reference Guide to the Literature of Travel*, 1948; Clarke, *Greek Studies in England 1700–1830*, 1945.

NOTES

1. Exact year unknown.
2. The city was renamed Palmyra by the Romans (meaning "the place of palms") but today has reverted to its former name of Tedmor.
3. Cust, *History of the Society of Dilettanti*, p. 81.

GLOSSARY

absolute chronology—Dating which is considered to be correct to within a twenty-five year period; established in the Aegean area by cross-dating with Egyptian artifacts for which there exists a reasonably certain chronology.

Archaic period—A historical period following the Geometric period. The Archaic period in Greece spans the mid-eighth century to the end of the sixth century B.C.E.

Attic—Something originating in ancient Athens or the surrounding area (i.e., within the *deme* of Attica, as in county).

atrium—Forecourt of a Roman house.

bee-hive tomb—A large, round, architectural structure built into a hillside and accessed by a *dromos* (long passageway). It has a pointed, cantilevered roof resembling a bee's hive.

Bronze Age—The historic period in which bronze artifacts predominate for the first time. In the Aegean area the Bronze Age begins c. 2800 B.C.E. and ends c. 1050 B.C.E. The Bronze Age begins in Italy c. 1800 B.C.E. and ends c. 1000 B.C.E.

cella—The innermost room of a Greek temple.

chamber tomb—A tomb cut into bedrock and accessed by a *dromos* (long passageway).

chronology—A historical framework designating various stages of cultural development.

coin hoard—A large deposit of ancient coins.

cuneiform—A script produced by pressing a stylus with a wedge-shaped end into a wet clay tablet. It was developed by the Sumerian culture in Mesopotamia during the Bronze Age.

Cyclopean walls—Strong fortification walls constructed of large, unworked stones filled at the interstices with rubble and clay. These walls have such a formidable appearance that the ancient Greeks thought they must have been constructed by the giant Cyclopes. They are found in Mycenaean palaces of the Bronze Age.

Dorian invasion—An invasion of Doric-speaking Greeks who came overland from the north and who, according to Greek tradition, caused the total collapse of Mycenaean civilization.

entasis—A subtle convex curve in the shaft of a column.

firman—A formal authorization obtained from the Turkish sultan.

Geometric pottery— Greek pottery produced during the initial part of the Iron Age characterized by geometric patterns. Geometric pottery appears c. 1000 B.C.E. and is produced until about the mid-eighth century B.C.E. Proto-Geometric refers to the earliest forms of Geometric ware.

grave circle—A circular area defined by a wall containing several burials.

Helladic—A chronological term coined by CARL W. BLEGEN and A.J.B. WACE to designate the Bronze Age period on mainland Greece (c. 2800–1050 B.C.E.).

Hellenistic period—The period following the death of Alexander the Great (323 B.C.E.) down to the Roman defeat of Antony and Cleopatra at the Battle of Actium in 31 B.C.E.

kouros, kouroi—Large-scale, free-standing, sculpted nude male figure dating to the Greek Archaic period. *Kore* (*korai*) is the (draped) female equivalent.

Linear A—A Minoan writing system which has never been deciphered. It was written on wet clay tablets and thus far has been found only on Crete.

Linear B—An adaptation of the Minoan Linear A writing system which has been found at sites throughout the Mycenaean world as well as at Knossos on Crete. It was deciphered by MICHAEL VENTRIS who demonstrated it to be a form of ancient Greek.

Minoan—The term coined by Sir ARTHUR EVANS to denote the Bronze Age civilization of Crete (c. 2800 B.C.E.–c. 1350 B.C.E.). He derived the term from King Minos, the legendary ruler of the island.

Minyan ware—A distinctive gray pottery which first appeared in Greece during the Middle Helladic period. The term was first used by HEINRICH SCHLIEMANN who found one of the earliest examples of this type of pottery during excavations at Orchomenos in Boeotia.

mithraeum—A sacred area often found in a subterranean setting, established for the worship of the god Mithras who was particularly popular among the armies of the Roman Empire.

Mycenaean—Designating a Greek Bronze Age civilization, so named because the earliest Mycenaean artifacts were found in the area of Mycenae in the Peloponnese. According to Homer Mycenae was the most powerful of the Greek kingdoms and its king, Agamemnon, led the Greeks against Troy. Mycenaean civilization has been found throughout central and southern Greece.

necropolis—Ancient place of burial, literally meaning "city of the dead."

Neolithic period—A historical period characterized by the use of polished stone tools, settled villages, pottery, and weaving. In the Aegean area the Neolithic period begins c. 6500 B.C.E. and ends c. 2800 B.C.E.

nymphaeum—A cave with running water; a fountain, dedicated to the nymphs.

ostraka—Inscribed potsherds used for balloting purposes.

palaestra—An area used for wrestling or other sports training activities.

pictographs—A script made up of pictorial symbols.

propylaeum—A gated entranceway to a Greek enclosure.

prytaneion—A Greek building where the governing body of a city assembled.

radiocarbon-14 dating—A method of dating artifacts by measuring the residue of radioactive carbon (C-14) present in the object.

sequence dating—A method devised by FLINDERS PETRIE for dating pottery based on stylistic development.

shaft graves—Graves which consist of shafts dug into the ground and sometimes lined with stones. They usually contain a number of secondary burials.

stele—An upright slab of stone used to mark a burial place.

stratigraphy—The various layers of the remains of human habitation recovered during excavation of a site.

sub-Mycenaean—The period immediately following the collapse of Mycenaean civilization.

syllabic script—A script made up of symbols each representing a syllable.

tell—An area of repeated human occupation which has formed a mound. The term is associated with Near Eastern archaeology.

temenos—A sacred precinct, often around a temple.

tholos tomb—A circular structure used for the burial of the dead. See "bee-hive tomb."

Troad—The area surrounding ancient Troy (in northwestern Turkey).

ABBREVIATIONS

ABBREVIATIONS—BOOKS

Complete publication information on the following may be found in the bibliography.

Leekley and Efstratiou, *AECNG*, 1980.
Leekley and Noyes, *AEGI*, 1975.
Leekley and Noyes, *AESG*, 1976.
Meyers, *OEANE*, 1996.
Stillwell, *PECS*, 1976.
de Grummond, *EHCA*, 1996.

ABBREVIATIONS—JOURNALS AND GENERAL REFERENCE WORKS

AA	*Archäologische Anzeiger*
AAB	*American Authors and Books, 1640 to the present, 1982.*
AF	*Architectural Forum*
AJA	*American Journal of Archaeology*
AJPA	*American Journal of Physical Anthropology*
AM	*Mitteilungen des Deutschen Archäologischen Instituts, Athenische Abteilung*
AmAnth	*American Anthropologist*
ANSN	*American Numismatic Society Newsletter*
ANSNM	*American Numismatic Society Notes and Monographs*
AntJ	*Antiquaries Journal*
APSY	*American Philosophical Society Yearbook*
ArchDelt	’Αρχαιολογικόν Δελτίον

328 THE MAKERS OF CLASSICAL ARCHAEOLOGY

AS	*Anatolian Studies*
ASAtene	*Annario della Scuola Archeologka di Atene e dell e Missioni Italiane in Oriente*
AZ	*Archäologische Zeitung*
BIA	*Bulletin of the Institute of Archaeology*
BICS	*Bulletin of the Institute of Classical Studies of the University of London*
BJDN	*Bioraphisches Jahrbuch und Deutscher Nekrolog*
BPI	*Bollettino di paleontologia italiana*
BSA	*Annual of the British School at Athens*
BSAAnnR	*British School at Athens, Annual Report*
BSR	*Papers of the British School at Rome*
CA	*Contemporary Authors*
CANE	*Classical Association of New England Annual Bulletin*
CANRS	*Contemporary Authors New Revision Series*
CB	*Current Biography*
CBD	*Chamber's Biographical Dictionary*
CNR	*Classical Numismatic Review*
CR	*Classical Review*
DAB	*Dictionary of American Biography*
DAS	*Directory of American Scholars*
DNB	*Dictionary of National Biography*
EJ	*Encylopedia Judaica*
ILN	*Illustrated London News*
IWW	*International Who's Who*
IWWE	*International Who's Who of Europe*
JBAASR	*Journal of the British and American Archaeological Society of Rome*
JEA	*Journal of Egyptian Archaeology*
JHisS	*Journal of Historical Studies*
JHS	*Journal of Hellenic Studies*
JMünch	*Jahrbuch. Bayerische Akademie der Wissenschaften (München)*
JRS	*Journal of Roman Studies*
JSAH	*Journal of the Society of Architectural Historians*
Klio	*Klio: Beiträge zur alten Geschichte*
MonAnt	*Monumenti antichi*
MusJ	*Museum Journal (Philadelphia)*
NAW	*Notable American Women*
NC	*Numismatic Chronicle*
NCAB	*National Cyclopaedia of American Biography*

NDB	*Neue Deutsche Biographie*
NGSRR	*National Geographic Society Research Reports*
NSc	*Notizie degli scavi di antichità*
NYT	*New York Times*
OpArch	*Opuscula archaeologica*
OpAth	*Opuscula Atheniensia*
ONFRS	*Obituary Notices of Fellows of the Royal Society*
PBA	*Proceedings of the British Academy*
PBSR	*Proceedings of the British School at Rome*
PPS	*Proceedings of the Prehistoric Society* (London)
Prakt	Πρακτικὰ ἐν Ἀθηναις' Αρχαιολογικης 'Εταιρείας
RA	*Revue Archéologique*
RDAC	*Report of the Department of Antiquities, Cyprus*
RGPL	*Readers Guide to Periodic Literature*
RM	*Mitteilungen des Deutschen Archäologischen Instituts, Römische Abteilung*
SIMA	*Studies in Mediterranean Archaeology*
SIMA-PB	*Studies in Mediterranean Archaeology—Pocketbook*
TL	*The Times*
TRSL	*Transactions of the Royal Society of London*
WP	*Washington Post*
WW	*Who's Who*
WWA	*Who's Who in America*
WWWEEA	*Who Was Who Among English and European Authors*
WWWA	*Who Was Who in American*
WWW	*Who Was Who*
WWWorld	*Who's Who in the World*

BIBLIOGRAPHY

Absalom, et al. *A Tribute to Sir George Hill on his Eightieth Birthday, 1867–1947*. Oxford: Oxford University Press, 1948 (privately printed).

Albright, William Foxwell. *From the Stone Age to Christianity*. New York: Doubleday and Co., 1972, 2d. ed.

Allsebrook, Mary. *Born to Rebel: The Life of Harriet Boyd Hawes*. Oxford: Oxbow Books, 1992.

Arias, Paolo Enrico. *Quattro Archeologi del Nostro Secolo*. Pisa: Giardini Editori E. Stampatori, 1976.

Åström, Paul, editor. "Who's Who in Cypriote Archeology: Biographical and Bibliographical Notes," *Studies in Mediterranean Archaeology* 23, Göteborg: Paul Åströms Förlag, 1971.

Bacon, Edward. *Archaeology: Discoveries in the 1960s*. New York: Praeger Publishers, 1971.

Barber, R. L. N. *The Cyclades in the Bronze Age*. University of Iowa Press, 1987.

Bent, J. Theodore. *Aegean Islands: The Cyclades, or Life among the Insular Greeks*. 1885. Reprint, edited by Al. Oikonomides, Chicago: Argonaut, 1966.

Boegehold, et al. *Studies Presented to Sterling Dow on His Eightieth Birthday*. Duke University Press, 1984 (*Greek, Roman and Byzantine Monographs* series).

Brea, L. Bernabò. *Sicily Before the Greeks*. New York: Frederick A. Praeger, 1966, 2d. ed.

Brendel, Otto J. *Prolegomena to the Study of Roman Art*. New Haven, Conn.: Yale University Press, 1979.

Browning, Iain. *Palmyra*. London: Chatto and Windus, 1979.

331

Butler, Howard. *Sardis. Vol. I: The Excavations, Part I, 1910–1914*. 1922. Reprint, Amsterdam: Adolf M. Hakkert, 1969.

Carpenter, Rhys. *Discontinuity in Greek Civilization*. Cambridge: Cambridge University Press, 1966.

Casson, Stanley. *Ancient Cyprus: Its Art and Archaeology*. London: Methuen and Co. Ltd., 1937.

Cesnola, Luigi Di Palma. *Cyprus: Its Cities, Tombs and Temples*. New York: Harper and Brothers, 1878.

Chadwick, John. *The Mycenaean World*. Cambridge: Cambridge University Press, 1972.

Chandler, Richard. *Travels in Asia Minor and Greece* (2 vols.), Oxford: The Clarendon Press, 1825.

Christenson, Andrew L., editor. *Tracing Archaeology's Past: The Historiography of Archaeology*. Carbondale, Ill.: Southern Illinois University Press, 1989.

Clarke, M. L. *Greek Studies in England 1700–1830*. Cambridge: Cambridge University Press, 1945.

Clay, Edith, editor. *Richard Chandler: Travels in Asia Minor 1764-1765*. London: British Museum Publications, 1971.

Clayton, Peter A. and Martin J. Price, eds. *The Seven Wonders of the Ancient World*. London: Routledge, 1988.

Cleator, P. E. *Archaeology in the Making*. New York: St. Martin's Press, 1976.

Cook, B. F. *The Elgin Marbles*. London: British Museum Publications, 1984.

Cook, R. M. *Greek Painted Pottery*. London: Methuen and Co. Ltd., 1972, 2d. ed.

Cottrell, Arthur. *The Minoan World*. New York: Charles Scribner's Sons, 1979.

Cox, Edward G. *Reference Guide to the Literature of Travel*. Seattle, Wash.: University of Washington, 1948.

Cust, Lionel. *History of the Society of Dilettanti*, edited by Sir Sidney Colvin. London: Macmillan and Co., 1914.

Daniel, Glyn. *A Hundred and Fifty Years of Archaeology*. London: Duckworth Press, 1975, 2d. ed.

Daniel, Glyn and Colin Renfrew. *The Idea of Prehistory*. Edinburgh: Edinburgh University Press, 1988, 2d. ed.

Daniel, Glyn, editor. *Towards a History of Archaeology*. London: Thames and Hudson, 1981.

Dawson, Warren R. and Eric P. Uphill. *Who Was Who in Egyptology*. London: The Egypt Exploration Society, 1972, 2d. ed.

de Grummond, Nancy Thomson, editor. *An Encyclopedia of the History of Classical Archaeology.* Freeport, Conn.: Greenwood Press, 1996.

Dinsmoor, William Bell. *The Architecture of Ancient Greece.* New York: W. W. Norton and Co., 1975, 3d. ed.

Di Vita, Antonino. *Ancient Crete: A Hundred Years of Italian Archaeology, 1884–1984.* Rome: De Luca Editore/Italian Archaeological School of Athens, 1984.

Doumas, Christos G. *Thera: Pompeii of the Ancient Aegean, Excavations at Akrotiri 1967–79.* London: Thames and Hudson, 1983.

Dow, Sterling. *A Century of Humane Archaeology.* New York: Archaeological Institute of America, 1979.

———. *Fifty Years of Sathers: The Sather Professorship of Classical Literature in the University of California, Berkeley, 1913/14-1963/4.* Berkeley: University of California Press, 1965.

Dunbabin, T. J. *The Western Greeks: The History of Sicily and South Italy from the Foundation of the Greek Colonies to 480 B.C.* Oxford: The Clarendon Press, 1948.

Edwards, Edward. *Lives of the Founders of the British Museum; with Notices of its Chief Augmentors and Other Benefactors.* 1870. Reprint, New York: Burt Franklin, 1969.

Evans, Arthur. *The Palace of Minos at Knossos,* Vols. 1–4. 1921–36. Reprint, New York: Biblo and Tannen, 1964.

Evans, Joan. *Time and Chance: The Story of Arthur Evans and His Forebears.* New York: Longmans, Green and Co., 1943.

Fellows, Charles. *Travels and Researches in Asia Minor, more particularly in the province of Lycia.* 1852. Reprint, Hildesheim: Georg Olms Verlag, 1975.

Finley, M. I. *Early Greece: The Bronze and Archaic Ages.* New York: W. W. Norton and Co., 1971.

Fitton, J. Lesley. *The Discovery of the Greek Bronze Age.* London: British Museum Press, 1995.

Frazer, J. G. *Pausanias's Description of Greece.* 1898. Reprint, New York: Biblo and Tannen, 1965.

Furumark, Arne. *Mycenaean Pottery III: Plates.* (*Acta Instituti Atheniensis Regni Sueciae.* Series in 4°, XX:3 edited by Paul Åström, et al). Göteborg: Paul Åströms Förlag, 1992.

Gardiner, E. Norman. *Olympia: Its History and Remains.* Washington, D.C.: McGrath Publishing Company, 1973.

Gjerstad, Einar. *Studies in Prehistoric Cyprus.* Uppsala,

Sweden: Uppsala University Press, 1926.

Gjerstad, Einar. *Ages and Days in Cyprus*. Göteborg: Paul Åströms Förlag, 1980.

Glyptothek Museum. *The Munich Glyptothek: Greek and Roman Sculpture*. Munich: Verlag C. H. Beck, 1974.

Goring, Elizabeth. *A Mischievous Pastime: Digging in Cyprus in the Nineteenth Century*. Edinburgh: National Museums of Scotland, 1988.

Graham, James Walter. *The Palaces of Minoan Crete*. Princeton, N.J.: Princeton University Press, 1972.

Grmek, Mirko D. *Diseases in the Ancient World*. Baltimore: Johns Hopkins University Press, 1989.

Harden, D. B. *Sir Arthur Evans 1851–1941, "A Memoir."* Oxford: Ashmolean Museum, 1983.

Harris, David R., editor. *The Archaeology of V. Gordon Childe: Contemporary Perspectives*. Chicago: University of Chicago Press, 1994.

Harrison, Jane Ellen. *Reminiscences of a Student's Life*. London: Hogarth Press, 1925, 2d. ed.

Hibbard, Howard. *The Metropolitan Museum of Art*. New York: Harper and Row, Publishers, 1980.

Hibbert, Christopher. *Rome: The Biography of a City*. New York: W. W. Norton, 1985.

Higgins, Reynold. *The Archaeology of Minoan Crete*. New York: Henry Z. Walck, 1973.

———. *The Greek Bronze Age*. 1970. Reprint, London: British Museum Publications, 1977.

Holloway, R. Ross. *The Archaeology of Ancient Sicily*. London: Routledge, Inc., 1991.

Houlder, Christopher. *Wales: An Archaeological Guide*. London: Faber and Faber, 1978.

Howe, Winifred E. *A History of the Metropolitan Museum of Art: with a Chapter on the early institution of art in New York*. New York: Arno Publishing, 1974.

Karageorghis, Vassos. *Cyprus: From the Stone Age to the Romans*. New York: Thames and Hudson, 1982.

Karageorghis, Vassos, et al. *Studies Presented in Memory of Porphyrios Dikaios*. Nicosia: Zavallis Press Ltd., 1979.

Kraus, Theodore. *Pompeii and Herculaneum: The Living Cities of the Dead*. New York: Harry N. Abrams, Inc., 1973.

Lanciani, Rodolfo. *The Ruins and Excavations of Ancient Rome*. 1897. Reprint, New York: Bell Publishing, 1979.

Leekley, Dorothy and Nicholas Efstratiou. *Archaeological Excavations in Central and Northern Greece*. New Jersey: Noyes Press, 1980.

Leekley, Dorothy and Robert Noyes. *Archaeological Excavations in the Greek Islands*. New Jersey: Noyes Press, 1975.

Leekley, Dorothy and Robert Noyes. *Archaeological Excavations in Southern Greece*. New Jersey: Noyes Press, 1976.

Leppmann, Wolfgang. *Winckelmann*. New York: Alfred A. Knopf, 1970.

Lord, Louis. *A History of the American School of Classical Studies at Athens, 1882–1942*. Cambridge, Mass.: Harvard University Press, 1947.

Ludwig, Emil. *Schliemann: The Story of a Gold-seeker*. Boston: Little, Brown, and Company, 1931.

Lullies, Reinhard and Wolfgang Schiering. *Archäologenbildnisse: Porträts und Kurzbiographien von Klassiscchen Archäologen deutscher Sprache*. Mainz am Rhein: Verlag Phillip Von Zabern, 1988.

MacKendrick, Paul. *The Greek Stones Speak*. New York: W. W. Norton and Co., 1981, 2d. ed.

MacKendrick, Paul. *The Mute Stones Speak: The Story of Archaeology in Italy*. New York: St. Martin's Press, 1960.

Maiuri, Amedeo. *Roman Painting*. Geneva: Skira, 1953.

Malecos, Andreas. *Studies in Cyprus*. Nicosia: Cultural Centre Cyprus Popular Bank, 1994.

Matz, Friedrich. *The Art of Crete and Early Greece*. New York: Crown Publishers, 1962.

McDonald, William A. *The Discovery of Homeric Greece*. New York: Macmillan and Co., 1967.

McFadden, Elizabeth. *The Glitter and the Gold: A Spirited Account of the Metropolitan Museum of Art's first Director, the audacious and high-handed Luigi Palma di Cesnola*. New York: Dial Press, 1971.

Meyers, Erik M., ed. *Oxford Encyclopedia of Archaeology of the Near East*. Oxford: Oxford University Press, 1996.

Michaelis, Adolf. *Ancient Marbles in Great Britain*. Translated by C. A. M. Fennell. Cambridge: Cambridge University Press, 1882.

———. *A Century of Archaeological Discoveries*. Translated by Bettina Kahnweiler. London: John Murray, 1908.

Miller, Helen Hill. *Greece Through the Ages: As Seen by Trav-*

ellers from Herodotus to Byron. London: J. M. Dent and Sons Ltd., 1972.

Mitten, David Gordon et al, eds. *Studies Presented to George M. A. Hanfmann*. Mainz: Verlag Philipp von Zabern, 1971.

Moncune, James A., editor. *Research Guide to European Historical Biography, 1450–Present*. Washington, D.C.: Beachman Publishing, Inc., 1982.

Morris, Christine, editor. *Klados: Essays in Honour of J. N. Coldstream*. London: Institute of Classical Studies, University of London, 1995.

Mylonas, George. E. *Eleusis and the Eleusinian Mysteries*. Princeton, N.J.: Princeton University Press, 1961.

———, editor. *Studies Presented to David Moore Robinson on His Seventieth Birthday*, Vol. 1. St. Louis, Mo.: Washington University Press, 1951.

Mylonas, George and Doris Raymond, eds. *Studies Presented to David Moore Robinson on His Seventieth Birthday*, Vol. 2. St. Louis, Mo.: Washington University Press, 1953.

Myres, John L. *A Handbook of the Cesnola Collection of Antiquities from Cyprus*. New York: Metropolitan Museum of Art, 1914.

Myres, John L. and Max Ohnefalsch-Richter. *A Catalogue of the Cyprus Museum with a chronicle of excavations undertaken since the British occupation and introductory notes on Cypriote archaeology*. Oxford: The Clarendon Press, 1899.

Ohly, Dieter. *The Munich Glyptothek: Greek and Roman Sculpture*. Munich: Verlag C. H. Beck, 1974.

Pallottino, Massimo. *The Etruscans*. London: Allen Lane (Penguin), 1974, 2d. ed.

Palmer, Leonard R. *The Penultimate Palace of Knossos*. Rome: Ed. Dell Áteneo, 1963.

Palmer, L. R. and John Boardman. *On the Knossos Tablets*. Oxford: The Clarendon Press, 1963.

Parslow, Christopher Charles. *Rediscovering Antiquity: Karl Weber and the Excavation of Herculaneum, Pompeii and Stabiae*. Cambridge: Cambridge University Press, 1995.

Peacock, Sandra J. *Jane Ellen Harrison: The Mask and the Self*. New Haven, Conn.: Yale University Press, 1988.

Pendlebury, J. E. S. *A Handbook to the Palace of Minos at Knossos with an Introduction and Bibliography by Leslie Preston Day*. Chicago: Ares Publishers, Inc., 1979.

Petrie, Flinders. *Seventy Years in Archaeology*. 1932. Reprint, New York: Greenwood Press, 1969.

Platon, Nicholas. *Zakros: The Discovery of a Lost Palace of Ancient Crete.* New York: Charles Scribner's Sons, 1971.

Potts, Alex. *Flesh and the Ideal: Winckelmann and the Origins of Art History.* New Haven, Conn.: Yale University Press, 1994.

Powell, Dilys. *The Traveller's Journey is Done.* London: Hodder, 1943.

Renfrew, Colin. *The Emergence of Civilisation: The Cyclades and the Aegean in the Third Millennium B.C.* London: Methuen, 1972.

Rhodes, D. E. *Dennis of Etruria.* London: Cecil and Amelia Woolf, 1973.

Sakellarakis, J. A. *Herakleion Museum: Illustrated Guide to the Museum.* Athens: Ekdotike Athenon, 1979.

Sandler, Lucy Freeman, ed. *Essays in Memory of Karl Lehmann.* New York: Institute of Fine Arts, New York University, 1964.

Schuchhardt, C. *Schliemann's Discoveries of the Ancient World.* 1891. Reprint, New York: Avenel Books, 1979.

Sjöqvist, Erik. *Sicily and the Greeks: Studies in the Interrelationship between the Indigenous Populations and the Greek Colonists.* Ann Arbor: University of Michigan Press, 1973.

Snodgrass, A. M. T*he Dark Age of Greece: An Archaeological Survey of the Eleventh to the Eight Centuries B.C.* Edinburgh: University Press, 1971.

St. Clair, William. *Lord Elgin and the Marbles.* Oxford: Oxford University Press, 1998.

Stewart, Jessie. *Jane Ellen Harrison: A Portrait from Letters.* London: Merlin Press, 1959.

Stiebing Jr., William H. *Uncovering the Past: A History of Archaeology.* Amherst, N. Y.: Prometheus Books, 1993.

Stillwell, Richard, ed. T*he Princeton Encyclopedia of Classical Sites.* Princeton, N.J.: Princeton University Press, 1976.

Stuart, James and Nicholas Revett. *The Antiquities of Athens.* 1762. Reprint, New York: B. Blom, 1968.

Taylour, William. *The Mycenaeans.* London: Thames and Hudson, 1983, 2d. ed.

Tomkins, Calvin. *Merchants and Masterpieces: The Story of the Metropolitan Museum of Art.* New York: E. P. Dutton and Co., Inc., 1970.

Traill, David A. *Excavating Schliemann: Collected Papers on Schliemann.* Georgia: Scholar's Press, 1993. (Illinois Classical Studies, Supplement 4).

Travlos, John. *A Pictorial Dictionary of Ancient Athens.* 1971. Reprint, New York: Hacker Books, 1980.

Turner, Frank M. *The Greek Heritage in Victorian Britain.* New Haven, Conn.: Yale University Press, 1981.

Ubelaker, Douglas and Henry Scammell. *Bones: A Forensic Detective's Casebook.* New York: Edward Burlingame Books (Harper-Row), 1992.

Uppsala University. *Uppsala University; 500 Years: History, Art and Philosophy.* Uppsala: Faculty of Arts, Uppsala University, 1976.

Vermeule, Emily. *Greece in the Bronze Age.* Chicago: University of Chicago Press, 1972.

Waterhouse, Helen. *The British School at Athens: The First Hundred Years.* London: British School at Athens, 1986.

Weber, Shirley Howard. *Voyages and Travels in the Near East Made During the XIX Century.* Princeton, N.J.: The American School of Classical Studies at Athens, 1952.

Weinberg, Saul, ed. *The Aegean and the Near East: Studies Presented to Hetty Goldman.* New York: Locust Valley, 1956.

Wheeler, Mortimer. *The British Academy 1949–1968.* Oxford: Oxford University Press, 1970.

Winters, Christopher, general editor. *International Dictionary of Anthropologists.* New York: Garland Publishing, 1991.

Wood, Robert. *The Ruins of Balbec, otherwise Heliopolis in Coelosyria.* 1757. Reprint, Farnborough, Harts.: Gregg International Publishers, 1971.

Wood, Robert. *The Ruins of Palmyra, otherwise Tedmor, in the Desart.* 1753. Reprint, Farnborough, Harts.: Gregg International Publishers, 1971.

INDEX

208
Dimini, 301
DINSMOOR, WILLIAM BELL, 86–88, 155
Diocletian, 179
Dion, Greece, 21
Dionysus, 243
diseases, 24
Dodecanese (Dodekanese), 76, 194–95
DODWELL, EDWARD, 89–90
DOHAN, EDITH HALL, 91–92
Dolmens, 192
domestic architecture. See architecture, domestic
Dorian invasion, 39, 47, 49, 113, 302
DÖRPFELD, WILHELM, 40, 53, 74, 93–95, 144, 168, 222, 269, 281
Douris Painter, 247–48
DOW, STERLING, 96–97
drama, 36, 37, 243–44
Dunbabin, T. J., 33, 80, 232
Dura Europos, 263–64
Durkheim, Emile, 144

earthquakes, 135
Edessa, Greece, 22
Egypt, 134, 160, 233, 242, 264, 266, 317
Egyptology, 251
Eileithya Cave, 148–49
El Amrah, 251
Eleusinian mysteries, 211–12
Eleusis, Greece, 66–67, 121, 211–12, 289, 311
    calendar, 97
Eleuthera, Crete, 231
ELGIN, LORD, 67, 99–100, 137, 173
Elgin Marbles, 100, 173, 277
Ellis, S. E., 153
Enkomi, Cyprus, 83–84, 276
entasis, 71
Epano Englianos (Pylos), Greece, 38, 40
Ephesus, Turkey, 61, 162, 315
Epidaurus, Greece, 67, 89, 229
Epigraphical Museum, Athens, 206
epigraphy, 97, 102, 115, 206, 209, 296
Equus Domitianus, Rome, 13
Erechtheum, Athens, 87, 311
Eretria, 289
Erganos, 131
ERIM, KENAN T., 101–102, 279
Erini, Cyprus, 83

Ethiopia, 34
Etruria, 79, 304–305
Etruscans, 42, 78–79, 92, 139, 226–27, 252, 256. See also art, Etruscan
Etruscology, 227
Euboea, 229, 249
Euphrates River, 264, 318
Eutresis, Greece, 126
EVANS, ARTHUR J., SIR, 39–40, 65, 94, 103–106, 113, 131, 132, 134, 146, 149, 153, 159, 187, 192, 215, 234, 299–300
Evans, John, 105
Exekias, 47

Fairman, H. W., 234
Fayum, 159
FELLOWS, CHARLES, SIR, 107–108
Finocchito, Italy, 224
Fiorelli, Giuseppe, 204
Fitzwilliam Museum, Cambridge University, 71, 115
Florence, 71, 78
Fogg Art Museum, 140
Fortetsa, Crete, 231
Forum Romanum. See Rome, Forum Romanum
four styles (Pompeiian painting), 204
France, Visigothic, 304
Frantz, Alison, 290
Frazer, J. G., 116
French, Elizabeth, 302
French School at Athens, 46, 74
Frilford, England, 103
frontiers. See limes
Frothingham, A. L., 92
furniture, 152, 256
FURTWÄNGLER, ADOLF, 32, 70, 109–11, 186–87, 222, 225, 241, 248, 281
FURUMARK, ARNE, 106, 112–14, 300

Galba, Emperor, 176
GARDNER, ERNEST A., 56, 115–17, 242
GARDNER, PERCY, 30, 116, 118–19, 150, 157–58
Garibaldi, Giuseppe, 34
Gazi, 148
Gela, Sicily, 78, 224
GELL, WILLIAM, SIR, 120–21,